8 —

MISN

D0709483

BEYOND LITERARY THEORY

Literature as a Search For The Meaning of Human Destiny

Eduard H. Strauch

University Press of America,® Inc.
Lanham · New York · Oxford

Copyright © 2001 by
University Press of America,® Inc.
4720 Boston Way
Lanham, Maryland 20706

12 Hid's Copse Rd.
Cumnor Hill, Oxford OX2 9JJ

Library of Congress Cataloging-in-Publication Data

Strauch, Eduard Hugo.
Beyond literary theory : literature as a search for the
meaning of human destiny / Eduard H. Strauch.
p.   cm
Includes bibliographical references and index.
l. Literature—History and criticism. I. Title.
PN511 .S73   2001   809—dc21   2001027159 CIP

ISBN 0-7618-1992-4 (cloth: alk. paper)

⊖™The paper used in this publication meets the minimum
requirements of American National Standard for Information
Sciences—Permanence of Paper for Printed Library Materials,
ANSI Z39.48—1984

To my Austrian-born parents who taught me the meaning of European culture and who made it possible for me to be born in America.

CONTENTS

PART ONE:
THE HISTORICAL SEARCH FOR A
LITERARY AESTHETIC

PART TWO:
THE SCOPE AND LIMITS OF
RATIONAL LITERARY THEORY

ACKNOWLEDGMENTS

As a doctoral candidate at Indiana University, Bloomington, Indiana, I owed much to the wise counsel of Drs. Horst Frenz, H.H. Remak, and N. Stallknecht. I especially wish to express my gratitude to Professors Norbert Fuerst and Kenneth Gros Louis as my dissertation advisors for the Ph.D. in comparative literature.

I am also grateful to Professors A.A. Ansari, Magbool H. Khan, Farhat Ullah Khan, and S. Wiqar Husain of the Department of English, Aligarh Muslim University, Utter Pradesh, India, who so graciously published several of my essays in the *Aligarh Journal of English Studies*.

I wish to thank Dr. Frank P. King, retired Professor of History, both for his positive encouragement of my projects and his valuable observations about my past publications.

Then there is Professor Charles F. Herberger, who over the years commended the general direction of my academic efforts but also tirelessly gave me sound advice based on his own remarkable record of publications — literary, historical, anthropological, and philosophical.

Mention must be made of my oldest friend Lorenz Mundstock, Professor of Philosophy, who over the decades offered me fresh understandings into a wide range of thought. For his wife Lee and all his friends, Lorenz's wit and wise insights often brightened a somber day.

I am especially grateful for the moral support, comprehension and caring of Ofelia P. Villagomez.

Last but not least is my debt to Susan Peabody of the School of Law, University of California, who prepared the final manuscript of *Beyond Literary Theory*. Her patience, conscientiousness, initiative, resourcefulness and professional work made possible the completion of the book.

Otherwise, whatever failings the manuscript may have are entirely my own.

PERMISSIONS

Chapter 2, The Obsolescent Critical Language of Today: Permission granted by the Editors of *Orbis Litterarum, International Review of Literary Studies*, Munksgaard, International Publishers, Copenhagen, Denmark to reprint "The Obsolescent Critical Language of Today," originally published in 1975, 30, 125-135.

Chapter 4, Image, Metaphor and Symbol: Permission granted by S. Wiqar Husain, Editor of the *Aligarh Journal of English Studies*, to use the article "Image, Metaphor and Symbol," AJES (1976), Vol. I, No. 2., 157-167.

Chapter 5, The Neo-Aristotelian Analysis of Literature and the Limits of Logic: Permission granted by the University of Chicago Press. Brief excerpts and paraphrases taken from Ronald S. Crane, et al., in *Critics and Criticism, Ancient and Modern* (Chicago: the U of Chicago P, 1952). Permission also granted by S. Wiqar Husain, Editor of the *Aligarh Journal of English Studies*, to use the article "The Neo-Aristotelian Analysis of Literature and the Limits of Logic," AJES (1978), Vol. 3, No. 1, 1-23.

Chapter 6, European Criticism of Anglo-American Formalism: Permission granted by S. Wiqar Hussain, Editor of the *Aligarh Journal of English Studies*, to use the article originally published as "The New Criticism and its Limits," AJES (1996), Vol. 18, No. 1, 1-11.

Chapter 7, The Search for a Science of Literary Criticism: Permission granted by S. Wiqar Husain, Editor of the *Aligarh Journal of English Studies*, to use the article "The Search for a Science of Literary Criticism," AJES (1983), Vol. 8, No. 1, 1-14.

Chapter 8, Scope and Limits of the Freudian Psychoanalytical Interpretation of Literature: Harcourt and Brace, Routledge, England, grants permission to use excerpts and paraphrases taken from C.G. Jung's *Modern Man in Search of a Soul* (A Harvest Book, 1933). Permission also granted by S. Wiqar Husain, Editor of the *Aligarh Journal of English Studies*, to use the article "The Scope and Limits of the Freudian Approach to Literature," AJES (1980), Vol. 5, No. 2, 125-143.

Chapter 9, C.G. Jung's Archetypal Approach to Psyche and its Implications for Interpreting Literature: Princeton University Press grants permission to reproduce the Princeton UP copyrighted material from C.G. Jung's *The Archetypes of the Collective Unconscious*, ISBN 0 691 097 615. Copyrighted 1959 and 1969. Harcourt and Brace, Routledge, England, also granted permission to use excerpts and paraphrases taken from C.G. Jung's *Modern Man in Search of a Soul* (A Harvest Book, 1933). Permission also granted by S. Wiqar Husain, Editor of the *Aligarh Journal of English Studies*, to use the article "The Implications of Jung's Archetypal Approach to Literary Study," AJES (1982), Vol. 7, No. 1, 1-17.

Chapter 10, Paul Diel's *Psychology of Motivation*: Subconscious Fate versus Supraconscious Destiny: Permission granted (in French) to reprint extracts from Paul Diel's *Psychologie de la Motivation*, copyrighted by Presses Universitaires de France, collection "Biblio- thèque de Philosophie contemporaine." Permission also granted by S. Wiqar Husain, Editor of the *Aligarh Journal of English Studies*, to use the article "Paul Diel's *Psychology of Motivation*: Subconscious Fate versus Supraconscious Destiny," AJES, No. 1, 1998.

Chapter 11, Dante's *Vita Nuova* as Riddle: A Medieval Meditation on the Numinous: Permission is granted by *Symposium, A Quarterly Journal in Modern Foreign Languages*, originally published as "Dante's *Vita Nuova* as Riddle" in *Symposium*, 1967, winter issue, 324-330 by Syracuse University Press, N.Y., now under the auspices of Heldref Publications, Washington, D.C.

Chapter 12, Four Dimensions of Signification in *The Old Man and the Sea*: Permission granted by Lydia Zelaya, of Simon and Schuster, to print scattered excerpts totaling approximately 160 words of *The Old Man and the Sea* by Ernest Hemingway. Copyright 1952 by Ernest Hemingway. Copyright renewed in 1980 by Mary Hemingway. Excerpts used by permission of Scribner, a Division of Simon and Schuster, N.Y.

Chapter 13, The Mystical Dimension of J.P. Sartre's *Nausea*: Permission granted by S. Wiqar Husain, Editor of the *Aligarh Journal of English Studies*, to use the article "The Mystical Symbolism of J.P. Sartre's *Nausea*," AJES, (1977), Vol. 2, No. 2, 194-220.

PREFACE

Beyond Literary Theory is not representative of any particular school of critical thought. Rather, it reviews the scope and limits of the rational, scientistic and psychological premises of the past three centuries. However illuminating past paradigms may have been, the great academic writers of the 20th century recognized the shortcomings of logic and scientific methodology to analyze literary works adequately. Moreover, purely intellectualist strategies failed to interpret the elemental power inherent in great literature. Neither knowledge extrinsic to the study of literature nor methods considered intrinsic were able to seize the holistic sense of the literary work or penetrate its inner sanctum. In other words, interpretation needs to go beyond academic theory so as to find the emotional intelligence in literature, which tests our understanding of the meaning of our own lives.

Today we understand that 20th century literary criticism tended to narrow the scope of our comprehension of human experience. This awareness not only leads us to question the viability and validity of the rational and scientific methodology used. More importantly, this perception impels us to discern deeper dimensions of meaning in literature.

The purpose of the first four parts of the manuscript is to demonstrate the scope and limits of distinct academic practices. Beyond these, the text proposes that the individual seek to discover his or her own sentient-spiritual response to the literary work.

As a guide to encouraging the reader to discover an original epistemology and corresponding methodology, *Beyond Literary Theory* offers more than concise summaries of major movements in 20th century theory. The book suggests maxims and methods by which to originate sound and creative criticism of one's own.

By going beyond conventional academic procedures, beyond the common knowledge of literary specialists, and beyond skepticism, agnosticism, and atheism, we begin to perceive spheres of significance which reveal the ultimate meanings of human experience. Such insight opens up an inner spiritual world beyond any orthodox religion or school of academic thought. Study in such depth and breadth can elicit a metamorphosis from academic self-assurance to a sense of awe at humanity's search for the meaning of human destiny. It is time for intellectuals to realize that our emotional intelligence includes acceptance of the mystical dimension of existence.

Eduard H. Strauch, Ph.D.
Mangilao, Gaum, 2000

GENERAL INTRODUCTION

Over the years, the student of literature is exposed to a whole range of literary theories, methods, and terminology, which are believed to enhance his ability to analyze and interpret literature. To be sure, much of this knowledge is useful as a general background for literary study, but there is the danger that such studies, for one reason or another, lead him away from the reason-for-being of literature. That is, the conscientious student may become infatuated with the technical and academic attractions of the discipline to leave forgotten his initial reason for studying literature: to learn about life. *Cl, This true*

In general, a literature student reads to learn vicariously from the lives and experiences of others, their joys and sorrows, their bewilderment at tragedy and their delight in moments of happiness. Through these adventures, the student seeks an epiphany of mind and emotion. The seeker hungers for the passions of life and insights into their significance.

Often the young reader is not sure he can survive the tests of life. Instinctively, he senses that writers have discovered truths that can help him overcome whatever life may bring. If living is a venture, the learner wants to master its meaning.

Yet, ironically, with the growth of his academic knowledge, the student often experiences a loss. The young scholar is no longer ingenuous and untutored. There is the probability he will aspire to scholarly "omniscience." In the name of specialization, he may begin to shut out all experiences which do not lead him directly to academic distinction. Because of this ambition, he may inadvertently shut out his original purpose for studying literature: to come to understand the meaning of human life.

Unfortunately, by becoming primarily a theorist, the budding scholar endangers himself as a species, for over time, literary fashions succeed one another, and theories come and go. A later generation of literature specialists overshadows the earlier ones, depreciating and undervaluing the contributions of the past because, in their new eyes, only up-to-the-minute theories deserve serious attention and respect. To be sure, a denigrating attitude simply shows how naive their literary world view still is. Only when they themselves are surpassed will they understand that the seasoned study of literature entails something deeper than cerebral theory.

Perhaps at this point in their careers, they begin to sense the need to become again a seeker of earthly truths, to search once more for the meaning of a human life.

To be sure, some students never feel the need to underrate or disregard their elders. Perhaps these young scholars share the same respect for the complexity of life. For the seeker of wisdom, the study of literature can mean finding the reason for life in the face of death.

On the other hand, the modesty of some may lead them to fear they will never know enough, never be adequately prepared to analyze and interpret literature until they know all the theories, all the terminology, all the methodologies. Such devotees may spend decades emulating the patience, thoughtfulness, and learning of their scholarly elders. Yet that pursuit may prevent them, finally, from accepting their own originality and insights.

In time, they grow aware of the obsolescent critical language in use and of the shortcomings of erudite descriptions of literary works. To broaden his understanding, the individual may survey yet again the history of western literary criticism from antiquity to contemporary literary theories. He may even undertake to formulate a science of literary studies by utilizing methods and breakthroughs of the emerging sciences. Nevertheless, as rewarding as those experiments might prove to be, he may finally come to realize that he yet needs to fathom literature as the expression of the human mind.

Perhaps he discovers psychoanalysis and analytical psychology. Later, he might delve into existential and humanistic psychology. For a while, the view of literature as psyche seems to hold promise of entering the inner sanctum of human imagination until one day, to his dismay, the student discovers that psychological theories themselves often are no more durable than literary theories. The reason for his keen disappointment is that he began his exploration of this inner realm with all the fervor of someone who had found a new faith.

Gradually, the searching scholar may move into studies of anthropology, numerology, mythology, religion and mysticism. These enrich him by extending and deepening his comprehension of mankind in general. Yet as fascinating as they are in their own right, he is not sure they satisfy his need to understand the essence of the human experience in literature.

One day he recalls the Pro and Contra of Peter Abelard, French philosopher and theologian, medieval professor at the University of Paris. Abelard's work juxtaposed arguments for and against accepted concepts and dogmata. The young scholar of today decides in like manner to review man's amassed knowledge of the past 2,500 years. From the ancient philosophers and medieval theologians, he gleans not a body of knowledge but an accumulation of self-contradictory interpretations of human destiny. Their early wisdom now seems to him a compendium of conflicting world views: monism versus dualism, theism vs. atheism, free will vs. fatalism, Epicureanism vs. Stoicism, hedonism vs. asceticism, etc. Similarly, he discovers the "knowledge" of recent centuries is an ensemble of antithetical theories as: idealism vs. materialism, indeterminism vs. determinism, essentialism vs. nominalism, nominalism vs. realism, vitalism vs. the laws of chemistry and physics. In the 20th century, biologists rejected the law of causality and denounced the reductionism of the physical scientists. Yet the searching scholar believes, nonetheless, there must be something incontestable beyond all this uncertainty, beyond erudite cerebration and beyond all antinomies. But what?

With determination he re-examines the diversity of literary theories he has been exposed to. From antiquity to the end of the 20th century, he studied poetics: the mimetic, pragmatic, expressive, objective, the empirical, the transcendental, the realist, and idealist. Moreover, he contemplated successive literary cultures moving through their distinguishable periods and movements: the classical, the medieval, humanism, the Renaissance, the neoclassical, romanticism, naturalism, symbolism, impressionism, expressionism, etc.

In the 20th century, he noted how, in linguistics, synchronic studies contended with the diachronic. The old antinomism also appeared in the distinction between intrinsic and extrinsic literary criticism. Similar antinomies from the past became *Zeitgeist* studies versus *Geisteswissenschaften* teachings. Hermeneutics mutated into *explication de texte*, semantics led through nominalism to deconstructionism.

Eventually, the earnest student of literature looked upon this accumulated mass of theory with consternation and a sinking sense of despair. The antagonisms between these opposing, competitive, divergent, and incompatible interpretations of literature led him to sense that what supposedly represented man's knowledge per se actually added up to a reductio ad absurdum. The search left the student dissatisfied with any set theory or any eclectic point of view.

Reviewing the stories and poems he had read over the decades, the student-scholar reflected on his own response to the genuine experiences they evoked. He became aware that they too offered contradictory views of life and the world. If so, what did all such contradictions mean in the end? Do they too simply cancel out each other so that the final sum is zero? Does the sum mean that truth simply is relative to time and place, psyche and human contentiousness?

Or does it mean there is no ultimate sense to life and no real meaning to human destiny? Like the message "Vanity of vanities" from Ecclesiastes, that seemed the desperate conclusion.

In that case, has the scholar's life been a senseless game — searching for the meaning of life when there is none? That conclusion is also a real possibility. Yet like Job afflicted by all the ills and evils that man can be heir to, there might remain a tiny glow of light at the center of his dark doubt. If so, what would that infinitesimal flame of faith mean in the vastness of a dark world without meaning?

That dot of light could mean only one thing. It was the secret key to life itself. It moved the scholar to think, to feel, to try to make sense out of human experience.

Why was he still alive? Why did his heart still yearn to discover life's meaning? Throughout the ages why had mankind created myth, religion, philosophy, literature? Was existence, after all, just pure contingency or happenstance?

Could that be? Man is not merely endowed with a brain superior to his animal kindred. Man's mind senses there is a meaning beyond the single life, perhaps beyond the human species.

Finally, another day the seeker awakens to a single, universal law beyond all dualisms and beyond all antinomies. Man is endowed with a teleological instinct. His creation myths, religions, and mystical experiences are evidence of this instinct. Today man understands that all along nature has taught him how all life processes proceed according to some design shaped by some mysterious purpose. Man's ageless instinct teaches him that our knowledge has some purpose, despite the self-contradictory inferences men have drawn over succeeding ages.

The true seeker sees a parallel between his single life and the intellectual history of mankind. Despite the final paradox that death will end the individual's life, man's teleological instinct, nevertheless, guides the individual to search out a purpose to his personal existence. Clearly man's purpose is to seek, to learn, to live. Clearly the individual's knowledge brings him strength, man's wisdom brings him consolation.

At this point the solitary scholar realizes he must leave behind much of the academic theory and analytical practice of the past. He must do so to rediscover his own novitiate intuitions into life's experiences.

As he looks directly and deeply into the mirror of literature, what does he see? There he sees neither fool nor sage, neither devil nor angel. His own image is as full of mystery as human destiny itself. He sees an intelligence in quest of an ultimate truth to live by.

An inner voice asks a final question. "Why are you here?" After a long silence, the same voice answers "You are here as your own Center. You are your own Purpose, your own Meaning." That is what literature teaches us. That is why we study literature.

This may be true for him & me & may others, but not as a general law of lit.

PART ONE:
THE HISTORICAL SEARCH FOR A LITERARY AESTHETIC

CHAPTER 1
THE TRADITIONAL PERSPECTIVE: LITERATURE AS BEAUTY, TRUTH, MEANING AND THE SUBLIME

I. INTRODUCTION

Twentieth Century thinkers and academicians are acutely aware of the fragmentation of knowledge due to the intensive specialization going on in fields of research. We all know there is an urgent need to discover a unifying epistemology, which can explain holistically how all the fragments fit together into some great truth or meaning. It is with this need in mind that I undertake to present my paper, for I intend to try to discover if four distinct and at times seemingly disparate critical traditions do not, in fact, embrace a single vision, which might explain the reason-for-being of literature.

Across the past twenty-five centuries, critics and philosophers have generally thought about literature in terms of four distinct traditions: literature as beauty, as truth, as meaning, and as expressing the sublime. Each critical tradition has centered its attention on a salient aspect, which has been emphasized over and above all the others. However, no contemporary critic has yet scanned those 2,500 years either to decipher the distinct pattern of each tradition as such or to juxtapose these patterns so as to perceive the grand design behind them all. My general purpose then is to scan the four traditions.

Yet how can the development of literary thought be of any interest to mathematicians, scientists, or even humanists in other disciplines? There will be no such interest — if we assume it is not necessary to grasp the other man's point of view, no need for mankind to understand each other, no need for a meeting of minds among branches of knowledge, nations, religions. and peoples. However, as has been so clearly manifest in theories of science, ignorance of one theory may be ignorance of the keystone to knowledge itself. It is my belief that literature is one such keystone to understanding the heart and mind of mankind.

Hence it is my humble hope that my worthy colleagues may catch a spark from this presentation of literary thought, a tiny, true idea which may illuminate in their own minds a series of fresh and creative conjectures about their own fields of knowledge. In sum, I hope I am able to bring you some light about our ways of thinking about life and literature where — before in your minds there may have been obscurity, misunderstanding, or complete indifference.

II. LITERATURE AS BEAUTY

Our understanding of literature as beauty comes from the ancient Greeks and Romans, who provided the Occident with what is called the classical tradition. To the ancients, all art and thought was modeled on the rationally ordered and harmonious universe in which all parts were manifestly interrelated as a living totality. The search of ancient thought was to discover the universal forms and principles governing that universe. Hence the artist was concerned to discover persisting and objective forms and to imitate the essential in nature. As a consequence, the by-products of the artist's endeavour to imitate the orderliness of nature became the classical ideals of balance, symmetry, and unity.

The tradition of literature as beauty is largely upheld by certain key figures in the history of literary thought. Thus we will focus our attention on the following men who have contributed most significantly to the tradition: Plato, Aristotle, Horace, Longinus, John Dryden, Alexander Pope, William Wordsworth, S. T. Coleridge, and T. S. Eliot. We shall also briefly touch on the intrinsic approach to literature which so distinctly characterized literary study in the 20th century.

Plato (427-347 B.C.)

In his *Republic*, Book X, the Greek philosopher, Plato banished poetry from his ideal state because she could exercise such a wanton appeal to men. However, Plato's Puritanic sternness resisted in vain the sheer beauty of poetry. Later relenting his earlier severity, he declared he would let poetry return to his ideal state if she proved herself as useful as she was enticing and beautiful. So although Plato's philosophy failed to describe in any detail the beauty of literature, he was, nevertheless, keenly affected by her powers. The irony of Plato's position is that his own philosophical writings are the most poetical of all philosophers.

Aristotle (384-322 B.C.)

Since Plato was Aristotle's teacher over many years, Aristotle is the spiritual son of Plato, but as an intelligent son, he thought out his own philosophy of life and literature. Indeed, Aristotle probed more deeply into the beauty, truth, and meaning of literature than anyone before him.

In contrast to Plato's abstract Pythagorean view of reality, Aristotle's own view of the universal forms was that of a biologist. He saw natural forms working through the concrete and material to fulfil themselves. For Aristotle the "ideal" was the way things would be if the form or principle functioning in animate beings were carried out to its logical conclusion.

Hence Aristotle saw reality as a process of becoming or developing. Form in poetry shaped and developed experience into unified meaning. Thus as Aristotle explains in his *Poetics*, the plot of a tragedy is a chain of events which moves through cause to effect. In other words, plot or tragic form shows the way things would be if they followed the law of probability or necessity. In sum, to Aristotle, beauty was not the result of some static, geometric form as a temple; rather, beauty was the result of dynamic forces at work in nature and in human beings as they worked out their individual destinies.

In aesthetic terms, Aristotle's *Poetics* is the first treatise to speak of the organic unity necessary to a literary work, where all the parts are organically related and united. The proper structure of plot was to have a beginning, middle and end with the whole made up of a given order and magnitude. Thus to Aristotle, a piece of literature must manifest living beauty.

Horace (65-8 B.C.)

Horace's treatise on the *Art of Poetry* provides any writer with sound advice as to which literary qualities to pursue. The writer should strive for clarity of outline, a clear cut sense of technique, prudence, good sense, and urbanity of taste. The first requirement of a literary work was to have simplicity and unity. Such simplicity and clarity let the beauty shine through.

Longinus (First Century A.D.)

Although Longinus centered his attention on the emotional transport a piece of lofty writing can evoke, his treatise *On the Sublime* also dealt with beauty *per se*. To Longinus, stately composition required harmony of language, because such harmony served both to convince us of the rightness of the argument and to inspire us to accept the noble passions expressed. Hence word and thought must be arranged in perfect harmony. Thus beauty is needed to organize, express and evoke man's noblest thoughts and most sublime feelings.

John Dryden (1631-1700)

Dryden's *Essay on Dramatic Poetry* (1668) concerned itself with neo-classical ideals as refinement, correctness, strict unity, and simple clarity. His key term "propriety" meant in part the elegant adaptation of thought and word to the subject. More importantly, propriety meant "proportion," that is, the subordination of the parts of a composition to the totality and the means to the end. Propriety assured the total harmony and unity of the artwork.

In drama, certain rules must be followed to attain the degree of unity necessary in a proper drama — hence the famous three unities of time, place, and actions. A play must take place in twenty-four hours;

the same basic scene must be kept throughout the play; and the drama should have one great and complete action. The conscientious use of the three unities was to achieve greater beauty of form.

However, at the same time, Dryden defended modern English dramatists particularly against French tragic writers. To Dryden, English drama gave greater pleasure through mixing comedy and tragedy and through its greater variety of characters and plots. Hence English drama not only had greater truth to life; its greater variety enhanced the beauty of the dramatic experience.

Alexander Pope (1688-1744)

Pope's *Essay on Criticism* (1711) echoed the basic thoughts of Horace but expressed the ancient ideas in fresh, graceful, and elegant lines of verse. Pope's essay is largely dedicated to defining the general qualities a critic needs, and the essay gives the particular laws the critic should follow. For instance, Pope urged the literary critic to judge a piece of writing as an entity and in the spirit the author wrote it. In addition, Pope had worthwhile things to say about literature as beauty. A work should be judged for its total beauty and not for striking parts, conceits, or language as distinct from the whole.

Pope also advised an author to use true expressions to clarify and improve his subject. Let the style suit the subject and let all the parts of a piece of writing be subordinate to its purpose. Hence truth and clarity of style make the beauty clearer.

William Wordsworth (1770-1850)

Wordsworth considered man's most distinctive trait to be his emotional and imaginative capacity to respond to the eternal forms of nature and to the meaning of our orderly universe. Consequently, as a poet, he wanted to awaken in his readers a keener awareness of the beauty in nature and a greater appreciation of the wisdom inherent in our common experience. As a poet, he wanted to educate our feelings to the exquisitiveness of life. His ultimate aim was to broaden and deepen our sympathy with mankind and with the natural world we live in.

S.T. Coleridge (1772-1834)

Coleridge was an original and somewhat eccentric poet-critic much influenced by German philosophy in general and Immanuel Kant in particular. For this reason, Coleridge's interpretation of beauty was in certain ways richer and more complex than the interpretation of the critics who preceded him.

Influenced also by Aristotle's world view, Coleridge's conception of beauty derived from his understanding of nature as an organic, unfolding process. The reality of nature is an activity wherein the universal and the particular fulfill each other. In a similar way, art should seek to emulate the processes of nature by reconciling the universal and the particular. Put another way, beauty represents the perception of the universal form omnipresent in the world's multiple phenomena and parts.

Coleridge's conception was most clearly stated in his *Biographia Literaria*, Chapter XIV, where he distinguished a poem from all other compositions in that it provides delight in each tiny part as well as in the entire entity. Furthermore, a legitimate poem would have organic unity such that all its parts mutually sustain each other. Correspondingly, the ideal poet will activate the whole soul of man so that all the reader's own faculties are subordinated to the whole effect of the poem. The poet achieves this effect by suffusing a spirit of unity and harmony throughout the poem. Ultimately it is the poet's synthesizing and magical imagination that fuses everything into exquisite beauty. Hence imagination is the ultimate power to create beauty as it reconciles such opposites as the general with the concrete, the idea with the image, and the representative with the individual. If imagination subordinates art to nature, beauty itself unites the fragments of experience into meaning.

In a public lecture on Shakespeare, Coleridge distinguished between mechanic and organic form. Mechanic form was a predetermined form superimposed on raw material, not growing out of the properties of that material. On the other hand, organic form shaped itself from within, and its full development was reached when the outward form was one and the same with the inner. Such is the life, such is the form. What Coleridge means is that the literary work should aspire to organic beauty by emulating the perfect beauty of natural forms themselves.

T. S. Eliot (1888-1965)

Eliot's criticism is concerned with the problem of form and style. He is interested in the formal qualities intrinsic to literature as a distinct craft. In reviewing the best tradition of English poetry, he came to have high regard for hard clarity of outline, the sure sense of structure, and sparseness of style.

In his famous essay "Tradition and the Individual Talent," he stresses the point that it is not "sublimity" of the subject matter of a poem that counts, nor "greatness," nor intensity of emotions. Rather, what counts is the intensity of the artistic process *per se*. Hence his concern is with literature as artistic beauty. However, as we shall see later, his essay has much more to say about literature as truth..

The Twentieth Century Study of Literature

We have seen that Coleridge considered a literary work to have a life of its own because the work embodies organic unity. A literary work is organic in that all its parts interact harmoniously and work together efficiently to form one total meaning. Similarly T.S. Eliot considered the poem a single organism with its own meaning.

Out of such understandings, there arose in the Twentieth Century the intrinsic study of literature, which came to concentrate on the aesthetic qualities of the individual work. This concentration meant that knowledge exterior to literature was avoided in order to concentrate the explication on the literary work itself.

In the 1930s and 1940's, the so-called New Critics held the credo that poetry itself is a source of knowledge to be communicated in its own terms. Through a close reading of individual texts, they studied single parts to discover the intimate inter-connections among the poetic elements. However, the critics were themselves were criticized for isolating parts of the artwork and neglecting to take account of the poem's totality. Be that as it may, the intrinsic study of literature shows that Twentieth Century criticism has concerned itself with literature as a thing of organic and semantic beauty.

Summary

The tradition of literature as beauty may be summed up as follows:

1. Historically, the artist sought to discover the essential traits and eternal forms in nature. The intellectual model for literature has been for millennia the rationally ordered and harmonious universe.

2. A literary composition must aspire to the organic unity we find in natural forms themselves. Thus all parts must be subordinated to the living whole, and the means of expression must be subordinate to the end or aim of the writing.

3. Since literature aspires to retracing the education of the human being to the realities and demands of life, the literary work must shape the experiences it portrays into a unified meaning.

4. Beauty in literature derives not only from natural organic beauty but also from noble passion, artistic sophistication, deep sympathy with mankind, and a consistent moral outlook on life.

II. LITERATURE AS TRUTH

In classical antiquity, art strove to imitate nature objectively, that is, to duplicate the essential and significant in its model. The aim of classical thinking was to know the truth, and the purpose of classical art was to translate and transmit that knowledge. Ultimately the aim of classical imitation or mimesis was to decipher the total truth, character, meaning and form of the rationally ordered universe.

Plato

In reaction to the relativism of his time, Plato's philosophy was a search for certainty, for a reality that was absolute, fixed and perfect. To him, the tangible material world was a mere appearance of reality, an imperfect copy of the final and absolute reality he sought. To Plato, the persisting order of the universe was the sole reality to believe in. Hence for Plato truth was to be found in order.

Plato was opposed to art and poetry, since art deceived the senses and poetry encouraged human weakness by indulging the passions. On the other hand, imagination misled us to believe what was not true. By contrast, reason and reason alone could conceive true ideas. Hence in opposition to the rich literary heritage of his culture, Plato insisted that philosophy, not poetry, aimed at ultimate truth and was, therefore, the ideal teacher of mankind. To Plato, ultimate truth transcended the changing flux of material things to attain the idea of absolute Being.

Aristotle

In Aristotle's *Poetics*, he discussed both the beauty and truth of tragedy. Because tragedy shows us the fundamental truth of fate and human destiny, Aristotle firmly believed literature offers its own great measure of truth. To Aristotle, literature not only represents the true but also it has a distinct moral effect on the mind. Indeed, the tragic poet's task is to show what may happen to human beings according to the law of probability governing human nature. For this reason, poetry is more philosophical and higher than history, for poetry expresses universal truths about mankind whereas history dwells on particular events.

Horace

Horace provided us with a famous dictum. The writer's aim should be to teach and delight. In other words, the literary work must both please the reader and be applicable to his life. To be sure, the way for a writer to attain this goal is to choose a subject equal to his powers and to use a style appropriate to the subject. Put another way, the writer must write about what he knows and adopt a style which will explain that knowledge simply and effectively to his reader. Hence the knowledge he communicates is the truth as he sees it in a language that is true to the subject.

If the first requisite of the writer is to have wisdom and intellectual insight, a good critic must have comparable qualities. A good critic must serve as a whetstone capable of sharpening the mettle or steel of the writer by excising the weak and ineffectual in a composition and enhancing its strengths. Hence the role of the critic is to sharpen the truth that the author is attempting to communicate.

Sir Philip Sidney (1554-1586)

With Sidney the English Renaissance found a spokesman who renewed the great ideas of the classical tradition and added a new understanding of the role of literature in educating mankind. Sidney's primary concern was the quality of the truth literature gives us. If Aristotle's theory of poetry is the skeleton structure of Sidney's thought, his other sources are Plato, Horace, and Christianity. As regards literature as truth, Sidney believed the ideal aim of poetry was to present the reality of human experience. If poetry cannot be regarded as literal truth since it is not rooted in actual historical happenings, literature does reveal general patterns of human interaction and their general meanings. Literature is more effective than philosophy because it provides vivid images of the general truths it discloses. In short, poetry provides examples with its generalizations.

However, Sidney is concerned with a greater truth than either philosophy or history can teach. To Sidney, the aim of all learning is virtuous action, that is, the ability to feel and react according to human truth. By portraying "ideal" types, in Plato's sense of perfect and absolute ideas, literature renders an image of the good that men can follow. In other words, by portraying convincing moral types of human character, literature encourages us to emulate such ideal human beings. Hence the great merit of literature is its portrayal of moral truth.

Alexander Pope

Pope's *Essay on Criticism* has many germane things to say about literature as truth. Echoing Socrates' injunction to "Know Thyself," Pope expresses the same truth more elegantly as in the following lines:

Be sure yourself and your reach to know,
How far your genius, taste, and learning go;
Launch not beyond your depth . . ..

(lines 48-50)

Obviously truth in literature begins with the author knowing what he is talking about.

Moreover, Pope has an ultimate criterion for truth: Nature. He writes:

First follow Nature, and your judgement frame
By her just standard, which is still the same:
Unerring Nature, still divinely bright
One clear, unchanged, and universal light,
Life, force, and beauty, must to all impart
At once the source, and end, and test of art.

(lines 68–74)

Hence for Pope, Nature is the ultimate source, the purpose, and the final test of art that is true.

Furthermore, in order to clarify how neo-classical rules correspond to the ultimate truth of Nature, Pope explains:

Those Rules of old discovered, not devised,
Are Nature still, but Nature methodized.

(lines 88–89)

Pope also advises the critic to be true to his calling by analyzing and interpreting literature truly. The critic needs to be comprehensive, thorough, and meticulous in studying the script before him. Pope says:

You then whose judgement the right course would steer
Know well each ancient's proper character;
His fable, subject, scope in every page;

Religion, country, genius of his age.
Without all these at once before your eyes,
Cavil you may, but never criticize.

(lines 118–123)

As a final admonition to both critic and writer, Pope warns that truth cannot be discovered through ignorance nor explained with superficial knowledge. He concludes, "A little learning is a dangerous thing." (line 21 5).

Samuel Johnson (1709–1784)

Johnson is an Eighteenth Century man who broadened and deepened our understanding of the truth in literature. Holding to the classical conviction that the aim of art is the mental and moral enlargement of man, Johnson believes literature attains this goal through the moving and imaginative presentation of truth. A writer is to seek out the principles, characteristics, and values which are universal and enduring. Johnson wants the writer to seek out the objective knowledge of general human nature.

To be able to achieve this truth, Johnson advises the author to avoid prejudices and personal eccentricities. Johnson wants the poet to reveal the general truths which will always be the same for mankind, and the first criterion is truth to life, but this truth is not to be found in the unique and transitory. For this reason Johnson admires Shakespeare who portrayed the genuine progeny of humanity. Hence Johnson extolled the portrayal of the interior character of man, the inner truth, man as a psychological and philosophical being.

Furthermore, Johnson urged critics and thinkers to judge the present in the light of the past. He wanted authors to uncover those human experiences which have survived beyond any particular place or age. In addition, he encouraged authors to direct their minds by reason and by the intelligent use of experience. Hence he wanted literature to embrace the total truth about humanity.

Above all, Johnson wanted the author's imagination regulated by knowledge and one's writings to be directed and governed by sanity.

For Johnson, sanity represented the soundest, highest truth to life and literature. Pursuing this ideal, the poet will be a true interpreter of nature, the legislator of mankind, and a sane guide for the thoughts and manners of future mankind.

William Wordsworth

Wordsworth appreciably refined our understandings of literature as truth. In his Preface to the Second Edition of the *Lyrical Ballads* (1802), his aim in studying the "incidents and situations from common life" was to trace the "primary laws of our nature, chiefly, as regards the manner in which we associate ideas in a state of excitement," thus showing how external nature can mould and develop man's mental and emotional character. Hence literature is to discover that mankind is truest to itself when found in their natural environment. In other words, Wordsworth wanted to study how the primary and permanent aspects of nature influence the permanent and essential qualities of human nature.

However, Wordsworth pursues a more intimate truth as well, for he believes our thoughts are the representatives of all our past feelings. The reason the poet is able to express the truths of human nature is that the poet possesses a more than usual organic sensibility. Moreover, he has thought long and deeply about his own experiences. Poetry becomes the breath and finer spirit of all knowledge because its object is to portray the universal passions of men. Thus poetry is the first and last of all knowledge and truth.

S. T. Coleridge

Coleridge was much concerned with the human mind and how it deals with truth and reality. To begin with, he distinguished between the understanding and reason. For Coleridge, *understanding* is directed toward the concrete, real world through our senses whereas reason is direct insight into the universal. On the other hand, Coleridge's concept of imagination shows the complexity and richness of the way the mind imaginatively attains truth and reality. First, imagination fuses the insights of reason with both the impressions of the senses and the conceptions of the understanding. Second, imagination creates a balance between general and concrete, between the idea and the image, between the individual and the representative. Third, imagination is a repetition in the finite mind of the eternal act of creation. Fourth, imagination serves as the living Power and prime Agent of all human perception. In sum, without imagination, we cannot perceive human truth in all its complexity and richness, and we can only find the ultimate truth to life itself through emulating the eternal, creative power in nature and the universe.

Percy Bysshe Shelley (1792-1822)

Shelley's various views on literature are complex, but his concern with literature as truth is clear. His first premise is that the poet is a legislator and prophet because the poet discovers the laws of the present and beholds the future in the present. Shelley's second premise is that a poem is the creation of actions which correspond to the abiding forms of human nature. The role of poetry is to awaken and enlarge the mind by making it the receptacle of a thousand thoughts till then unapprehended. In other words, poetry awakens us to the thousands of implications in our commonly shared human experience.

Shelley also sees poetry as related to knowledge and science. Since poetry emanates from the mind of God, the Creator, poetry is divine; and since poetry is divine, it is at once the centre and circumference of knowledge, and thus it encompasses all science. Shelley closes his essay "Defense of Poetry" with the memorable thought "Poets are the unacknowledged legislators of the world." In short, poets show us the durable truths of our evanescent lives.

John Keats (1795-1821)

Keats died from tuberculosis at the age of twenty six so that he hardly lived long enough to leave us a coherent philosophy of literature. However, he left us with some penetrating insights into literature as truth and into the relationship between truth and beauty. To attain truth, an author or thinker must first assume a paradoxical state of mind, which Keats called the "negative capability." That is, a thinker must be able to negate or lose his own identity in his work so as to achieve something larger than himself through imaginative identification with his subject.

Furthermore, Keats was against logical analysis because mere abstractions and the passion for system for its own sake can distort organic beauty into preconceived notions or into pseudo-patterns of knowledge. In particular, emerging sciences would do well to listen to Keats, warning against false theories and pseudo-systems parading themselves as ultimate truths.

On the other hand, Keats' concept of "negative capability" offers a more profound truth as well. In a letter written when he was twenty-two years old, he cautioned that a man must learn to live with doubts, mysteries and uncertainties without trying to escape that state of mind. Keats means at least two things by this admonition: (1) that the chaotic state of things can nurture creativity since creativity means a true search for Beauty, and (2) that despite death and chaos, Beauty reigns supreme throughout the universe. That fact should allay our ephemeral fears, for there is a vast, superior order and truth to existence. As Keats so aptly said in the closing lines of his poem, "Ode on a Grecian urn":

> Beauty is truth, truth beauty — that is all
> Ye know on earth, and all ye need to know.

These simple words mean more than they say. Ultimately they imply that what is organically or intellectually beautiful has a superior order to it because it is sustained by a superior truth.

William Hazlitt (1778-1830)

Hazlitt also offers us valuable insights into literature as truth. For Hazlitt, the purpose of art is not to enable the artist to express himself. Rather, its goal is to express a heightened awareness and perceptive grasp of objective reality, which is located in the world about us. To Hazlitt, nature is in a state of flux as an interweaving of relationships. Similarly the human truth of our lives is to be found in the mutual interaction of our diverse passions, feelings, and thoughts. For this reason, Hazlitt holds tragedy in high esteem. Tragedy superbly expresses the dynamic truth of human nature in the fact of situations and events which challenge the hero's life.

Hazlitt uses a simple but striking metaphor to describe what art does. Art acts as a microscope for the mind by convening every object around us into a little universe itself. Hence a literary work intensifies our perception of truth and magnifies our power to compare vital infinitesimal truths.

Hazlitt's central concept *gusto* describes the power or passion used in defining an object. Put another way, gusto gives us the truth of human feeling. Consequently, gusto in literature enables an author to portray vividly man's nature, imagination, and passions. Thus poetry is an emanation of the innermost being of our nature.

Hazlitt illustrates his point by describing Shakespeare's genius. Shakespeare's originality came from his power to see every object from the precise point of view others would see it. Hence originality serves to express the truth by showing us what everyone had missed before. Therefore, originality means the capacity to discover new and valuable truths in human nature.

On the other hand, imagination enables us to absorb experience and transform it to enduring human truths. Indeed, imagination is largely the sympathetic identification with life around us so that we attain "a more intense perception of truth." This same sympathetic identification in turn enables us to apply our knowledge and experience to the lives of others. In sum, Hazlitt concludes, "In art, in taste, in life, in speech you decide from feeling, not reason."

Matthew Arnold (1822-1888)

Arnold is the most eminent 19th century critic to concern himself with literature as truth. Arnold was deeply concerned with seeing things as they really are and in acting according to the true and valid. Rather than seeing things according to a preconceived notion, he insisted on seeing things in their true nature.

Arnold also wanted man's various pursuits to be evaluated and ranked according to how successfully they developed man's receptivity to culture and truth. In other words, Arnold was clearly conscious that there are degrees of truth. Furthermore, he regarded literature as the vital transmitter of human experience, because literature refines man's emotional understandings and subtly instills knowledge. Put another way, Arnold felt that literature increases the scope and sophistication of the mind's imaginative horizons. Hence literature extends the range of truth by sensitizing us to the experience of all mankind. In sum, by teaching honesty and sincerity, literature shows us that the heart and mind are one because the heart teaches us what the mind alone cannot know. Hence literature completes intellectual truth with humane truth. Indeed, by its truth to life, literature teaches us "how to live." Thus literature ultimately teaches us how to apply human wisdom to human life.

T. S. Eliot

In his essay "Tradition and the individual Talent," Eliot makes a plea for objectivity and impersonality in writing poetry. To Eliot, objectivity means requiring the artist to submerge his personality to the technical process of refining a poem. However, of more consequence is his conception of tradition. On the one hand, because tradition shows what are the abiding truths, it enables us to realize which literary approaches and qualities continue to have a vital effect on us. Tradition encourages us to use this knowledge. On the other hand, Eliot points out that one aspect of tradition is often forgotten, that is, the tradition of *change*, of tradition itself adapting to the needs and conditions of changing times. Indeed, when a new work of art is created, something happens simultaneously to all the art works which preceded it. Hence the past is altered by the present as the present is directed by the past.

Eliot's conception of tradition is similar to that of Johnson. who believed the poet must divest himself of the prejudices of his age and country and attempt to disclose general truths which will always be the same. Eliot also stresses the need to discover enduring truths. To Eliot, the historical sense involves the perception of the pastness of the past and its presence. Hence the historical sense compels a man to write not merely with his own generation in his bones but with the whole of European literature in him. The historical sense is a sense of both the transitory and the timeless.

Eliot is keenly concerned with how the poet can attain larger objective truth beyond the poet's private mind. The mind of his own country or of Europe is more important than the poet's private mind. The larger mind abandons nothing on the way.

In addition, Eliot regards the poetic process as a means to attaining truth. As he uses the concept "objective correlative" in his essay "Hamlet and his Problems," the artwork must have a set of objects, a situation, a chain of events which correspond to the particular emotion defined by the artwork. Hence rather than poetry being a means of self-expression, Eliot advocates that the process of writing be one of continuous self-sacrifice, a continual extinction of personality. Clearly his outlook is akin to that of the modern scientist since Eliot considers it possible to attain objective truth only through self-abnegation. This is the meaning behind Eliot's definition of poetry as an escape from emotion, an escape from personality. Eliot expects from us a selfless truth-seeking.

I. A. Richards (1893-1982)

Richards is another eminent figure in the century. His concern with literature as truth is perhaps most striking when he discusses the lessons he has learned from Confucius's *Chung Yung (The Doctrine of the Mean, or Equilibrium and Harmony)*. To Confucius, sincerity is the secret of the good life and the way to Heaven. The superior man seeks out self-completion in order to complete other men. The superior man effects a union of the external and internal, striving towards a more perfect order. From Confucius's point of view, Richards concluded that true intuition derives from sincerity because sincerity seeks to create a more perfect order within the mind. To be sincere is to act, feel and think in accordance with one's true nature.

In Richard's essay "Doctrine in Poetry" *(Practical Criticism)*, he prescribes a way we can test our response to a poem. The test of a poem is its sincerity and the feelings it arouses in the context of certain existential truths centered on man's eternal human condition. We may test the sincerity of a literary work by seeing if the poem deals with any of the following truths and human concerns:

(1) Man's sense of isolation and loneliness in the Universe;

(2) The inexplicable paradox of birth and death;

(3) The inconceivable immensity of the Universe;

(4) Man's place in the perspective of Time; and

(5) The enormity of man's ignorance.

To Richards, these are the most incomprehensible and inexhaustible objects of human meditation.

From reflecting on such existential truths, Richards draws a bold conclusion. If man is ignorant, it is his own fault. The reason is that man has not sought to make his thoughts truly sincere. Put another way, man has yet to fathom the paradoxical truths omnipresent in great literature and in life itself.

The Extrinsic Study of Literature

Parallel to the development of the intrinsic study of literature, the Twentieth Century witnessed a clear, corollary development of the extrinsic approach to literature.

The suspicion that studying literature alone might be an inadequate means of grasping the truths it contains led some critics to draw on other academic disciplines to illuminate the multiple truths in a literary work. Those critics who consider a piece of literature the product of an individual artist use biography and psychology as a means to explain the presence of facts and experiences in the work. On the other hand, critics who consider a literary work as determined by the author's economic, social, or political environment look to sociology, history, economics, and anthropology for insights into the substance and sense of the work. Critics of a more humanistic inclination will connect the literary work to the history of the arts or to the history of ideas. Still other critics find a literary work embodies a *Zeitgeist* or the spirit of the age which produced the work. All these extrinsic approaches assume literature encompasses truths either as an expression of its environment or as an example of the culture from which the literary work sprang.

Summary

The tradition of literature as truth may be recapitulated in thirteen summations:

1. The classical tradition, inherited from antiquity, embraced the faith that the rationally ordered universe concealed and revealed some eternal truth and meaning. Thus the aim of classical thought and art was to discover the knowledge the universe reflected.

2. After Aristotle, critics felt that literature dealt with universal truths about human nature and, as such, literature produced a positive moral effect on the human mind.

3. The writer must have knowledge and skill to translate and transmit the truth as he sees it. By using clear language true to the subject, the author can truly teach and delight his audience.

4. Literature seeks to discover the general meanings to characteristic human actions. By vivid examples, it both teaches great human verities and inspires men to virtuous action.

5. However, to attain verity, the writer must know himself and how far his intelligence and knowledge go. If truth to nature is the first criterion of true writing, true judgement is the result of comprehensive and thorough knowledge of the subject.

6. The aim of literature is twofold:

    (a) the mental and moral enlargement of mankind and
    (b) the moving and imaginative presentation of the true.

    The way to achieve this twofold aim is:

    (c) to rid oneself of personal biases and prejudice and
    (d) to seek, instead, to discover the universal and enduring truths of mankind. Above all, let sanity be your guide in word,

thought and deed.

7. The writer must discover the permanent and essential qualities of human nature. He must come to terms with his own feelings as educated by his own sensibility and by his own past. In addition, he must think long and deeply about the veracity of his own experiences. Only in this way can the writer learn to portray truly the universal thoughts and passions of mankind.

8. Imagination alone enables us to perceive the complexity and richness of human truth, and only through imagination can the poet learn to emulate the eternal, creative power at the heart of the universe.

9. The successful writer will awaken in us the thousands of implications to our commonly shared human experience. Because of poetry's truth to human nature, it is the centre and circumference of all knowledge.

10. The author must learn to live with the terrible facts of life — the sickness, the suffering, the death — without trying to explain away their awful mystery. On the other hand, life teaches one invariable law — that beauty is truth and truth is beauty. Indeed, that knowledge is reason enough for a writer to go on living. The true writer senses that the superior order of beauty comes from a superior truth somewhere at the centre of life.

11. Furthermore, sympathetic identification enables the writer to transform his ephemeral experience into viable human truths. Literature ultimately teaches him how to apply human wisdom to human life.

12. If one truth of tradition is to learn what is of lasting worth, a corollary truth is that tradition shows us the wisdom of creative change. In another light, truth should transcend the personal to incorporate the whole of one's culture. Put another way, an author must dedicate himself selflessly to seeking the true.

13. Finally, the writer should test his understanding of the truth against man's sense of isolation and loneliness in the universe, against the paradox of life and death, and against the enormity of man's ignorance.

III. LITERATURE AS MEANING

The Classical Tradition

Since to the ancient thinkers the universe was a meaningful process, in which all parts were interrelated in a living whole, and since ancient philosophers sought out the pattern of meanings to human experience, the search for the significance of existence, life, and human destiny was central to ancient Greek thought, art, and literature.

Plato

By contrast to the Greek tradition which believed literature served to probe into the meanings of human experience, Plato questioned the moral and educative effect of poetry. Plato maintained that poetry appealed to the inferior nature in man rather than to his higher nature. If anything, poetry offered inferior truths and consequently inferior meanings.

Aristotle

When Aristotle wrote on tragic plot, he was referring to the meaning of human experience. The inner coherence or structure of a plot arises from what characters do out of the inevitability of their natures. In tragedy a man decides his fate by the decisions he takes or the actions he pursues. He shapes the meaning of his life by embracing or avoiding some moral purpose.

Aristotle splendidly brings out man's sense of destiny when he discusses simple and complex plot. In simple plot, the hero experiences a change of fortune from prosperity to adversity simply through a tragic flaw in his nature. In complex plot, the change of fortune is accompanied by a reversal, a change to an opposite fate, subject to the necessity of the hero's character. The change can also be accompanied by recognition, that is, by a change from ignorance to knowledge, producing love or hatred between persons destined for good or ill fortune. Hence we witness in tragedy a charactor's misfortune which comes about through some error of judgement or frailty in his character. In the best tragedy, the tragic incident arises out of a family situation.

In sum, the perfect tragedy teaches us the consequences of our pride, injustice, rashness or blindness. Seen in this context, literature teaches us the meaning of self-knowledge, the need for sound decisions, and the profound reasons for different human destinies. To Aristotle, literature teaches man the higher meanings of life.

The Hebrews and the Church Fathers

To the ancient Hebrews, a poet did not simply create a poem but was led to discover the Truth by the guidance of God. Such was the clear case of the prophets. Hence Scripture embodied the living Truth. Indeed, the Hebrews saw God Himself as Creator, and the shadowy world was his poem. In the miraculous instance of Christ, God gave us light and Logos.

The Church Fathers felt impelled to write interpretations to the Holy Scriptures, which became one basis for literary exegesis down through the centuries. They believed the masses could only understand the literal meanings whereas the elite were gifted with the insight to apprehend the true meaning deeply imbedded in words and in eschatological events.

Saint Jerome, who translated the Holy Scripture, wrote thoughtful commentaries on nearly every book of canon. In addition, he wrote tracts on literal and figurative meaning. Other Latin Fathers in turn emphasized the meanings of images and figures. So from this heritage of Biblical exegesis we see that a piece of writing may contain literal as well as figurative implications.

Furthermore, in the hermeneutics of the Bible, there are at least four interpretations or meanings possible to Holy Scripture:

(1) the literal or historical sense;
(2) the allegorical;
(3) the moral, and
(4) the anagogical or mystical sense. (Anagoge is the mystical or spiritual interpretation of words, figures or events in the Old and New Testament.)

Similarly, as Islamic Scholars well know, there is possible a four-level exegesis to the Holy Qur'an. Indeed, there is thought to be no Koranic verse which does not have four meanings:

(1)   the limited sense (hand);
(2) the exoteric (zahir);
(3) the esoteric (Batin); and
(4) the divine plan (mottala).

Hence from these two hermeneutic traditions, we learn that there may be strata of significance in any given scriptural or literary text since literature embodies within it both a philosophical and religious heritage. Certainly literature can bridge the most mundane meanings and the most sublime meanings language is capable of.

The Problems of Meaning

Modern critics argue as to whether or not literature can make significant statements. Indeed semanticists still dispute the very meaning of meaning. In part, the problem centres on whether a communication is a literal statement of some reality or whether it is an idealized statement of some universal.

This debate leads us to recall Samuel Johnson who thought poetic imitation should not be of the individual but of the species. Put another way, what is representative in a poem should point to a universal with a significant objective reality behind it. We are also reminded of Sir Philip Sidney who considered poetry as superior both to history and philosophy. Hence if literal meaning can be compared and contrasted to some ideal meaning, then there is not simply more than one kind of meaning; there is also a whole range and spectrum of meanings —

perhaps even degrees of meaning.

This fact may explain why for most critics neither reason nor empirical evidence can attain the quality of significance they are seeking. Rather, they consider imagination as the means of reaching superior or transcendental meaning. Even skeptical Plato in his "Ion" believed the gods chose the poet to intuit the highest truths and meanings in existence.

F. W. J. Schelling (1775-1854)

Schelling is of particular interest to us because he strongly influenced Coleridge's conception of imagination. Because Schelling saw the universe as monistic with the divine essence located in every particular object, he considered imagination a superior cognitive power because it perceives this essence even in the mundane. Put another way, if the whole guides and controls every single part, then only by penetrating the meaning of every part can we imagine the significance of the whole. Through the use of imagination, we penetrate a seemingly lifeless object to perceive in it the dynamic essence of the universe. Hence imagining is an act of cognition, perhaps the most vital cognitive act the human mind can enact. For Schelling, literature incarnates the ultimate truth and the multiple meanings to life.

The Intrinsic Meaning of Literature

Twentieth Century "New Critics" were preoccupied with more than aesthetic concerns. They also tried to get at the meanings. To cite but two examples, David Daiches studied the interrelationship of minute structural elements in a poem for their subtle meanings. In turn, William Empson explored the multiple connotations of words in a text to seek out their patterns of meaning. Both critics examined how the complex unity of a literary work brings about a total significance. Furthermore, Anglo-American "New Critics" studied the denotative and connotative facets of words as well as their etymological depths to show the ever widening implications to a literary text. Their aim was to recover the total experience of the poem. Evidently, then, the overriding goal of their criticism was to explicate literature as meaning.

Carl Gustaf Jung

Twentieth century depth psychology oriented critical thinking to new dimensions of understanding as to the meanings of literature. One of Jung's key concepts is the "collective unconscious." Beneath the individual's personal identity and personal unconscious, there lies in every man a collective unconscious, which in effect is the reservoir of his racial memory. Out of these depths, the creative artist discovers primordial images or archetypes. These arise in him as patterns of meaning which go beyond individual experience and reflect the writer's deep cultural heritage.

As Northrop Frye describes the concept in his *Anatomy of Criticism*. literature embodies archetypal subjects, such as birth, coming of age, love, guilt, redemption, and death. There are archetypal themes as the conflict between reason and imagination, between free will and destiny, appearance versus reality, and the individual versus society. There are also archetypal characters as the braggart, the fool, the hero, the seductress, the maiden, the witch, and the like. In addition, there are archetypal images and situations.

In sum, archetypes are universal symbols which communicate the same basic messages to all mankind. These archetypal images reflect the countless typical experiences of our ancestors and of ourselves. They are the "psychic residue of numberless experiences of the same type." They have a common meaning to all humanity, and their appearance in literature shows how we all are indeed of the same family of man.

Summary

This brief sketch of the tradition of literature as meaning provides us with significant clues as to the meanings of meaning.

1. If the universe itself is a meaningful process in which all the parts are interrelated in a living whole, then probably human experience

and life itself may be understood as a pattern of meaning, As revealed in tragic literature, human destiny itself is such a pattern of meaning. However, experience itself reveals there are inferior and superior meanings to what we perceive and understand.

2 Tragic literature also shows the way a man shapes the meaning of his life by the decisions he takes, the actions he pursues and the moral purpose he embraces or avoids. Hence one key to life is found in moral choice. In other words, there is moral meaning at the center of every word, decision, and action as portrayed in literature.

3. Simple and complex plot in tragedy imply that simple and complex meanings derive from simple and complex experiences which lead one to recognize the truth about oneself and others.

4. The centuries-long undertaking to understand and interpret Holy Scripture has shown that the uneducated can only comprehend literal meanings. However, to grasp supernatural and sublime meanings to Revealed Truth, an educated elite is required to interpret the images, figures, and symbols of the esoteric meanings. Subsequently, Biblical and Koranic interpreters discovered at least four strata of meaning to every scriptural text.

5. When we make references to individual or species, it becomes clearer that more than one kind of meaning is meant. Indeed, there is a whole range of meanings and even degrees of meaning to a word, a figure, a passage, a text.

6. With our recognition of the true power of human imagination, we come to see it as a superior cognitive power. Because it sees the world as monistic, and not dualistic, imagination finds meaning in every part and significance in the whole. Imagination sees beyond the multiple meanings of this world to the dynamic essence of the universe and to its superior or transcendental significance.

7. In sum, beneath the patterns of meaning to human experience —

beneath simple and complex meanings; beneath inferior and superior meanings; beneath moral meaning; beneath the strata of exoteric and esoteric meanings; beneath multiple meanings, degrees of meaning, and the whole range of meanings possible to a given text — literature has still larger meanings to it. If, on the one hand, the mind is drawn to transcendental significance, on the other hand, it is drawn to the meanings derived from man's archetypal experiences. Man's universally shared psychic experiences point to the underlying sense and significance of life shared by all the races of man. Hence *literature deals with a quality of truth undreamed of by any science or mathematics.* Literature as meaning teaches us that mankind itself has a reason for being because life itself has meaning.

IV. LITERATURE AS THE SUBLIME

The Classical Tradition

In ancient Greece, the aim of the fine arts was to enlarge and nourish human awareness and insight. Art had the power to develop human feelings and motivations, and this power was known as *psychogogia*. Hence the power of art was in its capacity to educate human character to achieve its highest excellence.

Plato

In Plato's "Ion," he said that poets composed their poetry when they were not in their right minds, but when inspired and possessed. They sang by divine inspiration, not by art. Inspired by the Muse, the poet inspired others through his poetry, and his hearers were suspended like iron filings upon a lodestone or magnet. To Plato, because poetry had the power to portray the weaknesses and evils men are heir to, which power awakens similar passions in other men, poetry was dangerous to a well-ordered state and should be banished. Hence poetry or literature exercises an undeniable and at times irresistible power over the human mind, imagination, and feelings.

Aristotle

Aristotle held a diametrically opposite view of literature as regards its emotional impact and psychological effect. He defined tragedy as an imitation of an action that is serious and of a certain magnitude, which through pity and fear brings about the purging of these emotions. Pity is aroused by unmerited misfortune of someone like us. Aristotle's key idea is that tragedy effects a catharsis in us, which purges our emotions and re-establishes a state of healthy, psychic well-being.

Longinus

Whereas Plato and Aristotle were concerned with the contagious or healthful effects literature had on us, Longinus is the first thinker to draw our attention to the uplifting power of writing. Longinus's treatise *On the Sublime* is primarily concerned with the ways and means the writer can express the sublime and evoke it in others. His treatise deals with emotional rapture, imaginative grandeur, and the sympathetic response they arouse in us. Although his treatise technically deals with rhetoric and elevation of style, he is primarily concerned with our emotional response to what we hear or read.

He defines sublimity as a certain distinction and excellence in expression. A clear knowledge and appreciation of the sublime comes from understanding the two principle sources of elevated language. The first source is the writer's power to form great conceptions. The second source is the vehement and inspired passion he used to express his ideas. These powers are inborn in the writer and hence are due to human nature. In addition, there are three other sources of elevated language, which are technical and may be acquired by study and habit:

(1) the adroit use of figurative language;
(2) the skilled choice of "noble diction"; and
(3) the rhythmic and elevated arrangement of words.

Longinus makes sure to distinguish the sublime from other passions, such as pity, grief and fear. For Longinus, "Great accents fall from the lips of those with deep and grave thoughts," or again he says, "Sublimity is the echo of a great soul."

Hence greatness of soul is the prime requisite for great writing, and that greatness can be nourished by an enthusiastic imitation and emulation of previous great poets and writers. "We grow by what we imitate and emulate." In contrast to Plato who feared the contagion of literature, Longinus believed the great souls of men of old can inspire us to nobler deeds. Longinus believed greatness, nobility, and sublimity are fostered by contact with the great minds of the past and present.

Longinus's treatise was to have a significant influence on literature eighteen centuries later with the birth of European romanticism. In the nineteenth century, lofty feelings such as admiration, transport, enthusiasm, vehemence, even awe and terror were identified with the sublime. The aim of Longinus's treatise was to lift us out of our mediocre lives and to inspire us to the immortal in us.

Sir Philip Sidney

As we learned under the discussion of literature as truth, Sidney argued that poetry is the most fruitful knowledge because it teaches and moves us to virtue. Furthermore, the poet speaks the truth since he tells not what is, but what should be or should not be. Finally, since literature shows poetic justice at work in human life, literature guides us to see the deeper truths in human experience. Yet the profoundest truths in literature are intimately interwoven with man's sense of the sublime.

Sidney tells us that among the ancient Romans the poet was regarded as a diviner, a seer, a prophet who could give us heart-ravishing knowledge. Literature dealt with more than matters natural and historical, philosophical and moral. Literature imitated the inconceivable excellencies of God.

Sidney's final argument must confound the gainsayers of the worth of literature. He argued that since poetry is the most ancient learning, since its use even among primitive peoples is universal, since the ancients had divine names for it, since the poet surpasses the philosopher and the historian, and since Christ Himself used poetry to teach mankind, literature embodied the highest form of truth open to man. For these reasons, literature teaches and delights us and moves us to virtuous action. Like learning itself, literature draws us to as high a perfection as our souls are capable of. Hence literature awakens the noble and sublime in each of us.

Edmund Burke (1729-1797)

Burke's treatise on aesthetic was inspired by Longinus's treatise *On the Sublime.* If Longinus regarded the sublime as arising from the great conceptions and vehement and inspired passions of a noble spirit, Burke made a psychological analysis of the way the great and terrible in nature and literature affect us.

In the treatise *A Philosophical Enquiry into the Origin of Our Ideas of the Sublime and the Beautiful* (1757), Burke describes how the great and sublime in nature cause astonishment in us, that state of soul in which horror overwhelms us. To Burke, no passion so effectually robs the mind of its powers of reasoning and of acting as the fear aroused by our apprehension of pain and death. Hence terror is an important cause of the sublime. If dangerous animals arouse terror, so do obscurity and darkness, especially at night. Indeed, in nature — dark, confused and uncertain images arouse a greater power in us to express the grand passions.

Burke also discusses how the idea of pain, in its highest degree, is stronger than pleasure, in its highest degree. However, there is a power which inflicts the greatest pain so that strength, violence, pain, and terror rush in upon the mind together. It is the pain brought by some great power over which we have little or no control so that it overpowers us. No creature on earth has that power as the Deity above us. God as the ultimate power is a force which nothing can withstand. As seen in the Psalms of the Old Testament and in references to David, the sublime aroused is due to the presence of God in the scriptures. Hence we associate in our minds a sacred and reverential awe with the idea of the Divinity.

Burke then proceeds to compare the sublime and the beautiful. He states that the sublime is vast in dimension, the beautiful comparatively small. Beauty should be smooth and polished; the great should be rugged and negligent. Beauty should not be obscure; the great ought to be dark and gloomy; beauty should be light and delicate; the great should be solid and massive. If the beautiful evokes pleasure, the sublime evokes pain.

Because we share the passions of others, and since words can fully express the circumstances of most passions, words can evoke a deep impression on us. For example, John Milton in *Paradise Lost* describes the journey of the fallen angels as a descent from heaven to hell, that is into a "universe of death." Here a single phrase "universe of death" makes a deep and vivid impression on us. The example illustrates Burke's point that if a clear expression describes a thing as it is, a strong expression awakens our feelings and passions. Indeed, by the contagion of our passion, the reader catches the fire kindled in the soul of a great writer.

Edward Young (1638-1665)

As with Burke, Edward Young also concerned himself with inner man and the experience it is to be human. Young believed man's emotional nature is good and trustworthy. Indeed, a writer can disregard rules, traditions, and customs if he learns to look into his heart and write. Young's greatest concern was to avoid slavish imitation of past writers in order to be oneself an original writer. If one is to discover one's own genius, one must set free one's organic and vital spontaneity. He asked all of us a deeply troubling question: "How is it that we are born originals and die copies?" Blind zeal in worshiping the past or not knowing how to use our knowledge creatively turns us all into mindless memorizers.

The Development of Modern Criticism

As seen in Burke and Young, there arose in the eighteenth century a rejection of the systematic rules of neo-classicism in order to embrace a new ideal based on feeling. A new moral sense also arose based on one's capacity to respond with emotion. Indeed, certain traits were felt to be natural to man, such as spontaneity and originality. It followed as a consequence that originality and genius could be achieved primarily through self-expression. Hence human experience through our senses and sensations came to be the new criterion for literature. Eventually critical theory turned inward to the mind itself.

So the shift passed from belief in reason as man's distinctive nature to the belief that man is most natural in his feelings. As Goethe's Faust said, "Feeling is all." Consequently, there developed a new interest in "natural" man who lived in communion with nature as described by Wordsworth. J. J. Rousseau wrote effusively about the "noble savage" unspoiled by civilized life. W. Blake poignantly portrayed the natural innocence of the child.

Correspondingly, there was a shift from the generalizations called "universals" to fascination with the particulars of the concrete world. As the philosophers Locke and Hume maintained, man learns through his senses and through concrete experience. Along with this new naturalist emphasis, the romantic writers, by concentrating on particular details and specific character traits were able to evoke a sense of awe, strangeness, and magic in the reader.

S. T. Coleridge

Coleridge was influenced by romantic transcendentalism as can be seen in his definition of the "primary imagination." He defined that imagination as the "living Power and prime Agent of all human perception, a repetition in the finite mind of the eternal act of creation in the infinite I AM." The reference "I AM" refers not only to the Godhead or Deity but also to the sublime, present and potential, in the human mind. In Coleridge's essay "Shakespeare's Judgement Equal to his Genius," there is a strong hint that Shakespeare intuitively directed a power in him that was deeper than ordinary human consciousness. In other words, Shakespeare probably directed, guided and developed sublime powers in him because he was aware of the sublime in nature and in the soul.

Percy Bysshe Shelley

There appear to be two indirect allusions to the sublime in Shelley's "A Defence of Poetry." The first is his description of the mind during the heat of creation. The mind is as a fading coal, which some invisible influence has awakened to transitory brightness.

Unfortunately, when the actual composition begins, inspiration is already on the decline. Historically, inspiration was thought to be communicated by some divine or sublime power.

The other reference to the sublime is in Shelley's memorable definition of poetry. Poetry is the record of the best and happiest moments of the happiest and best minds. Poetry makes immortal all that is best and most beautiful in the world. Poetry redeems from decay the visitations of the divinity in man. Thus poetry reminds man of the sublime soul he has inherited from the divine.

William Hazlitt

Like Wordsworth and Coleridge, Hazlitt was concerned with human psychology. He was interested in the emotional excitement evoked by art and literature and in the effect of gusto or sympathetic identification with others. He believed that sympathy enabled us to enter into the feelings of others. What is dynamic in ourselves (the self) seizes what is dynamic in others and in the world. Indeed, our human destiny is largely determined by our imagination, for if our past and present identity is known by sensation and memory, our future identity is known primarily through imagination. Hence great art, literature and philosophy or great moral action comes from the capacity to sympathize with others; in short, imagination and sympathy point to man's largeness of soul.

Thomas De Quincey (1785-1859)

De Quincey distinguished between two types of literature. The first, the *literature of knowledge*, is largely embodied in historical and scientific works which later works surpass and supplant. Its function is to teach. However, it speaks through *mere* discursive understanding. The literature of knowledge passeth away.

The second type is the *literature of power*, which represents the enduring works of the creative imagination. Its function is to move us. It speaks to the higher reason or understanding, but always through affections of pleasure and sympathy. More rare than truth is power, that is, deep sympathy with truth. In contradistinction to the literature of knowledge, the literature of power concerns itself with the great moral capacities of man. The Holy Scriptures do not speak of understanding, but of the "understanding heart."

Similarly, tragedy, medieval romance, fairy tales, and epic poetry restore to man's mind the ideals of justice, hope, truth, mercy, and retribution. These literary forms give us examples of poetic justice. Hence the literature of power teaches us the meaning of our human passions of love and hatred, of admiration and contempt. The literature of power influences us toward the good and away from the bad. The emotions it arouses mould us through life and educate us to the moral way.

Matthew Arnold

If Arnold had striking things to say about literature as truth, he has equally telling truths to give under literature as expressing the sublime. Arnold's central concern was with the humanities and especially with literature as "the most effective means of informing and developing ... the 'whole man,' that is man as a total process of desiring, feeling, and thinking. . . ." Literature is particularly able to heighten the mental activity Arnold called *culture*. Literature should be understood as central to man's desire to integrate and perfect himself. In Arnold's essay "Sweetness and Light," he says our first motive ought to be to augment the excellence of our nature and to render an intelligent being yet more intelligent.

Arnold also discusses the origin of human culture. Culture is the love of perfection, and it is the study of perfection. Furthermore, its two distinguishing features are that it is possessed by scientific passion and by the passion for doing good. Beyond the desire to learn the universal order of the world, culture is the endeavour to make the will of God prevail.

Both religion and culture have the common aim of ascertaining what perfection is to make it prevail. Culture and especially literature listen to all the voices of human experience. Religion believes the kingdom of God is within you, and culture believes human perfection is an internal condition, which harmonizes all our powers to be beautiful and worthy human beings. Put another way, human perfection consists in becoming something rather than in owning something. Human greatness is a spiritual condition worthy to excite love, interest, and admiration. Sweetness and light is beauty and intelligence in harmonious perfection in the human mind. Culture and literature seek to make known everywhere the best that has been thought and known everywhere. Those with knowledge must let it shine as God's stars in heavens. There is need for light because an old order is dying and a new order being born.

Walter Pater (1839-1894)

In his book *Studies in the History of the Renaissance* (1873), Pater makes some apt remarks about literature as the sublime. When he speaks of human experience, he recognizes that everything is a matter of impressions and subjectivism. Since everything in life is evanescent and transitory, what then is of enduring worth? He answers the question with memorable lines, "To burn always with this hard, gem-like flame, to maintain this ecstasy, is success in life."

But what do those lines mean? Since everything melts under our feet, we must seek any exquisite passion we can. In the awful brevity of life, we hardly have time to make theories about things we see and touch. Pater wants us to embrace a passion which will quicken a multiplied consciousness — the poetic passion. We should love art for art's sake. In sum, let yourself be inspired by the sublime qualities in life and in literature.

Abraham H. Maslow (1908-1970)

In Maslow's *Religions, Values. and Peak Experiences* (1964), we have a description of literature as the sublime in contemporary psychological terms. In Maslow's inveighing against religious liberals and 19th century positivists, he states they are mistaken in making no place in their systems of thought for the mysterious, the unknown, the unknowable, the dangerous-to-know or the ineffable. They entirely ignore the rich, old literature based on mystical experiences. Put in a more forceful way, Maslow declares "An education which leaves untouched the entire region of transcendental thought is an education which has nothing important to say to human life."

He then goes on to describe his central concept, the "peak experience". To begin with, peak experiences characteristically perceive the whole universe as an integrated and unified whole. (It will be recalled how this insight is the central intuition of the classical tradition of literature as beauty.) Furthermore, Maslow says that it is peak experiences which give meaning to life itself. The peak experience achieves this because it reveals eternal verities, the highest human, spiritual, and religious values. This world is not merely a matter of fact but is a sacred place. In the peak experience, people report such emotions as wonder, awe, reverence, humility, surrender, and even worship before the greatness of the experience. The peak experience is a kind of reconciliation to and acceptance of death. Furthermore, in the peak experience, there tends to be a temporary loss of fear, anxiety, inhibition, perplexity, confusion and inner conflict. The profound fear of disintegration, of insanity, even of death all tend to disappear for the moment.

From what has been said so far on literature as expressing the sublime, it should be clear that the greatest literature offers to the sympathetic, serious and intelligent reader the possibility of vastly extending his mental horizons through such peak experiences. Literature dramatizes the fact that the sublime is omnipresent and immanent in earthy, human life.

Paul Diel (1893-1972)

Paul Diel's psychology represents our last illustration of literature as expressing the sublime. This eminent French psychologist has provided literature with a transtemporal and transhistorical understanding of psyche as it manifests itself in myth, Holy Scripture, and in great literature. Diel's basic premise is that soma and psyche form a biogenetic unity which developed as the human species evolved. Diel's key contribution ties in his extensive description of the *supraconsciousness*, which ancient myths and man's notion of the divinity foreshadow.

Intimations of immortality and intuitions of eternal truths in the Old and New Testament are mythical expressions of the fact that man is endowed with a supraconsciousness and that life has a biogenetic meaning. Hence Diel's psychology depicts how in myth the demons and powers of darkness are merely psychic manifestations welling up from the subconscious whereas the gods and powers of light are signs of man's supraconsciousness. It is the intimation of his higher mental capacity which motivates man to subordinate and harmonize all his material, sexual, and spiritual desires to obey the *essential desire* of his life, and the individual's deepest desire is to find the essence, meaning, and direction of his human destiny.

This effort requires that the individual not only seek to attain self-mastery by overcoming the exalted, non-sensical desires of his vanity. This effort also requires the individual, via sublimation and spiritualization, to surpass his past self by obeying the evolutionary promptings that both soma and psyche incarnate. Such is man's true biogenetic destiny.

In a major work, *The Divinity, The Symbol and its Signification* (1971), Paul Diel states clearly that the evolutionary goal is to live life according to one's own essential desire. That is, our supra-consciousness strives toward inner-outer harmony in such a way as to become eventually humanity's supraconscience. In fact, the supra-conscience arises out of our symbolizing imagination. In the myths of all peoples, the ideal to realize harmony and integration, within as without, finds its universal expression in the symbol of the Divinity.

Diel thus also regards the creative imagination as the direct manifestation of the supraconsciousness of man. Explicit and implicit in his analyses of the symbolism in Greek mythology, in the Holy Bible, and of the Divinity itself, Diel believes the manifestations of the sublime in scripture, in the arts, in literature are reflections of man's higher nature and his developing supraconscience.

Summary

As we have seen in our discussion of literature as expressing the sublime, great literature not only arises from great conceptions and vehement and inspired passion; it not only moves us to virtuous action; literature does not simply teach us to be our original selves; literature not only shows the creative artist to emulate the great I AM at the centre of the universe; literature not only shows that man has a sublime soul; not only does the literature of power foster the great moral capacities of man and speak enduring truths; literature not only educates and moulds us to follow the moral way; literature not only teaches us to pass our brief lives in ecstasy, burning with a gem-like flame; literature not only gives us peak experiences, which allay our confusions and fears and reconcile us to death itself; it not only is the expression of the sublime, but also it shows us, in addition, that the creative imagination of the greatest writers teaches us the need to find harmony within oneself and harmony between mankind. The supraconsciousness as manifest in the Scriptures and the great literary works shows man his future destiny. As the varying traditions which regarded literature as beauty, as truth, as meaning, or as the sublime, so with the varying ways cultures understand and interpret the purpose and meaning of life. Each supposes its truth is the only truth whereas its truth is but a part of the whole truth, which continues to grow and evolve throughout time.

Literature is sublime in so far as it teaches one elementary but immortal truth. In listening to the wisdom of the heart, man awakens to the prompting of his supraconscience. This has been the implicit lesson of sublime literature for well over 2,500 years.

PART TWO:
THE SCOPE AND LIMITS OF
RATIONAL LITERARY THEORY

CHAPTER 2
THE OBSOLESCENT CRITICAL
LANGUAGE OF TODAY

Mounting evidence indicates that traditional critical terminology is becoming obsolete. The modern critic is forced to use a vocabulary no longer capable of analyzing and interpreting literature in a precise and sensitive way. This predicament is not particular to criticism alone. Today the schism between language and intuition challenges thinkers in all fields of learning.

Man's opposing views of his own nature causes this quandary in contemporary knowledge. Either man is matter and a mere thing in a world of objects, or he embodies an essence. Either man is body or soul. In defining his experience of existence, he therefore speaks in terms of his objective and subjective self. Inherited from Plato, the Church Fathers and Descartes, this dualism is the reason that cognition today finds itself in a Gordian knot of self-contradictions. The vocabulary misused these past centuries now situates us in a linguistic and conceptual labyrinth from which there seems no exit. To date literary criticism appears to be using a language as incapable of conveying contemporary intelligence as would be Anglo-Saxon.

This heritage of dualism is seen not only in the language of criticism. It pervades our understanding of literary works, resulting in such pointless disputes as that centered on content versus form. Furthermore, it has led critical theories to go their separate ways, not to be reconciled without a serious revaluation of our perception and cognition. Recent efforts to overcome the subjective-objective antagonism proved this dualism to be the nuclear critical problem of the last century.

THE SUBJECTIVE
VERSUS THE OBJECTIVE

As extensively used, the terms *subjective* and *objective* are extremely ambiguous. M.H. Abrams points out that "from their earliest uses in criticism, the terms *subjective* and *objective* are both multiple and variable in their meanings." As an example he quotes John Ruskin, who in 1856 complained that they are "The most objectionable words that were ever coined by the troublesomeness of metaphysicians. . . No words can be more exquisitely, and in all points, useless."[2]

Wellek and Warren also stress the widespread misuse of the terms. *Objective* can mean: conceptual, succinct, minimizing, low, simple, tense, plastic, smooth, colorless, etc. *Subjective* can mean: sensuous, long-winded, excited, high, decorated, rough, colorful, etc.[3] With these expressions signifying so many different things, how may a critic conscientiously use them in literary study? The multiple meanings and the cross-purposes for which these terms have been used render them ineffectual for rational and sensitive discussion.

Nor has the proliferation of substitute terms solved the issue. Decades ago Ogden and Richards considered the distinctions *connotation* and *denotation* as artificial.[4] In place of these censurable expressions, the authors suggest the following alternative.

> Instead of . . . of an antithesis of prose and poetry, we may substitute that of symbolic and emotive use of language. In strict symbolic language, the emotional effects of the words . . . are irrelevant to their employment. In evocative language . . . all the means by which attitudes, moods, desires, feelings, emotions can be verbally incited in an audience are concerned.[5]

Both the distinction between the kinds of language and their effects is useful. However, the expression *symbolic* is troublesome because of its earlier semantic associations with 19th century literary symbolism.

In their own discussion of the literary versus scientific uses of language, Wellek and Warren state that: "denotative . . . scientific language . . . aims at a one-to-one correspondence between sign and referent"; literary language ". . . has its expressive side; . . . it conveys the tone and attitude of the speaker or writer."[6]

Bally of the Geneva school of linguistics divides language into "reasonable" and "affective" elements. However, he does not study texts as fiction or poetry but as examples of the functioning of language.[7] Such research leads away from the study of the literary text for its own sake and, therefore, has the misdirection of the extrinsic approaches delineated by Wellek and Warren in their *Theory of Litterature*. Similarly Paulhan of Geneva analyzes the "significative" and "suggestive" functions of language, which result in the significative and suggestive styles.[8]

The obvious advantage of such substitute terms is that they refine our *subjective* and *objective* vernacular, and their freshness prompts a closer inspection of old concepts. Furthermore, they direct our attention anew to the ability of language to evoke certain responses in us.

Obviously there exists an agreement concerning the general function and purpose of language. It may be either denotative, "scientific," reasonable and significative, or connotative, expressive, affective and suggestive. However, the very insistence on surrogate words suggests that scholars seriously question any universal viability to these special terms. Either out of caprice or conviction, the specialists seem unable to come to an agreement on terminology or methodology.

Due to their relativism, the terms *subjective* and *objective* have become so ambiguous as to be of questionable utility to serious literary criticism. Nor has the proliferation of substitute terms resolved the discord born of dualism.

Such ambiguity is bound to influence discussion of artists and their writings. In a *Dictionary of World Literature*, a literary piece is subjective because of the personality behind it. ". . . what a man feels and thinks, what he stands for, what he is lies at the heart of the work. The personality dictates the procedure; . . . in the measure of the author's personality, a work is original.[9]

Perhaps it is unnecessary to point out that emphasis on personality leads us away from studying the text itself. On the other hand, to stress

personality is to value uniqueness for the sake of uniqueness, originality for the sake of originality, and subjectivity for its own sake. That
such criteria are of dubious value is seen when we realize that the
unique may turn out to be eccentric, the personality unsound, and the
original — insane. Hence subjectivism *per se* can never be a sound
aesthetic criterion.

    In addition to critical theories accenting the "subjective," there are
a number of "objective" theories which consider the literary work as
a reality. Abrams observes that the "objective orientation" in criticism
requires the work of art to be analyzed "as a self-sufficient entity
constituted by its parts in their internal relations," and that it be judged
"solely by criteria intrinsic to its own mode of being."[10] This alignment
has enabled men with purity of purpose to make significant exegeses
of a great variety of texts.[11]

    In making a resumé of a well known, 19th century theory of the
novel, Herbert Seidler defines the opposing artistic ideals of the genre.
In "objective" narration the storyteller withdraws as completely as
possible from the tale. In "subjective" storytelling the reader senses the
presence of narrator in a number of ways.[12] Seidler points out that this
neat separation of styles is deceptive, for in such a work as Flaubert's
Madame Bovary, how otherwise may we explain our feeling for the
heroine? Despite the clinical objectivity of the style, the author has
subtly expressed his sympathy for Emma and evoked our compassion
for her unfortunate destiny.

    Another debate centers on the disadvantages of *telling* a tale as
against *showing* a story. Some critics observe that direct scenic
presentation is more in keeping with the way we learn things in real
life. When the narrator does not interfere with the narrative and
disappears behind his characters, the art becomes detached and
objective. Such artistic "objectivity" is supposed to lead the reader to
a more immediate and intensive experience than if he were merely told
about it. In other words, the more objective the manner of presentation
the more subjective or dramatic the effect.

    This is a most curious bit of reasoning, which puts at defiance our
notions of cause and effect, of logic, and of common sense. Such
inconsistent conclusions, lead us to infer that the old subjective-
objective ambivalence is behind the dispute of telling versus showing.

Franz K. Stanzel tried to resolve this argument by suggesting that different rhetorical styles or ways of narrating produce various effects on the reader.[13] To illustrate his point, Stanzel uses an excerpt from Quintilian's *Institutio Oratoria* that distinguishes between two narrative approaches: (1) the short report, which concentrates on the result of the sequence of the happening; and (2) the thorough, descriptive representation that gives the poignant particulars.[14] These represent the two fundamental forms of narration.[15]

As a bare statement of what took place, the first version reads approximately as follows:

> In the course of the war, even this city was conquered and destroyed. Nearly all the houses were turned to ashes by the fires set by the conqueror. The city inhabitants, mostly women, children and the old, were seized with panic. It was reported that the invaders first thought was booty. Presumably all of the temple's treasures were plundered. Eyewitness accounts affirmed that pillaging soldiers fought over the spoils. In accordance with the laws of war of that time, a good number of the inhabitants were deported as prisoners so that wives never again saw their husbands and many children lost their mothers.[16]

The second version represents the story scenically.

> From the roof of his house, which was not far from the eastern wall of the city, he could distinctly hear how the besiegers had succeeded in penetrating the city. The noise of battle drew closer as shown by the reflection of fire on the rooftops. In the streets below, people began to run everywhere without seeming to know where to find help. Directly before his own house, a group had gathered, weeping women and children and a helpless old man whose anxiety was etched in his face. Before they could reach a decision, the first enemy soldier appeared at the end of the street. He ran directly into the temple and began hauling out booty. Others came and immediately tried to tear his prize away from him. The noise,

the plundering soldiers, the anguished outcries of women and children, the crackling of the fire, which had seized the entire east end of the city, filled the air. From his hiding place he could observe how the inhabitants were bound and led away. A bewildered mother tried to find her child . . .[17]

Both versions seek to record an impressive event. The first version makes a "historical" statement of it. The narrator is distant, and the report aims at an unbiased communication. Put another way, this version contains three kinds of "objectivity" The first is that of style, where the author's attitude may be said to be stoical and where the purpose of the style is to translate faithfully what happened. The second kind of "objectivity" is that the characters and events are treated as matters-of-fact. The intention is to establish a true understanding of them. It follows that *the effect* ought to be more objective.

In the second version the reader is made an eyewitness to the event.[18] The goal of this account is to intensify the experience of the happening by the selection of exciting and pitiful incidents which stir one's emotions. Obviously this detailed rendition affects us more. This should mean that the second version is more subjective *in its effect.*

W.C. Booth gave another solution to the telling versus showing problem. He argued that the distinction between "showing," which is supposedly artistic, and "telling," which is supposedly inartistic, is unimportant because directly or indirectly the writer is telling us. The artist's judgement is always present to those who know how to look for it.[19]

True as this axiom may be, it does not really solve the conceptual confusion at the core of our minor altercation. We may see this by asking whether both versions are true. Or is one truer than the other? Some artists and critics insist that the second version is superior to the first. It must, therefore, represent to them a superior truth. Yet the first version has that sober, stable truth about it we find in history, maxims and proverbs. Indeed, it is in such dispassionate language that men record the enduring verities of life, of science and of philosophy. If so, then why should the second version be preferable or superior?

The fact is that both telling and showing are methods of "objectification," each aiming at a distinct representation of truth.

Furthermore, each version is both "objective" and "subjective." In the first version where the concrete and poignant details are stripped away, we have experience "objectified" into concepts and generalizations. Yet in the sentence "A city has been destroyed and conquered," there is clearly a "subjective" and "objective" interpretation of the events. The actual occupation of the city by foreign troops and the streets in ruins are sensorial and objective proofs of the reality. On the other hand, the words "conquered" and "destroyed" are evidently subjective because they appeal to the reader's empathy and feelings. Hence no abstraction can every refine away its empirical-emotional origin, nor can it attain the neutrality or unconcern required of absolute objectivity.

In similar way, Quintilian's second version with all the poignant details is both "subjective" and "objective." By the selection of details, its artistic method is objective. Put another way, in directing the reader's attention to the empirical and phenomenal, it is objective. However, by its evoking in the reader nearly the same feeling as the narrator felt, it is subjective. The second version is a *concretization* of events.

These realizations permit us to conclude that both abstraction and concretization produce dual effects in opposite senses — the "subjective" and the "objective."

Finally, we should observe that such abstractions as become maxims, laws and proverbs, which judge human situations, also become evaluations. For instance, as an "objectification" of tribal experience, Moses' Decalogue formulates laws which are both truths and injunctions. As commandments, they are subjective because they aim at motivating reverence and invoking obedience. To a lesser degree, the same is true of all maxims and proverbs.

In the light of common sense these aesthetic problems take on more pertinence if we relate them to man's habits of reasoning. *Telling* may be said to spring from man's inclination to theorize and generalize, i.e., to elicit useful abstractions from experience. A kind of inductive reasoning, *telling* aims at expressing experience "objectively" and efficiently. By contrast, *showing* rises from man's inclination to illustrate his ideas and to concretize his meanings. A kind of deductive reasoning, *showing* points to specific examples which require us to accept the author's conclusions.

Put another way, both telling and showing aim at a manner of "objective" truth — the one abstract and the other affective. This may also be seen in theories of literature. For instance, both Aristotle and Plato accepted the mimetic theory of poetry, that is, that art is imitation. In the "Poetics," Aristotle views the real and the empirical as "objective." To Plato, who believed in eternal Forms, the "objective" is the Ideal. Millennia later, the English romantic poets made comparable distinctions in their expressive theory of literature. To Wordsworth the "objective" is found in man's common experience as well as in the "spontaneous overflow of feeling" caused by recalled experience. To Coleridge, on the other hand, imagination itself is "objective" in its imitating God's creative process.

While these parallels in time are illuminating, they also serve to demonstrate the futility of utilizing the terms *subjective* and *objective* as criteria of excellence or performance. Literature is something beyond the "subjectives" and "objectives," the telling and showing, the tricks and techniques.

In our century, it is T.S. Eliot's distinction to have required that objects, situations and events correspond to the feeling the poet wishes to express if he is to evoke the same sentiment in the reader. The "objective correlative" bridges the separation between the artistic ideal of objectivity and the need of a personal voice to transmit and evoke experience.

Indeed, if that voice is not present, no technique can move us to understand and feel what has happened. Literature written in the name of "scientific objectivity" or "impersonality" pretends there is no such voice. Yet it does not matter whether we are shown or told, for we respond to the quality or pitch of the voice. A command snarled with hatred will awaken in us a different answer from one whispered with gentle love. It is voice which expresses our needs and calls for a reply.

Ogden and Richards describe this potency of voice as follows: (In language) "Under the emotive function are included . . . the expression of emotions, attitudes, moods, (and) intentions . . . in the speaker and . . . their evocation in the listener. As there is no convenient verb to cover both expression and communication, we shall . . . often use the term 'evoke' to cover both sides of the emotive function."[20]   Hence rather than busy ourselves with the merits of telling and showing, we may find more profit in seeking to describe in what ways the voice expresses the story and evokes our responses.

If we look at how the terms *subjective* and *objective* have been used to discuss artists and their works, we learn that such discussions are subject to the same vague semantics. To the "impersonal" artist the subjective implies a passivity before existence, an unmanly quietism before the heroic requirements of art. To the classical critic, "subjective" implies an artist's exaggerated, maudlin or hysterical response to experience or a lamentable pursuit of intensity for intensity's sake.

On the other hand, to the impartial artist, the objective mirrors scientific honesty and integrity, evinces moral forthrightness, and an active, masculine vision of life. To the purist critic, objectivity shows the artist's determination to come to terms with experiences; objectivity manifests self-mastery on the part of the author who does not permit his feelings to interfere with his judgements or even permit him to judge.

We see then how the terms *subjective* and *objective* have become prescriptive and moralistic — the subjective to be disapproved of, decried, discouraged — the objective to be favored, extolled, and emulated. If criticism is not to degenerate into preachment, such persuasions should be eliminated from critical terminology. What is needed is a distinctive description of imaginative literature.

From our discussion of the terms *subjective* and *objective*, we have learned many things. If anything, the extensive misuse of the words urges us to expunge these terms from literary criticism, except to point out how these terms were once used. Properly, they should become a part of historical criticism.

Clearly, the old mode of reasoning has come to a dead end, and if we are to transcend the dualism of the past, the critic must seek to recreate the lived experience of the imagined world. Human existence is a continuous fluctuation of pleasures and discomforts, a modulation of personal meanings. In real life, we do not sever the subjective from the objective, for we cannot sunder mind from matter or cut the soul out of its body and expect it to live. If we bear this simple verity in mind, we will eventually come to a more precise rendering of the *modus vivendi* of literature.

What is needed is a new language rooted in the very nature of man's monistic apperception. This language will be found in terms having etymological stability. In other words, for centuries the terms would have designated the same basic concepts and yet evaded a multiplicity of contradictory meanings. In addition, their widespread use in several Indo-European languages would prove their relative universality. Moreover, a catholic critical language would have to provide a means of healing the dualism of the past without itself being a needless proliferation of terms. Furthermore, the language should be descriptive, not prescriptive. If prescriptive, it would soon become obsolescent since values change. Finally, the language should be capable of application to all linguistic, formal and expressive aspects of imaginative literature so that every explication be consistent and complete. In these multiple criteria for a new critical language, the reader may find useful suggestions to pursue his own research.

CHAPTER 3
GENRE: KIND, FORM
OR MODULATION?

Although tradition has distinguished three major kinds of genre: the epic, the lyric, and the drama, the twentieth century has openly debated the finality of such absolute categories.[1] In their *Theory of Literature*, Wellek and Warren raised an objection to the concept of genre when they stated that, though suggestive, "Such exploration of the basic kinds . . . is scarcely promising of objective results." Indeed, the authors doubt that ". . . these three kinds have any such ultimate status, even as component parts variously to be combined."[2]

In opposition to this view, Emil Staiger subtly defends the supergenres when his *Principles of Poetics* maintains that genres derive from man's three basic ways of apprehending the possibilities of human existence.[3] Since genres arise from basic modes of apprehension, a literary work itself must reflect the sophistication of human apperception. For this reason an imaginative work, to a degree, participates in or manifests aspects of all genres.[4] From this, Staiger demonstrates the flexible nature of genre by his description of lyrical poetry. A lyrical poem is not simply lyrical, for it encompasses all genre possibilities; however, it is the preponderance of the lyrical quality which decides us to call the verse lyrical.[5] Moreover, in larger genres, as in narrative literature, shifts of emphasis may take place from the lyrical to the epic to the dramatic. Staiger even admits that the less a literary work corresponds to the ideal of "purity of genre" and the more it achieves an interpenetration of genres, the more perfect it may be.[6] Wolfgang Kayser in *The Verbal Artwork* also questioned the homogeneous nature of genre because the principles of grouping literary works vary greatly.[7] At times the outward *form* determines that a work is a different genre.[8] Even though Ferdinand Brunetière argued ingeniously for a "biology" of genre, Kayser believes the concepts of genre have emptied themselves of meaning.[9]

Kayser also dwelt on Benedetto Croce's refusal to accord any importance at all to the distinction among genres. Indeed, Croce regarded "aesthetic classification of the arts as absurd."[10] To be sure, Croce's extreme rejection of the concept of genres provoked a reaction, and since 1950 there has been a strong revival of interest.

> The problem of genres . . . this perhaps oldest problem of the science of literature, has moved, so to speak, into the centre of scholarly interest . . . To be sure, there manifests itself an almost bewildering wealth of disparate opinions.[11]

Among contemporary scholars, Herbert Seidler holds to the comprehensive view, accepting lyrical, dramatic, and epic as "enduring poetic possibilities. On the foundation of this loose system, we see the poetic forms analyzed today."[12] Seidler will not allow that the subject matter helps to determine genre, for such determination would leave a genre "without limit and artistically insignificant."[13] Seidler also tells us that pure forms seldom exist, that genres are not something immutable, and that they have fluctuated with historical situations. They are no more than vectors, which combine in concrete works in multiple ways. Generic tendencies evolve ever new combinations out of anterior possibilities.[14] Seidler believes that it is the fluid relationships between kinds that make possible the modifications from one genre to another.[15] By stressing the features which dissolve the rigid structure of kinds, Seidler makes us aware there are mixed genres, transitional genres, and even evolving genres.

We find a similar awareness of mixed and transitional genres among certain French investigators. For H. Bonnet "there exist veritable intermediary genres situated half-way between pure novel and pure poetry. From every novel there emanates a poetic atmosphere, and the novelist habitually seeks the tragic, the dramatic, the pathetic, the comic."[16] The novel is indeed not a genre, but it is a composite of several genres.[17] And "narrative poetry contains all genres, as a mixture, not as a synthesis."[18]

While Bonnet sees mixed elements in the genres, his compatriot Albérès calls attention to their evolutionary character. For Albérès the novel in 1950 was the expression of a metaphysic and ethic, whereas by 1966 it defined a manner of feeling, or an aesthetic, or a phenomenology.[19] Yet Albérès could cite Aldous Huxley's *Point Counterpoint* of 1928 as a forerunner of this new, polyphonic novel. There each character's problem resembles that of the others. The motifs of diverse personages intersect, unfold, and complement each other as in a fugue or musical counterpoint.[20] Similarly, P. Boisdeffre uses a musical analogy when he discusses the work of the novelist M. Butor: "From one end to the other; language is treated as musical materials, at the interior of which themes and variations unfold.[21] Obviously these eminent French critics see imaginative writing as transforming and transcending the old forms.

We may summarize the divergent trends in genre theory by citing one French and one German spokesman. A purist when isolating the essentials of each genre, Robert Champigny in his volume *Le Genre Romanesque* distinguishes the non-novelistic from the novelistic elements[22] by use of an effective similé. While insisting that ". . . the `pure novel' would consist only of the simple `novelistic' metal," he admits that the usual novel may have other ingredients, which ". . . form an aesthetically viable alloy."[23] Similarly in *Le Genre Poétique* Professor Champigny aims at isolating "*la poésie pure*," which is "the genre which carried farthest an aesthetic conversion of language."[24] Yet Champigny qualifies his aestheticism by declaring that in poetry "The modalities . . . emphasize an infinite plurality, not only of qualities but also of combinations, that is, of possible worlds."[25] On the other hand, in *Le Genre Dramatique*, Professor Champigny deplores the confusion between modern comedy, drama, and tragedy,[26] barely accepting any possible amalgam between poetry and drama[27] or between the novel and drama.[28]

If Champigny represents the closest approximation to traditional (French neo-classical) distinctions, G. Priesemann in the German Literary Lexicon states that literature represents the "ecumenical trend of the past three decades."[29]

> What constitutes a created genre is the object of contradictory opinions . . .In every definition of a genre there is need of ever growing differentiation . . . The theory of genres must admit borderline cases, transitions, and transgressions.[30]

The survey shows that no single classificatory principle is satisfactory . . . A scheme which would comprehend all possibilities remains so far, and perhaps for good, wishful thinking. This clearly confirms the fact that every classification is crude and arbitrary compared to the reality. From the viewpoint of the work, all schemes are unsatisfying. The work retains its individual life, its infinite nuances.[31]

Hence, from the above juxtaposition of conflicting views of genre, we are led to concluding along with G.N.G. Orsini, ". . . the field is littered with the ruins of past definitions which have convinced no one save their author . . ."[32]

The scholarly debate retraced thus far reveals how lexical and semantic distinctions have failed to delimit or define genre satisfactorily. Indeed, the inconclusiveness of the debate, however illuminating in itself, has served both to show the limited validity of definitions *per se* and to illustrate the need for a fresh epistemological start, which can only be begun by discovering the world views and systems of logic sustaining the discussions of genres.

The key to a more penetrating and satisfying interpretation of the literary work is provided by Northrop Frye's argument against the purist view of genre.

'Pure' examples of either form (romance or novel) are never found; there is hardly any modern romance that could not be made out to be a novel, and vice versa. The forms of prose fiction are mixed, like racial strains in the human being, not separable like the sexes.[33]

Frye's figurative language reflects our modern scientific understanding of form in nature, and this understanding must surely have a direct bearing on how we should apprehend genre. Herbert J. Muller illustrates this connection when he states that biologists have ". . . missed the most revolutionary implications of Darwin's theory, which undermined Aristotle's scheme of fixed objects, fixed categories, and fixed ends. It (Darwin's theory) emphasized process rather than the forms the life process happened to take, and natural selection suggests that these forms were not given in advance"[34]

Thus our knowledge of form in biological nature is distinct from the formal analysis of genres derived from antiquity, and this distinction requires us to take a historical view of the concept.

Jean Pucelle's *Le Temps* points out that in western civilization two basic outlooks have governed man's view of things. Hellenism gave us a philosophy of essences whereas Judaism gave us a philosophy of progress, contingency, and history. Inspired by Aristotle, medieval scholasticism visualized the world as basically static and thought in terms of qualities and genres. Henri Bergson in *The Creative Evolution* stated that, during the Renaissance, *laws* as the expression of mathematical functions became substituted for genres, thus permitting the descriptive translation of the curve of all phases of a process. Later, the 18th century developed sketchy evolutionary notions, which with Darwin's theory superseded the idea that species were fixed types.[35]

These historical, mathematical and biological facts justify posing two fundamental questions: (1) Is genre a physical object or mechanism to be dismantled into its workable parts, or does genre embody organic life processes which ought to be investigated and described as such? (2) Are purist notions of genre due to a culture or concept lag, as Bergson implies? For instance, the French neo-classicists argued for "pure" genres, even though the Renaissance had already begun the search for the laws which function in and through living forms. (On the other hand, Dryden and those who defended English drama did so out of a sense of the greater flexibility and freedom attained by "mixed drama" in which comedy and tragedy functioned together to achieve a greater life-likeness.)

We need not enter into a discussion of these two fundamental questions. Rather we need to discover a new epistemological basis for thinking about genre. We need to examine literature as human experience both as cause and effect.

It is my belief that all literary "forms" are governed by moods and states of mind which reflect modes of apperception basic to man. It is these modes that determine how we experience a poem or story rather than the genre form that decides what we experience.

These modes are shown in language. If it is true, as Roman Ingarden has said, that the meaningful unit of language is the sentence and not the word,[36] we ought to bear in mind that a sentence defines a state of being, an action, or the like. This simple fact permits us to make a generalization. It is highly probable that all sentences and therefore *all communication in language is expressed in either the indicative or subjunctive mode of apperception.*[37]

Grammatically the term *subjunctive* means that mode of a verb which represents a state or act as possible, doubtful, desirable, contingent, etc. The mode is used to describe a degree of emotion or feeling. As I would have the word used for the study of the human experience in literature, the subjunctive may be applied to all states, conditions, and actions which express or evoke an affective mood or state of mind. Everything in a story, poem, or drama which stirs the reader's anticipations, joys, sorrows, anguish or ecstasy participates in and evokes the subjunctive that is potential and operative in "genre."

Grammatically the term *indicative* means that mode of a verb which represents a state or act as so-called "objective" fact. The mode is used to make disinterested descriptions of places, persons, or events. It represents an extremely low degree of feeling or emotion. The term may, therefore, be applied to all actions and conditions in a linguistic communication which represent the noetic attitude. The indicative mode may be an "impersonal" style as in Flaubert or Stendhal. Or the indicative may be called forth by all sorts of comparisons among characters and their situations, by patterns of plot, description, character, and metaphor because such comparisons divulge the overall design of the "genre."[38]

Lest the reader think this distinction between the indicative and subjunctive functions of language (and genre) be a spurious one, let me remind him of what he knows well. Language embraces a "denotative" or "scientific" aspect as well as a "connotative" or emotive side. These aspects suggest there are a least two kinds of truth: the scientific and emotive. However, a third kind of truth is revealed in everyday reasoning. The third kind is contained in the special logic of the *if*-clause. "If this be true, then this is also true." What this reasoning represents is *conditional truth*. By the fact that we are dealing with a conditional world in any genre, we come to understand the practical use of the terms *indicative* and *subjunctive*.

In so far as conditional truth shows causal relations (if-then), it is indicative. In so far as that conditional world embodies and expresses feelings, doubts, and desires, it is subjunctive. In so far as this emotive truth is secured coherently in the conditional, it is indicative. Furthermore, in being ultimately grounded in universal human experience, the conditional is indicative. Hence the conditional world of the genre is indicative in its self-consistency as in its corresponding to actual human perception and to man's common sense.

Just how intimately the subjunctive and indicative modes are interrelated in any genre may perhaps best be illustrated by an analogy. In physics *cohesion* is the force by which molecules of the same kind are held together. Hence the syntax of a sentence, made up primarily of words expressing empirical or denotative meanings, is properly the *cohesive* link of language. *Adhesion* is the binding force exerted by molecules of unlike substance in contact with each other. Hence we may speak of the adhesion between sentences, i.e., of the mood or mode which binds together the elements, sensations or sentiments into a unified atmosphere or style. This properly is the *adhesive* link of language. Therefore, in imaginative literature we may speak of the cohesion of syntax and the adhesion of mood.

These understandings permit us to draw two important conclusions. First, the cohesion of sentence, paragraph and genre is expressed and evoked through the indicative mode whereas the adhesion of imaginative writing is communicated through the subjunctive mode. Second, we should always consider these modes as an interdependent subjunctive-indicative modulation. From word to word, from image to image, from sense to significance, this modulation moves through infinite variation toward a finalize entelechy of feeling and form. And this movement which realizes itself through the modulation of meaning acquires the nature of an ineluctable modality.

In contrast to the elaborate definitions of genre in the past, the description of literature as a subjunctive-indicative modulation may seem, to some, an inordinate simplification. Yet because my view has important eclectic affinities with Coleridge's penetrating concept of imagination, I feel that my interpretation of man's modes of apperception in literature is sound. Coleridge describes imagination as follows:

> The synthetic and magical power, to which we have exclusively appropriated the name of imagination . . . reveals itself in the balance or reconciliation of opposite or discordant

qualities . . . a more than usual state of emotion, with more than usual order; judgement ever awake and steady self-possession with enthusiasm and feeling profound or vehement . . . The sense of musical delight . . . with the power of reducing multitude into unity of effect, and modifying a series of thoughts by some one predominant thought or feeling.[39]

In the quotation the key words uphold the interpretation that a literary work is a modality. The phrase ". . . that synthetic and magical power . . ." testifies to the unifying and transforming power of the imagination. The ". . . balance or reconciliation of opposite qualities . . ." encourages the view that there is a fluctuating balance between the indicative and subjunctive. "A more than usual state of emotion . . ." shows the presence of the subjunctive mode whereas the phrase ". . . with more than usual order . . ." points to the indicative, which has transmuted the subjunctive into form and meaning. The subjunctive-indicative polarity is repeated in the words "enthusiasm" and "judgement." My thesis that a unifying modulation suffuses the literary work also finds kinship in Coleridge's "The sense of musical delight . . ." seduces "multitude into unity of effect . . ." and in his assertion that ". . . a series of thoughts" is modified ". . . by some one predominant thought of feeling . . ." Thus does the indicative mode of truth, order, and insight inflect the subjunctive mode of uncertainty and emotion.

In literature these subjunctive and indicative modes are the means by which to evoke and express corresponding effects. In the similarities of space, time, character, plot and the like, the indicative is brought about. In their differences, the subjunctive is called forth. Literature may be considered a modality in the comprehensive sense that the similarities, differences, and modulations all interact to effect understanding.[40]

This chapter has reviewed genre for its mixed kinds, its intermediary states, its transitional types, its evolving forms, and the fluid relationships among them. In addition, the debate among literary scholars has shown that definitions prove inadequate to capturing the kinetic and self-transforming nature of literature. Beyond typology, beyond classical epistemology, the literary work manifests man's understanding of the meanings of human experience, and such meanings cannot be defined by formal analysis. The scholars who have modeled their reasoning on classical logic have come up against the limitations of the classical world view. The scholars who hold the ecumenical view have come up against the limitations of thinking by analogies, for one man's analogy contradicts another's and because any analogy can illuminate only one aspect of its object. In the final analysis, an analogy is only an analogy.

What is needed is a descriptive science based on a new epistemological understanding of man's fundamental modes of apperception. The modal method outlined in this article opposes any interpretation which breaks up the literary work into definable parts or categorizes it conventionally. As a sequence of perceptions and experiences, the literary composition may be studied more sensitively and scientifically through describing man's subjunctive and indicative response to life.

CHAPTER 4
IMAGE, METAPHOR AND SYMBOL

In the first half of the 20th century European fiction showed a marked mutation of feeling and expression from the past. If one mentions works by James Joyce, Marcel Proust, Andre Gide, D.H. Lawrence, Jean Paul Sartre, Albert Camus, William Golding, Robbe-Grillet, and others, one is forced to acknowledge that metaphoric and symbolic stories occupy an eminent place. The affinities between novel and poem are so striking that they invite the critic seriously to study fiction for metaphoric patterns and variations.

However, such an etude is easier called for than accomplished since, in order to pursue it, we must first probe the meaning of image, metaphor and symbol. Let us explore these three concepts of poetics.

A classical distinction is ". . . that images may be conceptual as well as perceptual . . ." and ". . . that the proper basis for classification and analysis is their logical function."[1] Perceptual images are those which represent the world around us, objects associated with certain sensations. The confrontation of my sensations of an object with my idea of it is a transient and passive confirmation of the sensation-image. The moment I actively use the image to define my experience, the image becomes a concept which both represents a thing and re-evokes my attitude toward it. Therefore, the user's intention determines whether the image is employed to communicate a sign with denotative meaning or used to suggest feeling.

An image is not only visual. There are tactile, auditory, olfactory, and kinesthetic images as well. Indeed, there are as many images in the world as there are animate beings with conditions and movements or inanimate objects with shapes and distinguishing marks. Hence, as in a formal definition, we find that an image is defined by class and *differentiae*, form and qualities.

This becomes clear when we point to a cumulonimbus in the sky and call it "a towering, thundering cloud." Hence the image is classified and differentiated. However, the attributes "towering, thundering" are sufficient to represent the motion of a cloud; thus the parts or qualities themselves can evoke the image.

This potential becomes clearer if we use their qualities as participles in the phrase "his towering, thundering rage." Here, nature associations are said to picture someone's emotion, and the image becomes metaphoric. That is, the image translates and evokes a specific mood. Although the class (cloud) has disappeared, the *differentiae* (towering, thundering) suffice to conjure up the image. In this active use of image, it has become conceptual. Therefore, we may conclude that there are as many *kinds* of images as there are senses, and there are as many *degrees* of image as those senses can detect in range and refinement.

It is probable that vision is mainly responsible for intensive and extensive perceptions. It perceives changes in light, space, and movement. However, it also senses delicate differences. If it first registers form, vision also detects gradations of brightness and nuance of color. This may be why we first classify and then differentiate. By contrast, the auditory, olfactory, tactile, organic and kinesthetic primarily detect and discriminate among delicate sensations.

We may conclude then that our noetic sense of things comes mainly from vision, although it too is quite capable of noting subtleties, while our affective awareness comes essentially from all our other senses.[2] This conclusion permits us to speak of the form and the feelings of a literary work, where feeling implies all at once: touch, emotion, and organic-kinesthetic state-of-being.

In intellection it is probable that both perceptual synesthesia and simultaneous perception take place concurrently. What I mean is that a concept is usually the result of synesthesia, i.e., the cooperative effort of all the senses to fashion the concept into form and feeling. Hence a concept is the result of the integration of perceptual images.

At the same time, an image becomes truly conceptual as a result of simultaneous perception. That is, in addition to synesthesia, the object perceived is compared trans-temporally with all objects like it that the mind can remember. This is what is meant by simultaneous perception, the verification of images in time. Without understanding the act of cognition, we can never hope to grasp the meaning of the temporal modulation in metaphoric fiction which finalizes into form.

The virginal and consummated history of the sensorial picture shows that images are conceived not so much spatially as consecutively. Since conceptual counterparts, like sensory images, are formed all at once through synesthesia and through simultaneous image-confirmation, this would suggest that what matters among images is their trans-causal or trans-temporal relations.

This suggestion seems borne out by the realization that the true power and purpose of images in literature is to conjure up memories and to arouse expectations. Moreover, the way images function reminds one remarkably of E. Lämmert's *Rückwendungen* (recollections) and *Vorausdeutungen* (foreshadowing) which as fictional techniques unite the past with the present and at times predict the future.[3] Hence virtual images in literature are used not only for their meanings, but also for their ability to evoke mystery, memory, intimation, and the aura of prophecy.

These powers become evident when we realize that images are experienced in two main ways: in retrospect and in prospect.

Certain representations magnetize our attention because they seem surcharged with special meaning. Once a poem or tale has been read, these images beckon us to uncover the reason they seemed to fulfill a particular purpose in the total experience of the story. Such we may call "images in retrospect." On the other hand, those images which impress us before the reading is completed are "images in prospect." These not only elicit expectations but also lead us to sense what the final experience will be. In other words, they seem signs and omens of a future significance. Both kinds of image are electric with temporal and transcendental meaning. Both modulate us through time till we realize they have changed us — either by intensifying our experience or by broadening our vision of the world.

Metaphor rests on the copulative *is* which has a deceptive semantic stability. Although the word *is* seems a perfectly clear basis for comparison in a sentence as "The circle is round," it is hardly so in such a statement as "My girl is beautiful." Obviously context determines whether this copulative is to be understood in a noetic or affective way.

Then again the word *is* may replace sense copulatives as *feel, look, smell, sound, taste*. This fact is important when we recall that they function in characteristic ways which are antithetical. For instance, in such sentences as: "The flower smelled sweet," "The milk tasted sour," "The man felt angry," the copulatives are "objective" in being rooted in the empirical, for the statements may be confirmed or denied by our senses. On the other hand, to the degree that these copulatives express doubt, opinion or feeling, they communicate vague notions and evoke ambivalent responses.

Furthermore, these copulatives vary in their so-called "objectivity" or "subjectivity" to the degree that they correspond to different senses. Words specifically associated with sight (*look, appear, seem*) express a degree of certainty in such sentences as "This seems right," "It appears unavoidable," "She looks well." However, these same sight words express doubt and evoke ambiguity because *seem, look* and *appear* also imply that there may be a very different reality beneath the appearance of things.

In addition to its ability to supplant sense copulatives, the word *is* embodies other properties and powers. It can indicate a transition or transformation from one state or condition to another as with the copulative *become*. In such sentences as "He became an artist," "She became a mother," and "The youth became a man" is the realization of a later, superior or more accomplished state, and the word *is* may imply this metamorphosis.

With the copulative *feel*, we have a term with a wide range of application, for it refers to the sense of touch, the visceral and to one's general state of being. Clearly the word *is* may replace *feel* in such representative declarations as "The material feels soft," "She feels sick" and "He feels melancholy."

Therefore, the word *is* is capable of taking the place of the copulatives of sight (*seem, appear, look*), those of sense (*taste, sound, smell*), that of process (*become*) and that of sensation-conception (*feel*). Whenever we use *is* to supersede other copulatives, we see that the statement is made more emphatic, more certain, more stable — in appearance almost fixed and unquestionable. However, since all the copulatives which *is* may replace also register a degree of doubt, condition or contingency, the word *is* evokes antithetical responses and actually communicates both noetic and affective notions.

Finally, we need to mention the fact that sense copulatives have the power to act reflexively ("She looked angry.") and transitively

("She looked at the flower.") Because of this potency, they possess a transformational power denied regular transitive verbs.

Since metaphor is based on the copulative *is*, metaphor expresses and evokes both noetic and affective modes of understanding.[4] Furthermore, since the copulative *is* embodies the translation and transformation of experience, metaphor has the same powers.

This fact becomes clearer if we contrast a comparison to metaphor. For example, in the comparison "The book is a dictionary," the statement serves logical purposes where the species (dictionary) refers back to, in contained and confirmed by its class (book). Here the word *is* functions to translate. On the other hand, in the metaphoric clause:

My beloved is a black lilac,
Scenting a Persian dream . . .

something out of the ordinary happens. Grammatically speaking, the word *is* functions differently here because it both *translates* a state or condition (the loved one is a flower) and *transforms* because the mysterious flower reveals some unforgettable quality of the beloved. In other words, metaphor sets up a *conditional* world. The poet is saying "If you were in love as I am, *then* this woman would seem as a black lilac to you." By the addition of ". . . scenting a Persian dream . . .," the poet means she seems this way in his exotic dreams.

However, the metaphor calls forth in us specific psychological effects as well. To begin with, the main image ("black lilac") creates a tension by upsetting our expectations, for no lilac in nature is black. Hence the image presents the reader with an enigma. Since the color black connotes night, death, or evil, why is the poet's beloved associated with these obscure or ominous forces? The metaphor requires a Janus glance such as "my beloved" ↔ "black lilac." The reader continuously attempts to equate "my beloved" with "black lilac" or unite concept with perception, genus with species. Obviously, they do not fit together logically.[5]

Metaphor disrupts expected context. This must mean that it is an intentional distortion tending to break up normal syntax. Indeed, metaphoric language appears a willful fragmentation and re-integration of language, a purposeful dis-association of sensations and images pulled together again by the adhesion of mood. This means then that metaphor not only records and transmutes experience; it embodies a vision which evokes a mutation of feeling in the reader because his own memories and responses are challenged. The reader must re-discover his own psychic depths if he is to recover the meaning of the metaphor.

We may say then that the meta-logic of the metaphor fuses the perceptual and conceptual images into a pristine synthesis of feeling and form held in balance by emotive adhesion and syntactical cohesion.[6] Since the conscious use of metaphor is to express feeling as much as idea, metaphor is an image metamorphized by mystery and mood into a psycho-semantic significance. Hence metaphor is a modality of mood-meaning. If, as we enter its world, there seems a trend to disorder, disruption and complexity in metaphoric language, we learn in the end that a retrospective vision has shaped, directed and realized it into a suggestive semantic. In the same way, the images and symbols in metaphoric fiction unite and fashion experience into its ultimate forms.

The term *symbol* is used to describe an object typifying a quality, abstract idea, or the like. Employed consciously in literature, the word *symbol* has a complex meaning. "This term . . . refers to a manner of representation in which what is shown . . . means, by virtue of association, something more or something else . . . Thus a literary symbol unites an image and an idea or conception which that image suggests or evokes . . ."[7]

If we are to seize a fresh understanding of the term, however, we must re-examine our own experience of it. Let us proceed from the example we used under metaphor.

> My beloved is a black lilac
> Scenting a Persian dream . . .

By reason of the unfamiliar associations it evokes, the phrase "black lilac" represents a more advanced state of meaning or a richer concentration of significance.[8] Everyday experience warns us that the flower either must be supernatural or one born of imagination. Through the flower the poet is obviously seeking to convey some emotional or mystical meaning beyond the empirical or literal realities. The multi-meaning of symbol challenges the reader's intelligence and vigilance because it transforms his expectancies and experience.

However, from metaphor to symbol, does a further transformation take place? To help answer this, a brief glance at Christian symbolism may serve our purposes. In the medieval period when illiteracy dominated the western world, the Church sought to instruct the people through a vast encyclopedia of symbols. Everything recalled or conjured up the most important event in the history of man — the descent of God upon the earth, his assuming flesh and bone, his terrible suffering as a human being, his death, resurrection, and final Ascension. This event or story is the context for nearly all religious symbols employed in the age.

To mention only the most familiar, Christian symbolism included: *animals* (the donkey, ox, dragon, fish, lamb, and dove); *plants* (the apple, tree, palm, rose, lily, and thorns); *colors* (blue, red, gold, green, purple, and white); *people* (the Christ child, Christ on the Cross, the four evangelists, fisherman) as well as *objects* and *concepts* (bread, fountain, books, demons, garden, hand, crib, nails, sword, staff, left and right, and numbers).

If we arbitrarily choose a few to search for a clue to the transformation they incarnate, we find the fish is a symbol of Christ because the Greek word *ICHTHYS* (fish) represented the early password *Jesous Chrisos Theou Hyios Soter*. The dove represents the Holy Ghost in its obvious associations with flight, gentle presence, and the angelic. The apple reminds us of the sin of Adam and Eve and God's law but also, in paintings where the Christ child reaches for the apple, it is a symbol of His readiness to take upon Himself the sins of the world. The crown of thorns worn by Christ represents the sins He must bear for mankind. Near the Virgin a lily symbolizes her immaculate conception. The   red garment Mary wears in medieval paintings symbolizes the blood of the sacrifice, and her blue garment recalls air, truth, the breath of life, and the Savior Himself. Ears of corn or sheafs of wheat depict the bread of life, the Eucharist bread or Christ's body.[9] Hence for the faithful, every symbol re-evoked the Event, his feelings for Christ and all the memories of those feelings.

What energizes these animals, plants, colors, people, objects, and concepts to become true symbols? What empowers an image to transform into a symbol so as always to call forth a certain context?

The change from image through metaphor to symbol occurs when an image becomes the sign of an unforgettable event. An image becomes memorable when it recalls the danger a man has passed through. It often reminds us of the power of death, and indirectly it reveals the cause and purpose of human destiny.

In order to survive and yet remain sane, the body imposes a hierarchy of vigilance upon us. Ordinary perceptual and conceptual images evoke a low degree of attention. We tend to ignore these, except if our need or their intensity puts us on the alert. An intense image automatically causes us to compare it with remembered bodily sensations. A conscious acknowledgment of the image means it has forced us to come to terms with it, and hence it produces a certain degree of danger or hope.

A metaphor does not equate a class with a species as in "My house is a bungalow." Rather, it affirms that two persons or things share a mutual quality, condition, or state. When a poet says, "My love is a burning sunset," he is equating what is common between two phenomena: their fiery intensity, the multicolored sensations they call forth, and the insight that the love, like the day, is slowly ending, never to return. The analogy emphasizes only what in the thing is powerful, striking, or indelible. If we take note of an image because of the imminence we associate with it, the metaphor illustrates the more immediate and impending.

A symbol is an image translated beyond metaphor into a complex, trans-causal and trans-temporal meaning. A conscious image calls forth an imminent degree of consciousness, a metaphor evokes an impending degree, and a symbol transcends these anterior states, freeing them from contingency and doubt, by having found its final destiny. Hence the imminent event has transformed the image and metaphor into a symbol with metaphysical meaning. Symbol is an image-metaphor which has attained its essence.

Symbolization means then that an image must affect us before we can arrive at a new noetic state. The symbol is noetic in its ability to convey the same general experience, the memory and meaning of the event, whereas it is affective in recalling the anxiety or sorrow which found release in the death, change, or transfiguration of the hero. The symbol realizes its entelechy by seeking out its teleological purpose.

The comparative and superlative transformation of image and metaphor to symbol greatly resembles the idiomatic use we make of adjectives (fine, finer, finest), or adverbs (swift, swifter, swiftest), and of verbs (walk, run, sprint). Such comparisons evoke degrees of the affective whereas the superlative affirms a noetic state has been attained. In a like manner, metaphoric metamorphoses bear a striking resemblance to verbal concretization. For instance, gradations from the abstract to the specific (as man, senator, President, John F. Kennedy) summon up corresponding degrees of interest and attention. Hence both literal and figurative language appear to function to evoke affective and noetic degrees of consciousness and understanding.

Therefore, the symbol is a superlative form by reason of its *complexity* (it is transhistorical and transcausal); by reason of its *intensity* (it can convey the same meanings to an event despite great spans of time); and by reason of its *completeness* (it is a final transformation).

This potency leads us to comprehend that an image may go through successive stages to find final realization in a symbol. Like the hero in fiction seeking his purpose in the cosmos, the reader too may discover the ultimate meaning of his life in an image, metaphor or symbol.

CHAPTER 5
THE NEO-ARISTOTELIAN
ANALYSIS OF LITERATURE
AND THE LIMITS OF LOGIC

Some students may be perplexed that an ancient treatise, Aristotle's *Poetics*, should still be considered authoritative and useful. Others may wonder how a mind in antiquity could have been so thorough and comprehensive that contemporary innovations in literary criticism hardly mark an improvement on that venerable work. For this reason, the Chicago critics vigorously championed Aristotle's esthetic in their day. If their attack on the New Critics is sometimes unfair, nevertheless the neo-Aristotelians were justified in so far as they did battle for a viable and durable philosophy of literature. They regarded Aristotle's *Poetics* as a model of methodology which for the past 2,300 years has repeatedly inspired worthwhile criticism.

For Aristotle, reality was revealed through the essential and persisting forms in nature. Because he conceived nature as that force which shapes life into significant forms, he thought a story to contain an entelechy which shapes human events into meaning. If ideal beauty to the ancient Greeks was described in terms of balance, rhythm, symmetry and proportion, for Aristotle that ideal expressed itself in literature through the integration of all parts into an organic whole. Thus Aristotle's esthetic reflected his view that the universe was a living being with its significance manifest in its wholeness and in its metamorphoses.

It is well known that the *Poetics* represents Aristotle's effort to justify literature on the grounds that any true imitation of nature is a form of knowledge and that such knowledge can produce a morally enlightening effect. In literature, form describes the direction events take if permitted to realize themselves, or put another way, form shows a character fulfilling his destiny in order to discover his ultimate identity. Since poetry imitates the nature of man, the main value of poetry is in its reflection of the universal truths in human experience.

With these preliminary understandings in mind, we may turn to the more technical concerns of the Chicago "school" of criticism. In addition to giving the format of *Critics and Criticism, Ancient and Modern* (1952), Ronald S. Crane introduces the reader to the underlying assumptions and aims of the so-called neo-Aristotelian movement in criticism. Among these assumptions, he separates the attitudes ascribed to the "school" from their actual, basic principles.

First, the Chicago scholars are not the proponents of a special system of criticism, but rather they wish to develop a general theory of literature. Second, they do not neglect to study the language of poetry nor do they adhere to a pseudo-formalism which reduces a poem to the architectural principles of a literary genre. Third, their attachment to Aristotle's *Poetics* is not a question of doctrinal conviction nor are they committed dogmatically to Aristotle's philosophy. In sum, they reject the charges of pedantry made against them.

Crane regards linguistics, history and the analysis of ideas of equal importance to literary and artistic criticism, and although he urges the investigation of methods employed in the other arts for their possible use in literary criticism, he is opposed to any poetics derived from psychoanalysis or anthropology. Similarly, he is impatient at the hollow rhetoric that characterizes so much critical writing, and he belittles the foolish attempt of contemporaries to solve problems long ago solved. What the contributors of *Critics and Criticism* want is to develop a reasoned discourse about literature.

Crane deplores the diversity of contemporary views regarding the aims, nature, form, structure, texture, and worth of poetry. Such marked differences among critics have led to skepticism, dogmaticism, or a flabby eclectic approach which maintains that all critical positions are partially false and partially true. The only counter to such confusion is to get behind the limitations of terminology to determine whether its conceptual scheme ". . . derives from principles that define poetry as a kind of philosophy, . . . as an effect on the audience, . . ." or the like. We must also find out what mode of reasoning the critics use. The critics infer causes, move from parts to whole, or use ". . . dialectical divisions and resolution . . ."[1]

Crane and his associates acknowledge that many distinct critical methods are valid in their own spheres and that each critic has the right to choose his own approach. However, the neo-Aristotelians reserve the right to question the efficacy of such methods, for every system has characteristic potentials and limitations. In particular, the Chicago scholars object to approaches which emphasize the part but neglect the whole or study the likenesses among poems but ignore the differences. Some contemporaries use one method of analysis for all poems, while other critics juggle pairs of dualistic terms but leave unanalyzed more important aspects of a poem.

The aim of *Critics and Criticism* is to show the methodological limitations of those critics who display an indifference to the lessons of the history of criticism. Only by drawing on critical principles which have effectively resolved the perennial problems of literature can one make universal statements that transcend the esthetic peculiarities fashionable at any given time. The Chicago critics feel Aristotle's *Poetics* provides them with the basis for a comprehensive critical method which will examine the way poetic wholes function together.

To these critics, Aristotle's treatise seizes ". . . the distinctive nature of poetic works . . ." as concrete artistic wholes.[2] Since definitions and devices utilized in the *Poetics* were derived from the examination of many literary works, the neo-Aristotelian approach is comprehensive for the following reasons: (1) it embraces all the elements which produce definite effects on the mind; (2) it transcends linguistic analysis and poetic techniques to account for the union and interaction of wholes; and (3) it uses a great number of principles of literary construction whereby a wide range of pertinent distinctions among poems may be made. In other words, the Chicago critics feel they study the representation of significant human actions whereas the New Critics miss these because of their narrow preoccupation with linguistic paradoxes.

Crane admits that Aristotle's method has been misused when applied to poems constructed on quite different principles from those of ancient epic and tragedy. He acknowledges the limitations of the Aristotelian approach and admits that other critical techniques are needed to supplement it. However, Crane is definitely against extrinsic studies of poetry as those arising from the poet's life or from the spirit of the time, although once a poem itself is analyzed, it may be situated in the history of poetry. Finally, he regards bibliography, textual criticism, philological exegesis, and the history of ideas as essential tools to the Aristotelian method.

In sum, Crane's main objection to other critical approaches is that they have only proliferated ineffectual methods, and the reason for this is that such approaches have neglected the real achievement of traditional poetics. If criticism is to develop a comprehensive system as that of Aristotle, it must be based on sound inductive reasoning which takes into account a wide range of literary examples. Only by such thoroughness will the concepts and methods of any system become truly viable.

THE PRINCIPLES OF THE
NEO-ARISTOTELIAN APPROACH

If one seeks the conceptual scheme behind the neo-Aristotelian polemic against the New Critics, one finds that the Chicago scholars have attempted to develop a logic of literature only to discover the limits of any such logic. If the neo-Aristotelians themselves aimed at combating pluralism, relativism, skepticism, and sophistry, their effort to evolve an absolute methodology resolved itself into three or four extremely simple epistemological principles. Behind their sophisticated arguments stands no genuine organon of their own. Nevertheless, the principles they have used have value in themselves.

PARTS-WHOLE

Crane's introductory article underlines the first principle embraced by a majority of the neo-Aristotelians. He states that the salient defect of other fashionable critical approaches is that they treat parts of a poem as if they were functional wholes. Such approaches are irresponsible because they fail to make ". . . distinctions of form and function . . ." between different kinds of literary work.[3] Such critics would commit fewer errors if they examined poetic works as concrete wholes rather than offer poetic theories based on parts of literary works. Thus the Chicago critics draw on Aristotle's concept of organic unity to point up the New Critics' inadequate exploration of the parts-whole relationship in a literary work.

In another article, "The Critical Monism of Cleanth Brooks,"

Crane regards Brooks's near total emphasis on irony and paradox as deplorable.[4] What criticism needs is an adequate hypothesis about the poetic whole, not about the parts of the poem. We cannot assume that ambiguity, irony, and paradox are common to all kinds of poetry. To test an entire poem according to a single part is to distort the importance of that fragment. One cannot elevate a particular into a universal. By the limited context Brooks has chosen, he has kept himself from developing an adequate critical apparatus. Crane, therefore, proposes that an adequate critical method must be supported by sufficient evidence as to its utility. The theory of poetry needs to be multidimensional, not unidimensional as pursued by the single-minded New Critics.

Crane's "I.A. Richards on the Art of Interpretation" also criticizes Richards for the same error of studying parts instead of the whole.[5] Moreover, Crane objects to Richards' belief in the duality of human nature as the basis of our equivocal use of words. Richards has oversimplified the whole problem of reading texts by reducing their complexity to the distinction between the referential and emotional uses of language. However, since Richards argues that meaning occurs when pairs of contraries mingle, he sees man as endowed with a natural will of interpretation or with an instinct for dialectic.[6] Crane rejects Richards' way of framing the problems of literature in terms of organic processes. Biological analogies and linguistics do not substitute for traditional grammar, logic and genuine criticism.

INDUCTION VERSUS
DEDUCTION

In addition to pointing out the New Critics' failure to properly explore the parts-whole relationship intrinsic to any literary work, the neo-Aristotelians stress the need to evolve critical concepts and methodology out of an inductive study of many literary works, as Aristotle himself had done. Furthermore, the critic himself should proceed inductively when studying a particular text.

Although Elder Olson and Keast both criticize the New Critics for using limited paradoxes, ironies and symbols to study a work deductively, the neo-Aristotelians themselves use Aristotle's *Poetics* deductively as a kind of philosopher's stone to test literary works and

come to certain conclusions. Crane's contention that critical problems
have been resolved by Aristotle and that there is no need to solve the
problems all over again proves the neo-Aristotelian approach itself to
be largely deductive and not inductive.

<h2 style="text-align:center">REDUCTIONISM AND
EXAGGERATION</h2>

The neo-Aristotelians embrace a third principle. They refuse to
reduce the significance of a whole work to any of its component parts,
or conversely, they avoid singling out any trait in order to exaggerate
its importance to the total meaning of a work.

Olson's article on Empson,[7] for instance, finds Empson guilty of
reducing all poetic considerations to diction and to problems of
ambiguities. Indeed, Empson's willful reduction of the text of Macbeth
to suit his narrow linguistic theory proves Empson's incapacity to
handle a literary work. Olson denies that ambiguity is universal to all
or even to the best poetry. It is not words which determine the
meaning, but everything else in the poem which determines that
meaning. What is needed is a discussion of the implications of human
action and plot rather than Empson's reduction of the play to linguistic
exercises as a universal method of literary interpretation. To counteract
such reductionism, Olson would enlarge the scope of criticism to
include ". . . philosophy of arts and sciences, a discipline establishing
and criticizing . . . principles."

R.S. Crane also objects to the reduction of the complexity of any
text to elementary critical concepts as irony, paradox, and the like. He
sees Brooks as reducing all effects in a text to a single cause and
censures Brooks's reduction of Coleridge's complex "reconciliation
of opposites" to a simplist formula. Ironically, then, although Brooks
is against the heresy of paraphrasing. Brooks himself is guilty of
reducing complexity to unsophisticated statements. In short, Crane is
against Brooks's monistic reduction of critical concepts. The multiplicity of Coleridge's approach collapses to Brooks's monism.

DEFINITION AND MEANING

A fourth principle of neo-Aristotelian thinking is concerned with proper definition and adequate meaning.

To Elder Olson, Empson's discussion of the seven types of ambiguity typifies the vagueness of the definitions of the New Critics. In Empson's use of the key term *sublimity*, he confuses potential significance (what a text might mean) with actual significance (what a text actually means). Indeed, Empson hardly seems aware of the distinctions among implication, inference and meaning. Furthermore, the classification into seven types of ambiguity is based on dubious distinctions.

What is dangerous in such vagueness is that it leads to parallel, indefinite understandings of the true aim and scope of literary criticism. What is worse is that the New Critics use their definitions as proofs of what they intend to prove rather than as tentative bases for further inquiry. In sum, Olson disapproves of definitions as deductive proofs to illustrate the meaning of a text. Rather, a definition should be used as a hypothesis for the inductive investigation of a literary work.

Elder Olson provides a deeper insight into the way language functions to effect meaning. With ancient tragedy in mind, Olson points out that language is used both to conceal and half conceal the significance of events. Clarity of language is in proportion to reader expectation, and any increase in implication increases the clarity of the text. Conversely, suspense occurs with every delay of meaning, and suspense is maintained until the meaning is found.

Elsewhere Olson states that metaphor contains a dialectic, and this observation makes us realize that language itself may be used dialectically. Indeed, the suspense Olson describes may be regarded as a dialectic between the known and the unknown (and possibly threatening). Meaning then is derived from the resolution of the dialectic between the understood and the not yet understood. This leads us to infer that definition, like metaphor, is the result of a dialectic.

DIALECTIC

Thus far we have seen how the neo-Aristotelians have been preoccupied with the parts-whole relationship in the organic unity of a literary work, with the use of induction and deduction as a general critical method, with avoiding the reduction of a total work to a few simple elements or the exaggeration of a few traits into a total interpretation. Similarly they have been concerned with concision of definition and meaning. However, Elder Olson's view that dialectic is the very essence of literary composition points out the awakening of the new-Aristotelians to the limits of logic. In other words, a literary work and its language cannot be completely discussed by using logic alone, for metaphor, definition and literary composition itself manifest dialectical processes.

In fact, Crane's objection to Brooks's monistic reduction of Coleridge's complex concept "the reconciliation of opposites" may be regarded as a criticism of Brooks's forced syntheses. Put in a larger context, Crane finds the New Critics' exploration of partial antitheses, such as "irony" and "paradox," to be an insufficient investigation of the overall dialectic inherent in a poem or play. This means that Crane is for an adequate dialectical study of literature.

The neo-Aristotelians thus show a distinct awareness of the relations between philosophy and literary criticism. Not only are they generally concerned with the limitations of systems of thought; they are also conscious of the limits of logic. Their increasing preoccupation with dialectical reasoning is evidence of this.

Elder Olson's article "An Outline of Poetic Theory" confronts the "linguistic and methodological Tower of Babel which characterizes literary criticism of the past decades.[8] Olson maintains that the differences among critical approaches should not be regarded as outright contradictions due to mutual incompatibilities. One must distinguish the truth and falsity of viewpoints from the methods used for formulating those viewpoints.

He sums up the four philosophical positions behind the diversity of critical approaches. The *dogmatic* position believes in one truth and discredits other points of view as false or false in part. The *scynretic* position considers all positions partially false and attempts to "synthesize" whatever is true in them. Such a forced reconciliation tends to distort whatever significance the original positions contained. The *skeptical* view dwells on the difference among systems of thought and tends to regard them all as false. Dogmaticism, syncretism, and skepticism are concerned with doctrine alone. On the other hand, the *pluralistic* position attempts to account for doctrine and method because it considers it possible to embrace a plurality of truths and philosophical directions. All discussions of technique, form and process are largely determined by both the subject matter and the philosophical view held by the critic.

The discussion of any subject ensues from its manner of formulation. The diversity of critical approaches is a consequence of the general tendency to concentrate on four areas of interest: (1) the art object as product; (2) the artist's activity; (3) the artist's mind or character as source of arts; and (4) the effect of art on an audience.

If anything is to resolve this diversity and its consequent multiplicity of method, it is the dialectical method. However, dialectical reasoning is an exceedingly complex matter. It requires Olson to distinguish between two basic kinds of dialectic. One kind is the *integral or likeness dialectic* which proceeds by combining like with like. When criticism centers on the art medium, integral dialectic tries to establish universal criteria for all aspects of literature, showing which properties poetry holds in common. Thus integral criticism tends to draw the analogy between artist and artistic process, nature and natural processes, God and the continuous creativity evident in the universe. If it concerns itself with the end of art, its goal, like those of man, is linked to the teleological purpose of the divinity.

On the other hand, *differential or difference dialectic* proceeds by separating dissimilars. When criticism centers on the art medium, differential dialectic seeks to discriminate appropriate criteria for each kind of diction and to discover which properties are characteristics of poetry alone.[9] The defect of both integral and differential dialectics is that each rests on a part, instead of a whole, so that each attributes everything to a single cause.

Olson finds that Plato and Aristotle illustrate these two basic kinds of dialectic.[10] Whereas each embraces likenesses and differences, Plato's approach is primarily integral and Aristotle's is differential. Plato's dialectic subsumes everything to a single cause whereas Aristotle differentiates causes. However, Aristotle aims at the differentiation and analysis of poetic form with the purpose of studying how causes converge to effect specific emotional responses. Put another way, Aristotle's method differentiates in order systematically to resolve composites into their simplest parts.

Olson is concerned with the kind of poetic which regards poetry as a system of actions. As such, he is mainly interested in dramatic form because it best exemplifies the problems inherent in general poetics. Anticipation and expectation play a vital role in the emotional effect a literary work will produce. Wherever we anticipate, the unexpected may well occur.[11] In other words, a tragedy must not only be integrated; its plot should effect a catharsis through reversal and recognition. Hence when anticipation meets the unexpected, there we have a dialectical confrontation. Thus, according to Olson, the dialectical interaction in tragedy calls for a dialectical study of poetic form.

In Richard McKeon's article "Literary Criticism and the Concept of Imitation in Antiquity," he not only traces the early history of "imitation" but also clarifies how Aristotle and Plato used different dialectical approaches to define the concept of imitation.

As is characteristic of many critical terms, the word has assumed a variety of meanings in history. In Plato's dialogues the term is ". . . left universal in scope and indeterminate in application. The dialectical method is used to determine its meaning in particular contexts . . ." Plato applies the term to human activities as well as to ". . . natural, cosmic and divine processes . . ."[12] Although the word *imitation* is defined, it ". . . receives no fixed meanings . . ." Through images and associations, the word ". . . suffers extensions and limitations . . ."[13] so that its meaning ". . . may expand and contract . . ." when applied to poetry or philosophy.[14]

Plato is concerned with the correspondence between being (as eternal Form or Idea) and appearance, between truth and falsity, between knowledge and opinion. Plato explores the process of imitation dialectically by dividing the visible from the intelligible and by dividing each part into two classes which in turn are divided. Plato's dialectic reasons by division and distinctions.

By contrast, Aristotle uses a different method for defining his terms, employs them in a distinct manner, and consequently, arrives at a different definition of "imitation." If Plato's concept undergoes (via analogies) ". . . an infinite series of gradations of meaning . . . ," Aristotle's ". . . term is restricted definitely to a single literal meaning."[15] Plato's examination of the implications of imitation reach outward over the whole domain of philosophy whereas Aristotle restricts his discussion to a limited sphere of philosophy. Although for Plato the dialectical process may aim at defining words, ". . . any word may have many definitions." On the other hand, for Aristotle the definition of terms begins as a scientific undertaking. Thus out of the many meanings a word may have, Aristotle formulates an unequivocal meaning for each key word. The term becomes a constant. Apparently Aristotle reduces its connotations to its single denotation whereas Plato evidently expands a term out of an abstraction to explore all the possible connotations of that original term.

McKeon makes some final comments related to Plato's mode of reasoning about literature. If each dialogue of Plato is itself a dialectic, there also seems a dialectical development among dialogues, so the context of Plato's statements shifts from dialogue to dialogue. For this reason no coherent doctrine of Plato can result from collecting quotations of what he has said poetry means. Because a definition may vary according to the kind of reasoning employed, we need to discover the larger method or system of reasoning behind a definition. As applied to literary criticism, we must learn to detect the critic's underlying philosophical attitude if we are to uncover the logical or dialectical devices he utilizes to formulate meaning.[16]

The aim of Richard McKeon's "The Philosophical Bases of Arts and Criticism" is to trace out ". . . the dialectical consequences of philosophical and critical principles . . ."[17] "The general patterns . . . in philosophic discussions . . ."[18] show that the status of facts varies according to the different principles used to interpret them.[19] For instance, critical terms as "form," "content," and "expression" are deceptively similar concepts, but as they are analyzed and interpreted differently, they acquire different meanings. Apparent distinctions and differences in critical approaches may be resolved by some pervasive dialectic.

Fundamental differences among modes of criticism go ". . . back to fundamental differences of philosophical principles." Furthermore, "What is essential in one approach may be accidental in the other."[20]

McKeon discusses six modes of criticism used in esthetic analysis.

There are five "literal" modes and one "dialectical".

Aristotle's scientific criticism represents the first literal mode. Rather than using dialectic or rhetoric to analyze tragedy, Aristotle used a scientific method to examine tragedy in terms of construction and parts, finding in plot the chief criterion for unity and structure. The second literal form of criticism, the "poetic" mode, derives from Longinus and Arnold, who used lofty ideas and passionate utterance as touchstones of universal beauty and greatness.

A third literal form of criticism, the "scholarly" mode, studies with care an author's entire work to reconstruct his significance. Historical documentation is used to illuminate particular textual meanings. The fourth literal form of criticism, the"technical" mode, as illustrated in Horace and Boileau, focuses on the devices which produce effects, including the structure and unity of a literary work.

The fifth literal form of criticism, the "formal" mode, used by I.A. Richards et al., classifies styles of language for the purpose of analyzing the effectiveness of parts or evaluating their appropriateness. Eventually this mode pursues a parts-whole procedure, beginning with words and syntax to ultimately analyze the composition as a whole.

As keystone to the five literal modes of criticism, the dialectical approach comprises ". . . a vast . . . series of forms which emerge or move from one emphasis to another . . ." This dialectical criticism opposes each of the forms of "literal" criticism in appropriate terms. Whereas the literal modes are concerned with clear-cut boundaries between their respective modes and aim at literal definitions, the dialectical approach proves that distinct definitions fail to correspond to anything real, or the dialectical approach broadens the distinctions into viable descriptions with feasible applications.

In general, dialectical criticism extends the context of a literary work by situating it among other esthetic and cultural phenomena. The danger is that the dialectic may freeze prematurely into a dogmatic stance. Although McKeon does not overtly advocate any single mode of criticism, his own essay uses dialectical reasoning in emulation of Plato's use of the dialectic. Without prejudice or distortion, McKeon has sought to account for the literal modes as well as the dialectical.

Dispassionately and dialectically, he has shown the virtues, failures, and perversities of each mode. Indeed, by being a dialectician in the manner of Plato, McKeon reveals not only the limits of literal criticism but the limits of logic as well. By precept and example McKeon has shown the need to surpass any esthetic based on logic alone, and he has demonstrated the scope and potential of a dialectical approach to literary criticism.

To more fully appreciate the achievement of the neo-Aristotelians, we need to visualize the parallel between the intellectual problems of antiquity and those of modern criticism. As Socrates had to reject the paradoxes of Zeno and the Sophists, so the neo-Aristotelians felt the need to reject the ironies and paradoxes of the New Critics, no matter what other merits the intrinsic approach brought to modern criticism. Similarly, as Socrates had to turn away from the inadequacy of the rhetoric and "logic" of his time to work out a dialectic of his own, neo-Aristotelians as Olson and McKeon became aware that logic alone cannot come to terms with the dynamic nature of the literary work.

It is important, therefore, to recall the situation in antiquity. Plato sought to resolve the paradoxical opposition between the Heraclitan view of the universe as in a state of constant flux and Parmenides's belief that the universe was permanent. Inspired by the Pythagorans, Plato sought a dialectical solution to the starkly different views of reality. The answer was in Socratic irony which discarded false, sensory appearances to reach upward to the ultimate realm of pure Forms and true Ideas. Put another way, Plato's dialectic used spatial reasoning when he distinguished between absolute ideas and truths.

By contrast, Aristotle's dialectic concerns itself with biological and spiritual being and becoming; hence the profound significance of his discussion of drama which concentrates on the actions of men. As seen in Aristotle's description of complex plot, which effects transformations through reversal and recognition, Aristotle regards plot as a dialectic between man's being and becoming, between a deceptively stable identity and the individual's true, dynamic destiny.

Thus when Aristotle discusses tragedy in the light of parts organically united into a whole, he is basically using a combination of inductive and deductive logic. In other words, one part of his *Poetics* provides a spatial definition of tragedy. On the other hand, when Aristotle describes the entelechy inherent in human actions and when he distinguishes between simple and complex plot, he is using dialectical reasoning. In short, he then gives a temporal definition of tragedy. Because men are motivated to move from being through becoming to a final being, tragedy represents a dialectic and can obviously be interpreted as such.

CONCLUSION

We may summarize the contribution of neo-Aristotelian thinking as follows. The main objection to other critical ventures is that they mistake the part for the whole and tend either to reduce the entire literary work to that part, in order to explicate the work, or they tend to use that part (e.g., ironies, paradoxes) as a universal key to all literature. In essence, the neo-Aristotelians are saying that the New Critics and those who employ extrinsic methods of studying literature have failed to use the logic proper to a whole literary work. Furthermore, where methods of literary criticism are logical, they tend to use deductive logic as if they have already found the truth, or, worse, such methods use a limited logic to give quite inadequate interpretations. In emulation of Aristotle and modern science, the neo-Aristotelians advocate the use of inductive logic so that sufficient evidence may be gathered to substantiate critical reasoning.

In contrast to the vague semantics and ambiguities of the New Critics, McKeon urges the use of a combined approach to the definition of critical terms. If Plato's dialectic shows us that a concept should be examined for its possible multiple meanings, Aristotle's reasoning guides us to aim at concision of concept.

Thus if we regard a literary work as a definition of human experience, that work must not only be defined as a logical system (organic unity) but also as a dialectic. Put another way, a literary work requires both spatial analysis and temporal interpretation. The limits of logic may be overcome by the use of a dialectic which can both reconcile opposite systems of logic, as the inductive and deductive, and arrive at the concise definition of a particular literary work. Such a dialectic will not only establish a hierarchy from partial to complete truth and from inferior to superior value; such a dialectic will also serve to remind the interpreter that truth itself gradually transforms in time.

CHAPTER 6
EUROPEAN CRITICISM OF
ANGLO-AMERICAN FORMALISM

A survey of major European critics for and against Anglo-American formalism reveals a plethora of conflicting critical viewpoints. Indeed, the diversity of aims, methods, and approaches they advocate is bound at first to confuse both student and scholar. Yet they provide the ground of being out of which grew the critical concerns of today.

Typical of the time, the dilemma was not restricted to literary criticism alone. Virtually all humanistic knowledge was going through a similar crisis of conscience. Although at times the critics disagreed vigorously, their diverse theories and studies allow us to infer certain attitudes and characteristics which foreshadowed the future of literary criticism. The insights of the Europeans may, therefore, prove useful as criteria, hypotheses, and principles to the reader seeking today to create a new, holistic system of his own.

In his article "Anglo-American New Criticism," Dr. Alfred Behrmann summarizes its preoccupations and aims, its achievements and defects.[1] The New Critics were preoccupied with the poem and the interaction of structure and texture, tenor and vehicle, meter and meaning, and other such entwining terms. Poetry offered a knowledge of existence and a degree of objectivity denied to scientific discourse. As Cleanth Brooks expressed it, a poem reflected knowledge of ourselves as we experience the world. As a consequence, New Criticism paid serious attention to poetry as poetry. Moreover, it concerned itself with theoretical problems, even if these proved merely a rerun of problems already dealt with by pre-positivistic and pre-impressionistic critics. On the other hand, through the New Critics' insistence on isolating the poem as an object of study, they approached the concerns of structuralism.

To better clarify the aims of the New Critics, Dr. Behrmann situated them in their historical context. He mentioned Benedetto Croce's *La Critica* (1903), which treated literature purely as an esthetic phenomenon. J. E. Spingarn, in turn, attacked the convention of genres because artists were concerned with expressing themselves rather than with writing a specific genre. Next Behrmann discussed T.S. Eliot's contribution to critical development in *The Sacred Wood* (1920). Eliot advocated that a poem be viewed as a poem and not something else. Moreover, the poet-critic stressed the need to overcome the "dissociation of sensibility," inherited from the seventeenth century, in order to create a unified sensibility. Indeed, Eliot's artistic goal was to attain the impersonality of the most masterful poetry of the past. His erudition and sense of history enabled him to demonstrate how the past and present were interdependent because the past is actual in the present. To Eliot, every new work necessitated a reassessment of the works of the past, and yet a critic's main goal was to understand first the poem itself and not permit any moral, social, or religious implications to interfere with its strict analysis. Such understanding was achieved by close reading — line by line, stanza by stanza.

I.A. Richards rivaled Eliot in importance by having provided the New Criticism with additional goals. Richards' concern was with poetic tradition in the light of his own ideals of poetic style. He advised critics to study the intricate problem of analyzing a poem in terms of its language, imagery, and metaphor. In *Principles of Literary Criticism* (1924), he drew attention to the imaginative and emotional impact of words whereas in his *Practical Criticism* (1929) Richards encouraged the psychological study of language as it bore on literary analysis.

To Dr. Behrmann, Richards' true importance was in the emphasis on the density and stratification of the poem where the parts interact to evoke something beyond their sum. Since the emotive expression of poetic language contrasted to its referential nature, this contrast delineated the difference between poetic value and propositional truth. Joined together as context, they constituted the particular mode of existence of a poem.[2] Thus the achievements of the New Criticism.

As to its defects, Professor Behrmann notes that the New Critics had no common program, no mutual philosophy, no organized method. At most, they had a common inclination.[3] Behrmann refers to Murray Krieger's study of their contradictions and their failure to deal with decisive questions, which led Murray to consider the New Critics as apologists for an amateurish metaphysics.[4]

On the other hand, Behrmann's article just faintly suggested the strong cross-currents of European critical arguments for and against Anglo-American formalism.

A Swiss scholar advocating the formalistic or ahistorical method of literary study was Wolfgang Kayser (1906-1960). In *The Verbal Artwork* (1948), he expressed the belief that poetry treated its own reality or objectivity because the integrating character of language structured thought and feeling into a unity.[5] Kayser acknowledged, however, that, since the eighteenth century, critics had realized that a literary work engaged deeper levels of the soul than merely the esthetic.[6] To account for such inner levels of meaning, they must be related to the reader's world and to the poet's heart. This concession notwithstanding, Kayser affirmed that the artwork should be studied as artwork, not as disguised biography.[7] The work itself must concern us more than the author.

In his own way, Kayser resolved the problem of dualism by regarding the artwork as a complex unity of "inner" and "outer" world. Based on his awareness that reality comprised the empirical and the abstract, Kayser viewed lyric poetry as the intensification of experience because outer reality reflected the inner world of the soul. In plainer terms, the natural events depicted in poetry were a translation of what was taking place in the poet's soul.[8] Yet, despite these allowances, Kayser insisted that a complete interpretation required a precise understanding of the inner and outer construction of the poem as evinced linguistically and stylistically.[9] His primary concern remained, therefore, with the formalistic (*textimmanent*) elements of the literary work. In general, then, Kayser himself pursued a systematic analysis of formalistic strata.[10]

Nevertheless, Kayser had his reservations about exclusively using any single approach. For example, he doubted whether any isolated method, which explored a particular side of a work, could understand the work as a whole or as a unity.[11] Furthermore, he cautioned against using those principles of form and construction taken from other arts since the literary artwork had its own principles.[12] He even warned against the unconscious use of modern literary concepts on older literature, thus admonishing critics against superimposing their sophisticated notion on works which might not really respond to their method of analysis. On the other hand, Kayser admitted that it might be meaningful and justifiable to examine a poem in the light of a Weltanschanung, the spirit of the epoch, or the meaning of life problems — if such methods did justice to the essence of poetry.[13] Late in life, he acknowledged the need to situate the artwork in the time of its inception, yet what remained most important for him was form (Gestalt) and the close reading of text.[14]

The Swiss theorist Emil Staiger discussed genres as related to formalistic analysis in his *Principles of Poetics* (1946). He distinguished lyric, drama and epic by the way they evoked our awareness of time. The lyric was unhistorical because it caused us to be in things and they in us;[15] the epic was historical; whereas drama demonstrated the tension between the present and future in the suspense it called forth.[16] However, Staiger was too sophisticated to rest satisfied with distinctions, and he admitted that, as a result of language itself, a literary work could participate in the lyrical, the epic, and the dramatic.[17] A work was all the more complete as it participated in all three genres.[18]

Although Staiger conceded that a knowledge of genres, of history, and the author's biography might help to understand a literary piece, he insisted that the vision in lyric poetry transcended the historical or social mode of contemplation. Rather, the true criteria of interpretation were to be found in man's perpetual capacity to be touched deeply, for understanding came from being moved emotionally. Since some eternal quality in human nature responded to the poem, true interpretation must contemplate what was timeless in the literary work . There was an ageless power in literature which somehow corresponded to the *sub specie aeternitatis* of Spinoza. In this respect; Staiger's ultimate orientation appeared to point the way to an ontology or a phenomenology of literary criticism.

In *The Art of Interpretation* (1955), Staiger continued to stress the need to concentrate on the literary work itself. In no way could a poem be explained from biography, the poet's personality, nor even from the history of ideas, for literary interpretation was the art of discovering the inner voice (*Stimmigkeit*), mood, atmosphere, or state of mind by which individual linguistic parts found their totality. Literary interpretation was not a striving toward the objective knowledge of science. Rather, as an art, interpretation grew out of immediate feeling and the empathic appreciation of the artwork. If there were any significance to the concepts lyrical, epic, and dramatic, the reason was that these literary terms reflected the fundamental possibilities of human existence. For this reason the history of literature manifested the existential possibilities of the human being.[19]

Karl Otto Conrady's *Introduction to the New German Study of Literature* (1966) represented continental criticism advocating a more ecumenical approach. On the one hand, he typified German interpretation concerned with the inner laws of the individual work, with its artistic peculiarity and totality.[20] On the other hand, he believed literary history was indissolubly bound together with the analysis and interpretation of individual works. Furthermore, he affirmed that a methodical cultivation of sciences was urgently needed to complement literary study *per se.*[21]

Similarly, Werner Krauss in *Fundamental Problems of Literary Study* (1968) asserted that a narrow relationship existed between literature and history.[22] Although he discussed the defects of positivism, he extolled the virtues of applying the history of ideas to literature. He also situated literary study somewhere between philosophical materialism and idealism. He went on to draw parallels between Anglo-American New Criticism and the formalism developed in France and Russia, concluding that their emphasis on ahistorical study inevitably proved untenable.[23] Even though he acknowledged that the analysis of style was important, he insisted that a sensible explication must be associated with factors largely outside language itself. Indeed, he urged critics to reconsider the full significance of mimesis. He asserted that form reflected the perceptible in an object whereas content (*Inhalt*) referred to ". . . the inner meaning of perceived reality." Ultimate reality was composed of ". . . spiritual values which lie within sensuous perceptions." Hence as context, content determined form.[24]

On the other hand, the French critics, Carloni and Filloux, with characteristic Gallic lucidity, viewed criticism as a genre itself with its own laws and with its own implicit and explicit methods. The authors' aim was to confront theory and its application.[25] In their book *Literary*

Criticism (1966), they reviewed (1) the historical attempt to judge literature in absolute terms and according to doctrinal rules; (2) the rise of the positivist effort with its emphasis on strict determinism; (3) the reaction of impressionistic criticism, which the authors considered a pseudo-method because of its subjectivism and superficiality; and (4) the erudite criticism of professors.

Carloni and Filloux's comments on the academic critics were illuminating as to the actual method pursued by scholars. As scrupulous and thorough as scientists, as passionate for facts, academic critics made use of documents and information which served the intrinsic explanation of literary works. The merit of such criticism was its rigour and precision.[26] However, the danger in the method was the frequency with which it stagnated into compilation, ending in arid erudition rather than in meaningful syntheses.[27] In the monographs such professors wrote, the literary work was related to literary history, and the author's own evolution of thought was confronted with his work.[28] Their central activity, then, was documentation in which every reference or statement was backed by documentary evidence. As a means rather than as an end, this erudite display all too often lacked a philosophy to back up the method.[29] Hence academic critics eclectically selected extrinsic materials as evidence and used formalistic analysis to interpret and evaluate the work.

Klein and Vogt's *Methods of Literary Study: Literary History and Interpretation* (1971) reviewed the critical approaches in America, Russia and Germany. The preface made clear their belief that the concepts and techniques of literary practice were not possible without theory, i.e., without knowledge of the historical and ideological changes in method. The authors' aim was to make the student cognizant of these changes in method by confronting the historical and ahistorical views of literature.[30]

Among the five basic approaches Klein and Vogt examined with care, they dwelled at greatest length on the ahistorical or formalistic theory of interpretation. They restated the already well known view that the literary work was an esthetic product to be explained solely from the text itself. The rise of this technique in Germany came as a reaction to the propaganda of National Socialism, hence its practitioners renounced any ideological engagement, and they practiced the ahistorical approach rigorously so as to exclude the social, historical, or political implications of literature.[31]

The authors illustrated this formalistic approach in the figure of Karl Viëtor (1892-1954), who maintained that where literature is investigated as a by-product of political, social, intellectual, psychological, or cultural events, the critic had moved away from literature *per se.* Viëtor wanted the literary scholar to study the sensuous-spiritual wholeness of the work itself as sui generis, and not as a reflection of forces or influences outside it.[32]

However, by the 1960's the exclusive formalistic interpretation of literature had become forced, unnatural and exaggerated. To emphasize this change, Klein and Vogt quoted Benno von Wiese's 1963 argument that the separation of literary history from interpretation was senseless. As evinced in this development, critics were striving for the reintegration of esthetic, historical, and social influences on literature.[33]

Klein and Vogt themselves felt that the function of literature was to impress and change society. In fact, they believed society must be convinced of the educational worth of literature.[34] For this reason they advocated the inclusion of literary history because it was the mental construct by which a culture accounted for its past.[35] As such, literary history could show how literature had served to enlighten and emancipate the people of a culture. In short, Klein and Vogt saw literature as an influence to better society.[36]

Zdenko Skreb in his article "The Scientific Nature of Literary Research," discussed formalistic approach, especially the exegesis of lyrical poetry, which emphasized the specific quality of the poetical artwork. If this approach was effective at first, the overflow of individualistic interpretations gradually led to a malaise as to the exclusive use of the intrinsic technique. Moreover, the multitude and variety of differing interpretations resulted in a sense of bewilderment among conscientious critics. One sought in vain for a common methodical consciousness. No conceptual system for coordinating isolated efforts was evolved.[37]

Skreb cites Jost Hermand's *Synthetic Interpreting* which criticized the formal approach of both the Russians and the West, for to him the poetic artwork was in the middle point of steadily widening, concentric spheres of implication and meaning.[38] Hence if the literary work were to be explicated, he agreed with Hermand's contention that literary research should pursue such comprehensive analysis so that even the smallest detail be explored for its universal connections.

Furthermore, Skreb warned critics against relying on intuition, which was the "fatal error" literary interpreters too often yielded to. Rather, it was necessary to transform the researcher's subjective experience into objective understanding by learning to judge literary works *intersubjectively*.[39] Moreover, he warned originators of methodologies that it was senseless to speak of methods when they had no, solid, scientific, conceptual world to support that method.[40] Nevertheless, instead of regarding the formalistic or hermeneutic approach as unscientific, he considered it as one pole of the scientific method with its opposite pole rooted in the deductive method of reasoning. Thus literary study needed to pursue the rigour and exactness of the sciences, complemented by the strictly logical operations of deduction so as to establish a precise knowledge of the literary work.[41] If such precision of method were followed in the analysis of data, a historical synthesis of these analyzed phenomena could then take place.

Edgar Lohner, in reviewing the shortcomings of formalism, cited German scholars who felt the need of historical awareness in literary interpretation as a safeguard against *furor interpretandi*.[42] He noted Kurt Müller-Vollmer's observation that the work of art did not represent a closed and isolated world of its own because its symbols and signs related the poetic world to the world we know. In other words, if the verbal structure actually were autonomous, how could a literary work tell us anything about the world?[43]

Lohner also stressed the need of the historical approach as an ancillary aid to *explication de texte*. Analyses must be founded on historical erudition, and if literary analysis were to become a literary science, it must be situated in the psychological and cultural moment when the literary form was created.[44] Lohner expanded on this observation by referring to Emil Staiger's statement that poetics should become a kind of philosophical anthropology which revealed the human being in time.

As a final reference to European criticism for and against Anglo-American formalism, mention must be made of Guerin, Labor, Morgan and Willingham's *Handbook of Critical Approaches to Literature* (1966). The authors believed that a given work had a most suitable approach and that every approach had its advantages and limitations.[45] They objected to the purist approach of the New Criticism because literature did not exist in a vacuum and a work of art should not be judged as if disembodied from all experience except the strictly esthetic.[46] A global, catholic orientation was needed because each individual approach had its limitations. If "traditional" methods tended to overlook the structural intricacies of the work, the "formalistic" neglected the context of history and biography which could provide important insights into the meaning of the work. In order to get the total meaning of a literary work, Guerin et al. advocated using many methods, among them historical-biographical, textual linguistic, and moral-philosophical analyses.[47]

SUMMARY

The purpose of this chapter has been to elicit the common attitudes and characteristics of European critics dealing with Anglo-American formalism. We may summarize these findings as follows.

1. Certain European critics approved of formalism and maintained that the *ahistorical* study of literature should remain the critics' uppermost concern.

2. Other European critics averred that no *exclusive critical approach* should be used. They argued that, if such single-mindedness tended to ensure greater precision of observation, it tended, nevertheless, to miss other elements vital to understanding the literary work.

3. Another group of critics advocated the *eclectic application of multiple approaches*, including those intrinsic and extrinsic to traditional literary exegesis. Obviously, inclusiveness was the aim of such eclecticism.

4. Still other critics advocated a *total syncretism* of methodology in order to achieve the integration of what we know about the literary work, the author, the period he wrote in, and his place in literary history.

5. Still other European critics wanted to direct criticism toward the comprehensiveness of interpretation. The total meaning of the literary work could best be grasped by dealing with the ways it portrayed the existentialist possibilities of human destiny.

6. The last group advocated that literary study should look to ontology or phenomenology for its ground of being. Wishing to establish criticism as a branch of philosophy, these critics attempted to transform the discipline through a deeper understanding of the nature of literature and through a *higher synthesis* of the ways we understand it.

In sum, the antimonies engendered between the formalists and their determined opponents led to the development of even more trenchant positions in the decades that followed, but that is another story.

PART THREE :
LITERARY THEORY AS
HUMAN SCIENCE

CHAPTER 7
THE SEARCH FOR A SCIENCE
OF LITERARY CRITICISM

Although the scientific method has increasingly influenced academic thought during the past three centuries, few students have genuinely understood the nature, scope or significance of scientific methodology as it may apply to literature. Hence this chapter has three purposes. First, it will briefly review the key ideas of those early, methodical thinkers who influenced modern literary study. Second, the paper will retrace the search of 18th and 19th century theorists and critics who sought to transform criticism into a science. Finally, the conclusion will provide a list of maxims and methods that a contemporary scholar may use to more effectively pursue his own independent research.

If anything characterizes the scientific outlook, it is the effort to understand the *how* and *why* of natural phenomena. Commonly rejecting dogma and authority as the basis for theory, scientists check their daring hypotheses against evidence painstakingly collected through years of observation. In this way the facts advanced by science have increased man's actual knowledge of the world.

Francis Bacon (1561-1621) gave us an early definition of this approach. Opposing the extensive use of deduction in Aristotle's *Organon*,[1] Bacon proposed induction as a method of reasoning in his own *Novum Organum* (1620). Induction enables a researcher to infer a general truth from many particular facts by investigating a series of incidents or circumstances which appear to be governed by some probable relationship or pattern of occurrences. The investigator's aim is to detect just what connection exists among such phenomena, how they operate and why.

Bacon was wary of the very hypotheses which set off such investigation, for men all too often are misled by their "idols." Bacon warned against such idols as (1) bad habits of mind, (2) expecting more law and order in nature than can be found, (3) personal prejudices, (4) the tyranny of words, (5) the veneration of past systems of thought, and (6) deductive reasoning as used in Aristotle's syllogisms. In place of these, Bacon advocated the analysis, classification, and correlation of all data pertaining to a given problem. By testing one hypothesis after another, the researcher tries to uncover the law governing his facts. In other words, induction implies a patient search for patterns which divulge the shape and significance of empirical experience.

During the same period, René Descartes (1596-1650) was also seeking to develop a solid system of thought. To attain an indisputable foundation for his method of reasoning, he systematically doubted everything he once thought of as knowledge until he realized he could not doubt the act of doubting. As a result, he came to the conclusion, "I think, therefore I am." With this new insight into man's thinking self, Descartes founded modern philosophy, and his "Cogito ergo sum" made the discovery of mental processes as important as the inductive exploration of empirical phenomena.

Because Descartes regarded the essential faculty of human nature to be reason, he wanted to train the mind to reason well. In his *Discourse on the Method* (1637), he outlined the principles of his system:

1. First, never accept anything as true which you do not recognize as such.

2. Second, divide each of the difficulties that you wish to examine into as many parts as is possible and as will be required to better resolve them.

3. Third, conduct your thoughts by order, beginning with the objects that are simplest and easiest to recognize, and

4. Last, make enumerations so complete and reviews so general that you are assured you have omitted nothing.

By the circumspection that these four steps impose on thought,

Descartes methodized rational investigation. In the following centuries, Cartesianism, as his method came to be called, encouraged the systematic analysis of truth and logic. Thus Descartes provided posterity with a model of the way the mind can define and transform experience into knowledge.

Thinkers in all intellectual domains gradually felt the need to pursue the aims and methods of either Bacon or Descartes. As 18th century France became preoccupied with social, scientific, and philosophical questions, Fontenelle's *Conversations on the Plurality of Worlds* (1686) made science fashionable. During the century, Buffon popularized the natural sciences, and geology was born.

Lavoisier introduced the important concept of *analysis*, which is the chemist's technique for separating a substance into its elements, and *synthesis*, which is the recombination of those elements into their original state. Later, *analysis* came to mean dividing any whole into its parts and *synthesis* meant recombining those parts into the original whole.

A prominent influence on the future of literary criticism was Montesquieu (1689-1755). His *Spirit of the Laws* (1748) studied the relationship of law to the constitution of each form of government, to the country's climate, religion, commerce and the like. He believed that laws are relative to the physical aspect of the country and to the situation and size of the terrain. Furthermore, laws derive from the religion of the inhabitants, their inclinations, their wealth, their number, their mores, their manners, and from the interrelationship these conditions have among themselves. Montesquieu's intent was to examine all these connections in order to discover how together they formed what he called the spirit of the laws (I, 3).

Although Montesquieu's erudition was incomplete and at times inexact, his effort to introduce the spirit and processes of science into the study of society was a pioneering attempt. More than this, he largely achieved his goal, for it became the philosophy of French education: "It is not a question of making people read, but of getting them to think." (*Esprit des Lois*, XI, 20).

Eighteenth century France also saw the publication of the *Encyclopedia* (1751-72), which attracted such noteworthy contributors as Diderot, D'Alembert, Voltaire and Rousseau. It had two distinct objectives: (1) as an encyclopedia, it sought to demonstrate the range of human knowledge, and (2) as a *Reasoned Dictionary of Sciences, Arts and Trades*, it described each science, trade and art by depicting its essential characteristics. The encyclopedia showed the value of the careful examination of phenomena and laws, and it aimed at converting men's common ways of thinking to rational habits of thought.

Comte de Buffon (1707-88) represented certain other scientific inclinations. He stressed the need to describe things precisely, and accurate details were necessary if an adequate account was to be rendered. Yet the most important need was to discover that great hypothesis which unified and explained everything.

Buffon himself sketched in the basis for a transformist and evolutionist explanation of living creatures. Further developed by his disciple Lamarck, Buffon's hypothesis found its culmination in Darwin's theory of evolution. Darwin's two decade study admirably illustrated Buffon's admonition to science students: "Genius is only a greater aptitude of patience."

It was not long before persons interested in literature took up the scientific attitude. Among those seeking to apply the scientific approach to literary criticism was Madame de Staël (1766-1817), who undertook the analysis of the romantic soul. In her *Literature Considered in its Relation to Institutions* (1800), she makes use of Montesquieu's famous theory to study the influence of mores, laws and religion on literature as well as the influence of literature on society. She states, "Climate is one of the principal reasons for the differences . . . between images which please in the north (of Europe) and those which one loves to recall in the south . . ." Reflecting the joys of life and of the heart, the southerner (of Europe) expresses himself through passion and willpower. By contrast, the northerner shows the influence of foggy and solemn climate by his preoccupation with suffering. Furthermore, his melancholy stems from the sense that man will never understand human destiny.

In Madame de Staël's *About Germany* (1810), she studies the mores, arts, literature, philosophy, morality, religion and enthusiasm of the Germans . Her opposition between Northern and Southern Europe leads to a parallel contrast between classical and romantic poetry. Although a scrutiny of her information reveals it to be superficial, and even though her critical views are considered by some to be too subjective, her emphasis on inspiration and genius foreshadowed the development of 19th and 20th century psychology, as shown in her assertion, ". . . it is sufficient to show that the diversity of tastes . . . derive not only from accidental causes, but also from primitive sources of the imagination and of thought."

Francis-René de Chateaubriand (1768-1848) also explored the attributes of the modern mind. In *The Genius of Christianity* (1802), he contrasts Homer's epics to the sublime poetry of the Bible and praises Gothic art and chivalric virtue. In discussing the way the Christian religion inspired art and literature, he showed how it fostered genius, virtue, good taste and virility of concept. His review of works by Dante, Tasso and Milton introduced historical criticism because he was examining the influence of culture on the individual artist.

On the other hand, Chateaubriand's own ideal of beauty stimulated later critics to speculate on the role of the human mind in the production of literature. Chateaubriand's belief in the spontaneity of the imagination eventually led to a scientific study of the literary psyche.

Charles Augustin Sainte-Beuve (1804-1869) in such works as *Critiques and Literary Portraits* (1836-39) and *Monday Lectures* (1851-62) pursued his own scientific bent when he observes, "To be the disciple of Bacon in literary history and criticism seems to me the need of the time."[2] Indeed, he asserts, "I analyze. I botanize. What I should like to establish is the natural history of literature."[3] In the same vein, he is confident about the future of literary study. "A day will come . . . a day when the science (of criticism) will be established, when the great families of the spirit and their principal divisions will be determined and known. When the principal character of mind is given, one will be able to deduce several other characteristics."[4] At that future time, scientists will be able to find the great natural divisions that mark off different groups of minds. Thus the critic himself should become. ". . . someone who seizes the life and the mind . . . someone suitable to be a good naturalist in this vast field of minds."[5]

In addition to this wish to see literary criticism emulate the orderliness of the natural sciences, Sainte-Beuve also sought out the larger sociological connection between a man and his culture. "The relation between the work and the author, the author's background — family, nation, historical period, and his period in relation to other ages

— all these relations, in widening concentric circles, are necessary for the critic's estimate."[6]

Sainte-Beuve's third method was to examine the specific connection between literary works and the author who created them. Characteristically, he asks about the writer, "What did he think religiously? How was he affected by the sight of nature? How did he act as far as women are concerned — or in the matter of money? Was he rich — was he poor? What was his regimen, his manner of daily life? In brief what was his vice or weakness?"[7] Applying an old proverb, he remarks, "Tell me who admires and loves you, and I shall tell you who you are . . ."[8] In essence, by sympathetically yet objectively studying the personality of the artist, Sainte-Beuve in his monographs attempts to give a more intimate account of literary creativity. Thus he equated the creative power of the poet to the insight of the critic. "The Poet finds the region . . . where his genius can live and unfold: the critic finds the instinct and law of that genius."[9]

By employing these diverse methods, Sainte-Beuve was pursuing a critical ideal ". . . to go beyond the judgements of outdated rhetoric, to be as little as possible the dupe of phrases, words, beautiful intentional sentiments, and (to attain) truth . . ." Unfortunately, Sainte-Beuve did not always reach this ideal.[10]

Another important influence on literary criticism was positivist philosophy. Auguste Comte (1798-1857) advocated applying scientific methods to understanding humanity. In his *Course of Positivist Philosophy* (1830-42) and subsequent works, he viewed the human intelligence as going through three major stages: the theological, the metaphysical, and the positive. If man began by seeing gods everywhere, then abstract forces, he finally saw there are social laws to be discovered. At the positive stage, thinkers are no longer preoccupied with problems about the origin or destination of the universe nor interested in the causes of natural phenomena. Rather, thinkers are prepared ". . . through the combined use of reason and observation, to devote (themselves) uniquely to discovering" the effective laws governing mankind.

Hippolyte Adolphe Taine (1828-1893) developed a scientific philosophy of literature kindred to Comte's positivism. In Taine's *Introduction to the History of English Literature* (1863-67), he made clear, that his interest was in the racial mind and character of a people in its general process of thought and feeling. For instance, he wanted to arrive at the primitive disposition of the Germanic and Nordic race, its peculiar sensations, and its characteristic conceptions. He states, "Here lie the grand causes, for they are the universal and permanent causes, present at every moment . . . always acting, indestructible . . ."[11] These he attributes to "*race, milieu,* and *moment.*" When he studies a literary work, he situates it in the matrix of a national culture that produced it, the age or period of its birth, and the society into which it was born. Thus Taine sees a literary work as ". . . a transcript of contemporary manners, a manifestation of a certain kind of mind.[12]

In this conjunction Taine makes clear what he expects. "You consider his [the author's] writings, his artistic production , his business transactions or political ventures and that in order to . . . measure the scope and limits of his intelligence, his inventiveness . . . to find the order, the character, the general force of his ideas, the mode in which he thinks and resolves. All these externals are but avenues converging toward . . . the genuine man, I mean that mass of faculties and feeling which are the inner man."[13] Taine also spells out how this search is to be scientific in nature by adding, "Is psychology only a series of observations? No, here as elsewhere we must search out the causes after we have collected the facts. No matter if the facts be physical or moral, they all have their causes; there is a cause for ambition, for courage, for truth, as there is for digestion, for muscular movement, for animal heat. Vice and virtue are products like vitriol and sugar; and every complex phenomenon arises from other simple phenomena on which it hangs.[14]

Taine's injunctions show his effort was to discover the laws that Auguste Comte urged social scientists to find. By uncovering the circumstances of race, epoch , and milieu which constitute the moral conditions that created a given literature, Taine's literary study was an attempt to reconstruct the moral history of a civilization based on a knowledge of universal psychological laws. Thus Taine provides us with a method of finding out the psychology of the people that produced a certain literature.[15]

Claude Bernard (1813-1878) also influenced the search for a science of literary criticism. His introduction to the *Study of Experimental Medicine* (1865) introduced the experimental method to scientific research.. The two-fold aim of experimentation is: (1) to test "authoritative" assertions of the past for their validity and (2) to discover new facts about matter, nature and existence. As distinct from the science of observation, the science of experimentation can with absolute objectivity determine just what are the material, hereditary, or environmental conditions which produce an event. This determining of the causes of an occurrence became known as *scientific determinism.*

Emile Zola (1840-1902) used Bernard's approach in his own introductory essay to *The Experimental Novel* (1880). Zola suggested that the novelist and scientist perform similar experiments when the writer of fiction sets up his initial story situation to discover the causes and effects of human interaction. Indeed, Zola felt experimentation would one day be a part of literary criticism when he states, "I have only spoken of the experimental novel, but I am fairly convinced that the same method, after having triumphed in history and criticism, will triumph everywhere."[16] In other words, the critic will have a set of criteria and experimental techniques by which to examine a novel's correspondence to truth and cohesion of imaginative reasoning. In addition, the critic will not only be able to test a literary work in the light of past experimentation but also he will be able to discover the new elements, structures, and dimensions in innovative literature by which it surpasses the past.

Charles Robert Darwin (1809-1882) also influenced Zola. Darwin's *Origin of Species* (1859) propounded that organic life evolved from early and simple forms to the myriad of species that exist today. This evolution took place through "natural selection" wherein those organisms which could best adapt to their environment survived the struggle for existence. Zola adopted the view that man is similarly a product of heredity, environment and natural selection, and hence his novels portray characters who act in accordance with biological and environmental laws. Indeed, this way of looking at humanity engendered the 19th century literary movement called *naturalism*, where novelists adopted attitudes kindred to those of the physiologist, the zoologist, and naturalist in the fictional portrayal of mankind.

Although Ferdinand Brunetière (1849-1906) attacked literary naturalism in his work *The Naturalist Novel* (1883), he himself, drew heavily on Darwin's evolutionary theory in *The Evolution of Genres in the History of Literature* (1890) and his *Manual of the History of*

French Literature (1897). Brunetière regarded this history of literature from the genealogical standpoint, studying how an author's ideas evolved in his works. By emphasizing the literary work itself and de-emphasizing the author's personality or social background , Brunetière sought to demonstrate an inner causality in the history of literature by examining the influence of earlier literary works on later ones. Thus he draws an analogy between the development of a genre and the history of a species. "A genre is born, grows, attains its perfection, declines and finally dies."[17] However, René Wellek's objection to the analogy teaches that the adoption of any concept or method from one discipline to another is fraught with danger.[18]

Pierre E.M. Berthelot (1827-1907) in his *Science and Philosophy* (1885) opposed pure reasoning as a means of fathoming reality. Only positive science can coordinate and corroborate the facts of observation and experience. It does this by "A progressive generalization deducted from anterior facts . . . ceaselessly verified by new observations. . ." which ". . . conducts our knowledge from vulgar and particular phenomena . . . to natural laws." Thus positive science is characterized both by exact induction and the search for encompassing laws to account for as many facts and phenomena as possible.

Gustave Lanson (1857-1934) in *The Scientific Spirit and the Method of Literary History* (1909) stressed the need for exact methods of literary research. In addition, he advocated that the researcher have patience, a respect for facts and a dispassionate dedication to the task. Lanson's *Manual of the History Of French Literature* (1894) urged students to observe a strict methodology, and he himself demonstrated a judicious use of history and criticism, provided apt psychological portraits, and concentrated his discussion on literary works *per se*.

Although the search for a science of literary criticism is best exemplified by the writings of French critics and theorists, German scholars also made noteworthy contributions to the cause. The literary historian Wilhelm Scherer (1841-86) explored virtually every major aspect of scientific methodology, and in a sense his works represent a summation of the trend toward a science of literary criticism in the 19th century.

Scherer attempted to find a poetic based on the principles of the empirical sciences. Adopting the ideas of French scientific determinism and English positivism, Scherer even set himself the task of uncovering the interrelationships between extra-literary facts and those phenomena indigenous to the literary work. The isolated fact interested him only in so far as it manifested some literary law.[19]

On the other hand, Scherer warned against making hasty syntheses or arriving at grandiose conclusions as the history of ideas (the *Geisteswissenschaften*) school in Germany was prone to do. The true literary scientist must avoid the bad habit of seizing upon a few traits in a literary work and constructing a whole philosophical system out of these. In short, Scherer attacked the prevalent tendency to turn a limited accumulation of facts into sweeping generalizations about literature.

Scherer also described the ideal researcher and the goal he should pursue. He ". . . should undertake to organize his knowledge from the point of view of Causality." In order to do this, he needs to have ". . . a systematic head, . . . and knowledge of all peoples, in all times, (be) at home with all spheres of human life . . ."[20]

Adapting Taine's formula, Scherer studied such influences as "heritage" "experience," and "knowledge" (*Ererbtes, Erlebtes,* and *Erlerntes*) with the purpose of discovering the laws that condition the production of literary works. To such studies he added his own method of "reciprocal illumination" (*wechselseitige Erhellung*) which aimed at comparing certain human activities in diverse historical periods.[21] Best represented in his posthumous *Poetik* (1888), this approach used literary works as sociological documents to highlight the influence of literature on the history of a nation.

Scherer insisted on looking, ". . .upon history as an unbroken chain of causes and effects . . ."[22] In his *History of the German Language* (1878) he asserts, ". . .with Buckle [the English historian] we believe that determinism . . . is the cornerstone of all true comprehension. We believe that the goals of historical science are essentially kindred to those of the natural sciences . . ." and ". . .with the help of natural sciences, the physical forces [of nature will be] compelled to serve mankind." Included in this belief is an idea which not only hearkens back to Descartes but which also prophesies 20th century psychology and the ultimate aim of that emerging science: " . . .we seek to understand the powers of the mind in order to master them."[23] Thus faith in science extends to all spheres of human experience.[24]

From this short description of the key ideas of early methodical thinkers and from the effort of 18th and 19th century theorists to transform criticism into a science, we may derive the following truths and procedures.

A LIST OF MAXIMS AND METHODS: NEGATIVE AND POSITIVE

The following list of maxims and methods may enable the serious scholar to pursue his own research more effectively.

I   Negative Maxims

   (1) Beware of the tyranny of words, of hollow rhetoric, and of effete concepts.

   (2) Past systems of reasoning may be incapable of solving contemporary problems.

   (3) Be wary of analogies drawn from any science or any discipline outside your own. They may be attractive, but false. An unsound analogy may lead your research to worthless theories or unproductive methods.

   (4) Avoid making hasty syntheses or drawing grandiose conclusions based on a limited number of facts.

   (5) *Distrust answers that silence your sincere questions.*

II Positive Maxims

   (1) There are as many forms of reasoning as there are avenues to human knowledge.

   (2) A single fact may conceal a universal law.

   (3) No event occurs in isolation or without consequences. If literature is influenced by society, literature also influences society. If Christianity inspired art and literature, they in turn

modified and educated our appreciation of the meaning of Christianity.

III Negative Methods

(1) Examine your most cherished assumptions, for they may be rooted in prejudice, not facts.

(2) Doubt everything you think you know until you perceive the ultimate ground of your own thought processes. Thus did Socrates, Plato, Aristotle, Francis Bacon and René Descartes evolve new methods for discovering knowledge.

(3) *Don't give up your search for a sounder truth, a more effective method, a more satisfactory answer.*

IV Positive Methods

(1) Develop a step-by-step procedure whereby you can organize your ratiocination and systematically examine any intellectual problem.

(2) Have patience, a respect for facts, and employ exacting methods of research.

(3) Only through a genius for patience can one achieve accurate descriptions of phenomena and, with luck, discover the great hypothesis which can explain all the examined facts in a new, seminal way.

(4) Scientific problem-solving should be conducted in two successive stages: (i) the differentiation and analysis of materials into their basic elements, followed by (ii) the recombination and synthesis of these understood elements to see what they signify as a totality. In short, by the reversible method of analysis and synthesis, one can identify, test, and verify the findings of one's research.

(5) No creative artist or thinker lives in a vacuum. As his work reflects his mind, so does it reflect his time and culture. By studying his character and personality interacting with the knowledge of his time, you can grow more apt at discovering insights into his originality and competence as a craftsman or genius.

(6) If causality is used at all as an expository technique in literary analysis and interpretation, use it only to explain the influence of earlier literary works on later ones.

(7) Make use of complementary concepts (e.g., race, milieu, and moment) to try to discover the universal and permanent conditions of human creativity. However, adequate concepts are necessary to investigate complex phenomena adequately.

(8) Use a many-sided examination of the influences on the production of a literary work. By employing a variety of methods — psychological, sociological, anthropological, philosophical — you are more likely to gain a more competent and complete understanding of what you are examining.

(9) Be patient in observation and careful in experimentation. That is, first study a literary work for the facts: its subject, situation, characterization, patterns of meaning, style and theme. Then experimentally test these observations to see how far they coincide with your hypothesis as to the author's world view. By this method, you can better determine which details and events convey which meanings, and you can verify how accurate and complete is your understanding of the work.

CONCLUSION

If the legacy of positivism, scientific determinism, and experimentation from the 18th and 19th century overshadow all other forms of thought, the 20th century came to regard these contributions with dissatisfaction. In literary criticism, whatever real benefits had been achieved by the effort to transform it into a science, there ensued a distinct reaction against the domination of these specific forms of scientific thinking. By the 1930's, critics and theorists were seeking out a methodology with which to grasp the nature and laws intrinsic to literature itself. Ironically, the search of these critical thinkers was conducted with the same conscientious spirit which best typifies our scientific heritage.

CHAPTER 8
THE SCOPE AND LIMITS OF THE FREUDIAN PSYCHOANALYTICAL APPROACH TO LITERATURE

Although responsible scholars and psychologists have repeatedly challenged the precepts and methods of Freud's psychoanalysis, writers continue to use this psychoanalytical approach to literature in MA. theses, doctoral dissertations and post-doctoral papers. This chapter then serves three distinct purposes: (1) to define the scope and limits of Freud's science, (2) to examine how it has been used in literary criticism thus far, and (3) to test the most sacrosanct assumptions of Freudian psychoanalysis to see if they are valid when applied to literary works.

As given in any standard dictionary, there are three general definitions of psychoanalysis. The first definition describes it as a method of investigating the unconscious mind through the analysis of a patient's dreams or his free mental associations. A second definition describes psychoanalysis as a method of psychotherapy used on psychoneurotics. This method permits the diagnostician to examine a patient's unconscious patterns of resistance to reality or his characteristic projections of neuroses onto others. The third definition describes psychoanalysis as the interpretation of art, literature, or anthropology according to clinical theories of the psyche.

In such works as *The Interpretation of Dreams* (1900), *A General Introduction to Psychoanalysis* (1917), and *An Outline of Psychoanalysis* (1940), Sigmund Freud gave modern psychology a new understanding of the depths and dynamics of the human personality. As the matrix of personality, the *id* is the totality of what an individual has inherited psychologically, including the instincts. From this inner world of subjective experience, the *ego* and *superego* become differentiated. Because the organism must do business with the outside world, the ego comes into existence and becomes the means of communication with reality. If the *id* is preoccupied with the needs of our subjective reality, the *ego* distinguishes between what the *id* wants and what the external world requires. Thus in simple terms the *id* represents the *pleasure principle* whereas the *ego* embodies the *reality principle*. It should be borne in mind, however, that the ego is at the service of the *id* since the *ego* seeks to fulfill the *id's* needs in such a way as is acceptable to the environment. Indeed, the ego uses its energy to integrate all three systems.

A third system, the *superego*, is the watchdog of traditional values and ideals of society as we have learned them. Representing the ideal rather than the real, the superego seeks achievement and perfection more than anything else. It does this in three successive stages: (1) by inhibiting the sexual and aggressive impulses of the id; (2) by admonishing the ego to exchange moral goals for animal goals; and (3) by striving for perfection. In simple terms the *id* is governed by biological hungers, the *ego* by psychological satisfactions, and the *superego* by the need for social recognition.

Of considerable renown is Freud's discussion of the *life* and *death instincts*. Evidently the *libido* — characterized by the instincts of hunger, thirst, and sex — expresses the life instinct. Counter to this drive is the death instinct which is destructive by nature and may either turn outward against others or inward toward self and lead to suicide.

The human psyche is an interplay of driving forces (*cathexes*) which are inhibited by *defence mechanisms* or *anticathexes*. This opposition between these forces explains all personality conflicts. The tensions we feel are due to the counteraction between a drive and a restraining force. As a result of such conflicts, one experiences a variety of anxieties, which are warning signals to the individual to do something positive about his troubling situation. The person learns to resolve his tensions, conflicts, and anxieties in two basic ways: (1) by sublimations, i.e., by seeking to reach an admirable cultural achievement, or (2) by setting up *defence mechanisms*, by which to deny or distort reality so as to make it appear less threatening. There are two commonly known *defence mechanisms*. *Projection* is where one attributes one's own feelings or attitudes to others, such as "He dislikes me" for "I hate his guts." Another form of *defence mechanism* is to pretend warm emotions or concern for someone in order to disguise indifference or dislike.

Closely connected with Freud's psychoanalysis is the concept of the *Oedipus Complex*. Oedipus — the Theban hero — slew his father, married his mother, and begot children by her. In psychoanalytical reasoning, the feelings aroused by the *libido* are such that a male child develops a sexual desire for the mother, but represses it for fear of punishment from the father; and if the child's desire is recognized, the father may feel hostility toward the son. Sometimes the boy's fear develops into a *fear of castration*. The *superego* develops in the child and acts against his incestuous and aggressive inclinations.

The concepts of Freud naturally led to characteristic methods of research. These may be described as follows: (1) Since a patient's mind represents a totality, his psyche must be an interlocking network of experiences. Thus the diagnostician can explore all evidence of these experiences via the patient's dreams and free associations, comparing and contrasting part of the evidence against another and striving to discover the internal consistency of that inner world. (2) When Freud had a hunch as to the dominant tendency of a personality, he checked and rechecked it many times before deciding upon a final interpretation. (3) Freud was ready at any time to revise his hypothesis in the light of new evidence which might confute his earlier intuitions. (4) Of utmost importance, the information gleaned from the patient's free association of ideas was studied for the manner of stating those associations, and the psychoanalyst sought to fathom their meanings. Freud himself developed fine sensitivity to slips of the tongue, errors of memory, and mistakes of any kind, drawing astute inferences from these. Regardless of all the apparent contradictions or disconnectedness of evidence, Freud through infinite patience was usually able to decipher a logical or coherent pattern which revealed the secret of the personality.

What usually strikes the non-specialist's imagination is Freud's concern with the neurotic and psychotic. Writers usually associate Freud's psychoanalysis with uncovering *traumatic* experience which brings about regression to an earlier stage of development. Indeed, the clinical study of *traumata* reveals how the mind may vortex about a psychic wound, and a patient's free associations often reach back to the source of a forgotten grief.

Twentieth century American and British literature frequently portrayed the pathos or tragedy of traumatized victims. Sherwood Anderson's collection of short stories, *Winesburg Ohio*, presented intense psychological portraits of neurotic individuals. His novel *Dark Laughter* satirized pseudo-individuals abased by sexual neurosis. The playwright Eugene O'Neil combined Freudian psychology and expressionistic dramatic devices to awaken audiences to man's subconscious life. William Faulkner's use of "interior monologue" set forth memories which haunted the lives of characters in *The Sound and the Fury* and *As I Lay Dying*. Arthur Miller in *Death of a Salesman* depicted the figure of Willy Loman as every man pulled down into a whirlpool of psychotic self-pity. The English novelist D H. Lawrence used the Oedipus Complex in his *Sons and Lovers*. These representative examples clearly show that writers have consciously used Freud's theories as a means to explore greater depths of characterization and to reveal a philosophy of life.

When the psychoanalytical approach is employed to examine literary works with the pronounced and declared use of Freudian theory, one cannot really object to the employment of methods adopted from that science to analyze and interpret literature — if the critic conscientiously uses Freudian terminology and methodology.

A well-known disciple of Freud who made conscientious use of psychoanalytical concepts (in *Hamlet and Oedipus*) was Dr Ernest Jones. Jones examined Hamlet as if the personage were a real person, and through Hamlet he studied the psyche of the author Shakespeare. Jones limits his view of human nature to characteristic mental illnesses, and evidently he believes the destiny of a person is determined by inner and outer causes over which the individual has little or no control. Like Freud, he regards man as a victim of childhood *traumata*, uncontrollable impulses, and mental disease.

In his study of the play *Hamlet*, Jones clearly states the hypothesis for his analysis: "[T]his deterministic point of view . . . is the characteristic . . . of modern psychology."[1] If this determinism is his major premise, Jones's minor premise is to attribute Hamlet's suffering and inner conflicts to a psychopathological origin. According to this view, the play portrays the "hero's unavailing fight against what can only be called a disordered mind."[2] Jones considers the mystery of the play to center on Hamlet's delay in revenging his father's murder, and the "cause" of that inability to act is Hamlet's

Oedipus Complex; i.e., Hamlet's *superego* acts against his own incestuous drives to prevent him from striking out against the father image represented by the treacherous uncle Claudius.[3] Jones then goes beyond the psychoanalysis of Hamlet as personage to attribute the source of the play to Shakespeare's attempt to work out his own neuroses and psychoses. Thus the psychoanalyst ascribes the *Oedipus Complex* to Shakespeare himself and asserts that this complex is the psychic source of Hamlet.[4]

It must be said that Jones's general approach in *Hamlet* and *Oedipus* is thorough. Recapitulating the main interpretations of Hamlet of the past, Jones provides sufficient context for his own analysis and interpretations. He complements this erudite approach by showing how this Hamlet story relates to similar myths, and finally he explicates the play by extrapolating details from Shakespeare's little known life.

Despite Jones's methodical development of his thesis, there are a number of objections to his psychoanalytical study of Hamlet. First, Shakespeare had no knowledge of Freud or of modern psychological theory to consciously apply Freudian concepts in the creation of the play. Thus at best Shakespeare *unconsciously* represented the *Oedipus Complex* in Hamlet. To be sure, a counter objection would be that clinical patients themselves often lack psychoanalytical knowledge, which ignorance does not prevent them from being psychoanalyzed. Nevertheless, it is difficult to accept Jones's hypothesis that the presence of unconscious elements in any psyche necessarily and always finds expression in consciously controlled efforts and willed actions. Indeed, artistic selection would tend to exclude the psycho-neurotic and include the healthful and socially admissible in order that the communication be as successful and acceptable as possible. One's professional performance as compensation for one's private defects may sublimate these unconscious weaknesses or quite overcome their tendency to disorder. In fact, it appears axiomatic that where clarity and order reign supreme in artistic or literary composition, there all or nearly all personal imperfections have been overcome.

The second objection is to the assumption that Shakespeare himself was a victim of the very neurosis of his protagonist Hamlet. Were we to use that assumption on all Shakespeare's characters and plays, we would quickly discover the absurdity of Jones's pseudoscientific hypothesis. For if Shakespeare's mind reflected the supposed complexes, neuroses and psychoses of each and every hero or villain in the whole range of his histories, comedies and tragedies, Shakespeare would surely be the world's greatest case history of a multiple split personality. Rather than being a lunatic of the proportions of a genius, Shakespeare possessed the positive power to create characters who will continue to teach men good sense and the meaning of human destiny for centuries to come.

The third objection to Jones's study of *Hamlet* is that he willfully forces a psycho-neurotic model (the *Oedipus Complex*) on a basically sound-minded protagonist (Hamlet) and then selects all evidence from within the play which seems to corroborate the psychoanalytical point of view. However, the reason Jones's psychoanalytical interpretation is based on inadequate evidence from within the play is that he neglects or intentionally excludes evidence contrary to his supposition. Freud himself would hardly have committed such an error or allowed such an un-scientific procedure.[5]

For the purpose of illustrating the failure of Jones's psycho-analytical approach to explicate the play, let us provisionally accept the *Oedipus Complex* as *modus operandi* and apply it to another major figure in Hamlet.

If anyone may be said to suffer from this complex, it is King Claudius. Younger than the queen, Claudius was also the cadet to the elder Hamlet. Hence Claudius satisfies many of the conditions we might diagnose as the *Oedipus Complex*, for Claudius is the real usurper. By killing Hamlet Senior and marrying his elder brother's wife, Claudius psychologically killed the father figure in the older Hamlet. Since the Prince jeopardizes the benefits of Claudius's Oedipal murder and the continued sexual conquest of the Queen, Claudius acts to have the youth executed (in England) and that failing, he plots to destroy Hamlet through the rash Laertes, who is impelled to revenge the death of his own father Polonius. Contrary to Jones's reasoning, if the Prince actually suffered from the *Oedipus Complex,* that state of mind should have made it all the easier for him to kill Claudius as the usurper of his own and his father's position, rather than inhibit Hamlet's action against Claudius. Indeed, Hamlet may have been revolted by his perception of the *Oedipus Complex* exemplified by the hasty intimacy between Claudius and the Queen.

Such intuitive awareness would explain in part Hamlet's bitter reproach to his mother. Thus his anger with her may be regarded as his loyal representation of his father's memory to a faithless wife. Furthermore, Hamlet's antic disposition is contrasted to Ophelia's real insanity, and Laertes's hot-headed reaction to Polonius's death reveals just how rational and circumspect is Hamlet's own vengeance.

In sum, *if* we were to accept the *Oedipus Complex* as a viable concept with which to examine Hamlet, the complex would apply to the villain rather than to the protagonist. This difference is not without significance, for it would thus be recognized as an evil or as a sick inclination requiring sublimation. Just as a physician does not have every disease he diagnoses and cures and just as the psychoanalyst himself does not have every neurosis or psychosis he detects, so Shakespeare himself may have recognized the *Oedipus Complex* in his villain and portrayed it as a villainous propensity. In the same way Hamlet sensed the loathsome implications of the incestuous relationship between Claudius and the Queen. Indeed, the consequences of Oedipal action were shown by Sophocles to be rooted in *hubris* (overweening pride) and *hamartia* (blindness), which are more truly archetypal "causes." Their Elizabethan corollary, *ambition* and *unscrupulousness*, would seem to provide a more viable basis for the interpretation of Hamlet than the more restricted and less universally active *Oedipus Complex* which is supposed to be essentially limited to children between three to six years of age rather than to be characteristic of the adult.

In any case, the supposed psychic hiatus between Hamlet — *Oedipus Complex* — Shakespeare simply is not proved by Jones in the face of counter possibilities. The tenuous analogy of most psychoanalysts-turned-literary-critics is the romantic notion of the artist as neurotic, which in the entire range of literature must be limited to very few authors such as Nerval, Byron, Baudelaire, and Verlaine. With an assumption as questionable as that of Jones, Freudian literary criticism seems bound to fail.

FREUDIAN PSYCHOCRITICISM
IN FRANCE

In recent years there has emerged in France a Freudian school of psychocriticism which seeks out an author's involuntary association of ideas beneath his conscious structuring of literary texts. Whereas psychoanalysts like Ernest Jones had been preoccupied with the artist who created the works, French psychocritics like Charles Mauron keep the author's texts in view.

Representative of one important trend in *la nouvelle critique* (the French "new criticism"), Mauron's *Des Métaphores Obsédantes au Mythe Personnel* (1963) and subsequent works employ a psycho-critical method which pursues four main operations: (1) an author's works are superimposed in order to discover patterns of obsessional images; (2) the themes which thereby emerge are analyzed so that the author's personal myth may be revealed; (3) shaped by psychocritical analysis, the material is further sifted until a dynamic image of the unconscious personality is found; and (4) these psychocritical findings are tested by the author's biography

For Mauron, psychocriticism is different from psychoanalysis only in degree, and the method he pursues aims at being scientific instead of literary. He studies the poetry of Mallarmé, Baudelaire, Nerval and Valery in order to discover their personal myths, which he believes are often the manifestation of a superior self. This myth reveals how the personal unconscious reacts to circumstances as representative of *Homo sapiens*. To be sure, the psychocritical interpreter needs a scientific knowledge of the unconscious.

Although Mauron's viewpoint and procedure at first sight appear orderly enough, Professor Robert Emmet Jones in *Panorama de la Nouvell Critique en France de Gaston Bachelard à Jean Paul Weber* (1968) attacks the fundamental hypotheses of Mauron's approach.[6] To begin with, Emmet Jones questions whether Freudian complexes are indeed applicable to the whole human race (p. 162). He doubts the validity of using biographical materials to verify the intrinsic study of the literary work itself (p. 164). Furthermore, he discredits the assumption that one's every conscious act is dictated solely by unconscious influences (p. 166), and he asks ironically whether only psychiatrists are qualified to write literary criticism (p. 169).

Emmet Jones attacks in particular Mauron's psychic determinism because it limits the expressive significance of artistic creativity (p. 173), even though Mauron views the creative act as an effort of the individual consciousness to integrate the personality. Nor does Emmet Jones accept the psychoanalytical model as capable of describing the poet's mind.

Professor Jones sees the determination to find Freudian figures everywhere as tending to make literary works into psychological clichés (pp. 177-8). As a matter of fact, the jargon adds nothing to our understanding (p. 183). Worse, by reducing literary analysis to a unique formula, the psychocritical approach has narrowed the horizons of the literary work. Mauron's formula may work well enough with a few authors with a homogenous oeuvre, but any attempt to apply the psychocritical approach to major figures such as Victor Hugo, Honoré de Balzac or Molière is bound to reveal its limitations (p. 174). Indeed, Mauron's study of Racine has reduced the great tragedian "to a series of unconscious desires and traumatisms" (p. 185). Emmet Jones concludes that the psychocritical approach is based on a pseudo-science.

Professor Emmet Jones is not the only literary scholar to voice his objections to the psychoanalytical approach to literature. René Wellek in *Concepts of Criticism* (1963) disapproves of the view that the artist is a neurotic whose creativity keeps him from a nervous breakdown. Furthermore, Wellek finds the prevalent search for sexual symbols to be not only boring but also a violation of the meaning of the artwork.[7] In a broader context Wellek in the *Theory of Literature* (1957) doubts that the psychology of an author can be understood through assigning "the ideas, feelings, views, virtues, and vices of their heroes, to their author's personality. No such cause and effect relationship between the author's private life and the artwork exists."[8] Thus Wellek rejects the basic assumption of Ernest Jones's *Hamlet and Oedipus*. In effect the only psychology of literature Wellek finds admissible is the study of types and laws intrinsic to the literary work itself.[9]

Another scholar to question the validity of the psychoanalytical approach to literature is Herbert J. Muller. In *Science and Criticism* (1964), he regarded Freud's interpretation of psyche as a manifestation of dualistic reasoning. Muller contrasts Freud, who split mind into a fundamental opposition between *id* and *superego*[10] to Adler who "interprets behaviour as an organized striving toward a definite goal in which consciousness and unconsciousness are not antagonists but different means to a common end."[11] Furthermore, Muller explains why depth psychology has failed to truly account for psyche. When "Freud analyzed only a function of the total personality, he misinterpreted the whole because he tried to explain it in terms of the part; he misinterpreted the part because he ignored its organic relation to the whole."[12]

If the reader is reluctant to accept the judgment of Freud or the Freudian approach from someone outside the field of depth psychology, it should be made clear how Carl G. Jung's view of psyche has marked differences from Freud's. In the *Modern Man in Search of a Soul* (1933), Jung does not deny that many neuroses are traumatic in origin; he contests the assertion that they arise without exception from some crucial childhood experience.[13] He sees Freud's concept of sexuality as so elastic that anything happening to the individual can be interpreted according to that psychic prime mover (p. 21). Jung admits that the Freudian viewpoint corresponds to psychic realities, but it does not represent the sole truth (p. 66). In other words, Freud interprets man almost exclusively in the light of man's defects (p. 116).

To Jung, Freud's teaching is "one-sided in that it generalizes from facts that are relevant only to neurotic states of mind." Within these limits "Freud's teaching is true and valid," but it is "not a psychology of the healthy mind." "In short, Freud failed to examine his assumptions adequately (p. 118). Indeed, the contrast between Freud and Jung rests on the "essential differences in their basic assumptions" (p. 128). Thus Jung departed from Freud's way because Jung came upon facts which required him to alter his theory. Failure prompted Jung to change his perspective and his methods (p 57).

Jung challenges whether psychology can seriously be used as approach to literary criticism. He notes that the proliferation of psychologies in the twentieth century amounts to a confession that psychologists are perplexed as to what psyche is (p. 29). Furthermore, "the present state of development of psychology does not allow us to establish those rigorous causal relations which we expect in science" (p. 153). In fact, it may be asserted that creativity is the very antithesis of causality, and thus it is more or less useless to attempt to impose a causal explanation on an artwork.

Jung also finds it an error to try to explain artistic creation from personal factors found in the artist. As he puts it, "the truth is that it [such an explanation] takes away from psychological study of the work of art and confronts us with the psychic disposition of the poet himself (p. 160). Freud's *Leonardo da Vinci* sought to unlock the meaning of a work of art by exploring the personal experiences of the artist (p. 167). Jung categorically denies that such analysis accounts for the work itself (p. 168). The artist as a person must be distinguished from the artist as creator. Indeed, the ruthless passion for creation may override every personal desire (p. 169). It is his art which explains the artist "and not the insufficiencies and conflicts of his personal life" (p. 170).

By the 1970s Jung's arguments were joined by those of other eminent psychologists. H H. Murray, A. Angyal, A. Maslow, and V. A. Frankel have largely rejected the major hypothesis of Freudian psychoanalysis, i.e., scientific determinism.

SUMMARY OF OBJECTIONS TO FREUD'S PSYCHOANALYSIS

The objections to the Freudian approach stem from the consequences of Freud's assumptions, and these objections may be summed up as follows. Freud's psychoanalysis rests on the questionable assumption that psyche may be fully interpreted in the light of its weaknesses (neuroses, complexes, and psychoses). Apparently Freud thought that parts of the psyche represented the whole. Hence the psychoanalytical approach is bound to misinterpret a literary work expressly using Freudian theory, for this approach judges the whole meaning of a poem, story or play according to the restricted meanings of a limited number of psychic elements. In this way the significance of a literary work is violated by the psychoanalytical preoccupation with a few parts to the exclusion of others.[14]

A second serious objection to the Freudian approach is that psychoanalysis rests on the philosophy of scientific determinism. (The theory regards all natural occurrences as determined by anterior causes or according to natural laws. As applied to psyche, determinism is the theory that ulterior causes determine men's decisions.) Based on such an assumption, psychoanalytical criticism cannot possibly fathom the meaning of man's creativity. If anything accounts for the way an artwork coordinates and integrates human experience into a meaningful whole, it is creativity, not causality. Put another way, in so far as a literary work surpasses the conditions and influences of its time, causality is not effective, and the truly original work clearly manifests its inherent power to transcend the past. Thus genuine creativity cannot be explained by causality.

A third objection is the deceptively self-evident equation between author-hero-work. In fact, the fictional hero and the literary work always go beyond the author's life in some way. The reason for this fact is that personality prevents any perfect remembrance of past events, and in the literary world, personality and talent transform experience into as universal a meaning as possible.

Another reason that the equation between author-hero-work is deceptive is that it is based on a concept of causality derived from physics. According to the logic of physics, such symmetrical causation does not exist in the realm of psyche when effects are far less than the cause, as in the case of apathy, or far greater as with *traumata*. Thus in the world of psyche, if such symmetry is found in our aesthetic notions of balance, harmony, and unity, nevertheless, the psyche is ruled by asymmetry between cause and effect. Indeed, many techniques of poetry, drama and fiction are used to build up psychic expectations and suspense, to intensify experience, and finally to effect *catharsis* of pity and anguish. Literature provides such emotional gratification by reason of the fact that psyche responds sympathetically and imaginatively to cause. Thus the effect of literature is brought about by appealing to the asymmetrical nature of psyche. If, in the future, students wish to use a psychological approach to literature, they must find another method of analysis than that based on a symmetric concept of psychic causation.

One final comment on the capacities of psyche is necessary. If neuroses, complexes and psychoses show the negative effects of psychic asymmetry, man's creativity manifests the positive powers of the mind. In so far as a literary work transcends reality by organizing and intensifying the experience of it in a meaningful way, there we find causality subordinated, subdued, or transformed into a higher reality by some creative power in man. By shaping a tiny idea into a work of art, the mind constructively surpasses its own past, and any causal account of that process cannot adequately explain what has taken place.

PSYCHOANALYTICAL VERSUS
INTRINSIC STUDY OF LITERATURE

Let us now examine the most sacrosanct assumptions of the Freudian psychoanalytical school of criticism. By comparing and contrasting its premises and methods with those of the intrinsic study of literature, we can test the validity of Freudian hypotheses as applied to literature. The proposed comparison and contrast should demonstrate how erroneous postulates may lead us to misread facts, to misuse methods, and to lose precious years in futile research..

The assumptions that psychoanalysis and the intrinsic study of literature *seem* to share are the following:

1. Both the psyche and the literary work embody a self-contained, coherent order of human experience.

2. Both the psyche and the literary work are amenable to a method of investigation which will reveal the self-consistency of the manifest intrinsic order.

3. Both the psyche and the literary work deal with the human being at grips with life-and-death situations. Both deal with problems of anxiety, pain, suffering, and the elusiveness of happiness.

4. Both the psyche and the literary product show the infinite variety of human experience as well as reveal certain archetypal characteristics.

5. Both the psyche and the literary product aim at discovering some meaning to experience, and both shape or pattern experience in such a way as to give inchoate sensations and sentiments some kind of significance.

These apparent similarities between psyche and literature have led literary students to believe there is sufficient basis for psychoanalyzing literature and authors.

Unfortunately, to each of the above assumptions there is a serious objection which invalidates Freudian psychoanalytical theory and methods when applied to literature. These objections may be stated as follows:

1. Psychoanalysis studies the unconscious associations in a patient's dreams or in his semi-conscious associations when preoccupied with self. The study of these associations reveals the deeper preoccupations of the subconscious. By contrast, the literary product is the outcome of the conscious choice and artistic selection of experiences most important to convey meaning. Put another way, the revelations of a patient are due to a will-less state of mind whereas the artist's product is due to discipline, sustained effort, and a clearly conscious act of the will.

    There is also a difference in the self-contained, coherent order of human experience examined by the psychoanalyst and the experience portrayed by the literary artist. The psychoanalyst uncovers subconscious preoccupations and complexes whereas the creative artist has transformed subconscious materials via sublimation to a superior order of understanding. (This must surely be true of the greatest writers such as Shakespeare, Racine, Molière, Dante, and Dostoyevsky who are able to communicate human experience effectively across different cultures.)

2. Although the method of investigation pursued by the psychoanalyst is adequate to his purposes, it is inadequate in examining the intrinsic order and self-consistency of an artwork because the clinician is only looking for subconscious materials or complexes, not for the sublimated expression of experience. At least the Freudian approach does not look for any possible manifestation of the suprapersonality characteristic of the truly creative mind.

3. While both psyche and literature deal with life and death situations, and while both confront human suffering and the

elusiveness of happiness, only art and literature express a philosophy of life. That is, by reason of coming to terms with fate or destiny, the pessimistic artist or optimistic author manifests a superiority of sheer intelligence over that of neurotics and psychotics. Indeed, the attitude of mental patients is that of a victim whereas the outlook of the artist is basically heroic. In general, psychoanalysts show little interest in the heroic. Put another way, the artist's understanding and superiority, which are the result of creative thinking, simply surpass in every way the philosophical determinism at the core of psychoanalysis.

4. Whereas both psyche and literature reveal the variety of human experience, the psychoanalytical approach tends to dwell on an image of man as unstable, unpredictable (except in so far as being characteristically neurotic or psychotic), irresponsible, and unable to cope with the problems of life. It tends to make mores and ethics appear relative to individual biological and psychological needs. This psychic relativity is coupled with a view of human nature as in a state of perpetual flux because the psyche is eratically actuated by fears and anxieties. This is a kind of Heraclitan view of the inner world of the individual at war with himself, a battle between lower instincts and higher impulses, a victim of his own inner dualism since he is unable dialectically to resolve conflicts except through the agency of the god-clinician.

In opposition to this image of man, literature has provided us with an idea of man's more stable and enduring traits which enable him either to survive, to understand, or to solve the problems of life creatively. Moreover, mores and ethics count in literature and are the reason for noble actions. Although literature has pictured the pathos and tragedy of human existence, it has also shown mankind at grips with existence — in combat with that which would humiliate or destroy the individual. These heroic propensities in man are seldom if ever explored by psychoanalysts. In sum, in Freudian depth psychology, the archetype is man as victim. The archetype of man provided by literature gives humankind a choice between victimization and heroic resistance. Thus the Freudian psychoanalytical interpretation of literature must neglect much of what makes literature an art and a philosophy of life.

5.   While it is true that both the psyche and the literary work aim at discovering some meaning to experience, psychoanalysis has a distinct and different view of semantic sense from that of intrinsic literary criticism. For psychoanalysis, meaning is to be found in the chaotic, the diseased, or in the deceptively senseless. Psychoanalytical meaning is that which reveals the patient's inability to come to terms with himself or his world. In literature, on the other hand, the individual seeks his meaning in the world order or seeks out what makes life significant and worth living.

In so far as Freudian psychoanalysis is preoccupied with traumata and archetypes as psychic causes over which man has little or no control, this philosophy of mind is fatalistic. In so far as literature is preoccupied with human purpose, or even with the failure to find such purpose, literature is teleological. In other words, traditionally, literature has shown that mankind's deepest, most enduring instinct is to find one's place in the cosmic scheme of things and to synchronize the single destiny with the purpose manifest in the universe. If psychoanalysis reasons backward in time to the dark causes of human action, literature itself represents man as reasoning forward in time to the teleological meaning of human life. In so far as psychoanalysis neglects this vital awareness in man, this approach to literature must remain blind to the light that literature gives.

CHAPTER 9
C.G. JUNG'S ARCHETYPAL
APPROACH TO PSYCHE
AND ITS IMPLICATIONS
FOR THE STUDY OF LITERATURE

The names of Sigmund Freud and Carl G. Jung are so familiar to students of literature that one is tempted to assume that everyone knows with some precision the major concepts of psychoanalysis and of analytical psychology. However, the biased arguments one hears from partisans of one depth psychologist or the other makes one realize that ignorance or dogmatic opinion is all too prevalent in altercations. Since in Chapter 8 I discussed Freudian psychoanalysis, the present chapter will pursue three distinct purposes: (1) examine C.G. Jung's hypotheses and assumptions about psyche in contrast to Freud's; (2) describe and define Jung's analytical psychology; and (3) consider the implications of Jung's archetypal approach for the study of literature.

In the essay entitled "Sigmund Freud and his Historical Setting" (1934), Jung assesses the scope and limits of psychoanalysis. While Freud's system of thought does present a self-consistent whole, Jung considers it as limited to a few transparent principles which exclude all else.[1] Freud seeks neither to connect his thought with historical predecessors nor to show its affinities with contemporary concepts in other fields. Moreover, the peculiar terminology of Freud's theory further isolates it from other realms of knowledge.

Freud's fundamental tenet stresses the effect of repressed sexuality on mental health. Indeed, Freud appears to interpret all cultural phenomena as the result of the repression of the sexual instincts. Every positive gift or creative activity is a compensation for some negative, infantile experience.[2] In reaction to the overwrought sentimentalism, sickly morality and bogus religiosity in 19th century Victorianism, Freud laid stress on the natural facts associated with infantile sexuality in order to destroy the fraudulent virtues of that century.[3] Nevertheless, in Jung's eyes, Freud's theory has little, actual scientific value.

Freud's preoccupation with causality shows that his programme really is oriented backwards, instead of forwards as is Jung's own teleological viewpoint. Furthermore, Freud's system is dominated by his unconscious *Weltanschauung*,[4] and Freud himself is under the compulsion of the Victorian *Zeitgeist* into which he was born.[5] These factors limit Freud's interpretation of the human mind.

Therefore, it can hardly be said that Freud pursues truth in the impartial and unbiased way of science. In fact, Freud's dogmatism belies the rationalism he is heir to. Instead of the whole truth, he only offers us part truths. Because Freud's approach is largely confined to the 19th century view of psyche,[6] his interpretation is historically and culturally inadequate.

In a second essay "In Memory of Sigmund Freud,' (1939), Jung acknowledges the extensive influence Freud has had on contemporary thought, recognizing that the *Interpretation of Dreams* (1900) is an epoch-making work.[7] Nevertheless, psychologists have disputed Freud's technique and theory.

Freud's greatest weakness was his inadequate training in philosophy which resulted in a theory without sound philosophical premises. Confined as it was to materialism, Freud's psychology derived from clinical concepts about neurotics, and when these concepts were used to explain and interpret broader cultural phenomena, as in his *Totem and Taboo* and *The Future of an Illusion*, their insufficiency became self-evident. Thus Freud was first and foremost a clinician whose obsessive preoccupation with the neuroses of degenerate psyches led him to discover the diseased and defective and to ignore the helpful and healing powers within the unconscious. Freud's skepticism and pessimism led him to disbelieve in any genuine creative capacity in man, for even sublimation, the source of much of mankind's achievements, turns out for Freud to be like dreams — merely disguised wish-fulfillment.[8] [9]

In *Modern Man in Search of a Soul*, Jung makes clear other points of difference from his teacher. To begin with, Jung does not deny that many neuroses have a traumatic origin, but he does contest Freud's belief that all neuroses arise from critical childhood experience.[10] Moreover, Jung finds Freud's concept of sexuality so vague and elastic that it can be made to account for virtually any neurotic disturbance.[11] Because Freud interprets man almost exclusively in the light of the individual's neuroses, his generalizations are one-sided and delineate only neurotic states of mind. Within these limits ". . . Freud's teaching is true and valid . . . ," but it does not describe the psychology of the healthy personality.[12] Whereas Freud failed to examine his assumptions adequately,[13] Jung came upon facts which required him to alter his earlier use of Freud's method and which prompted him to seek out new methods and a new theory to account for the manifestations of man's sound, creative psyche.[14]

Basically, Jung questions one main assumption which Freud evidently never doubted. Freud believed that human events are the inevitable outcome of antecedent conditions. In other words, psychic and environmental factors determine how we react and what we do. Free will is a myth in so far as our psychic wounds inhibit our capacity to choose. To Freud, man is the psychically wounded animal. Therefore, man's actions are caused by subconscious impulses and forces over which the individual has little or no control.

Jung does not believe that the present development of psychology allows anyone to attempt to establish the rigorous causal relations expected of science.[15] Since Jung regards creativity as the very antithesis of causality, he finds Freud's attempt to impose causal explanations on art to be a more or less senseless exercise. Jung finds it an error to try to explain the artistic creation from the artist's personal history as Freud attempted to do in *Leonardo da Vinci*.[16] The truth is that it (such explanation) takes away from the psychological study of the work of art and confronts us with the psychic disposition of the poet himself."[17] Even when we study the poet himself, we must bear in mind that the artist as a person must be distinguished from the artist as creator since his passion to create may override every personal desire.[18] "The work in process becomes the poet's fate and determines his psychic development . . . not the insufficiencies and conflicts of his personal life . . ."[19]

To reinforce this viewpoint, Jung distinguishes between two modes of artistic creation. The psychological deals ". . . with the lessons of life, with emotional shocks, the experiences of passion and the crises of human destiny."[20] The poet often interprets these events. On the other hand, *visionary* artistic creation reverses all the conditions of the psychological. It comes from the hinterland of man's mind, the superhuman world of light and darkness. Out of timeless depths, it may be a vision of other worlds, of the beginnings of things before men, or an intimation of the future.[21] This vision is represented in works of Melville, Dante, Goethe, Jacob Boehme, Wagner, and perhaps Walt Whitman. It is out of this hinterland and out of the timeless depths of human experience that the archetypes well up and manifest themselves in literature and in men's lives. Beyond the limitations of any single life, these archetypes as images, situations, and figures in tales continue to convey over the eons, in the most varied cultures, man's insights into his existential condition.

Obviously, then, Jung saw Freud's theory and method of psychoanalysis as based on an inadequate hypothesis. Although all the instances Freud tested bore out his point of view, he failed to include evidence which might have contradicted his theory. For this reason, Jung thought Freud's approach lacked applicability to the many experiences which characterize the healthy, resourceful, and mature human being. By contrast, Jung sought to be more comprehensive by taking into account factors beyond his original hypothesis. So doing, he found himself broadening his perspective to include experiences widely shared by human beings who manifested no marked mental aberrations in their day-to-day existence. Such experiences, representative of mankind's psyche in general, he called *archetypes*.

At this point we may draw a parallel between Newton and Einstein, Freud and Jung. If Sir Isaac Newton's theory of gravitation explained deterministically one series of natural phenomena, Einstein's later theory of relativity, explaining the interdependence of matter, energy, and time, accounted for more natural phenomena. Similarly, if Freud's theory accounted for certain, deterministic psychic phenomena, Jung's theory evidently encompasses more mental phenomena. Jung's description of the polar tendencies of the mind is somewhat like Einstein's discussion of the interconvertibility of mass and energy, for to Jung there is a dynamic interchange between the personal ego and archetypal Self whenever the personality undergoes the process of individuation or the artist is truly creative.

For Jung, this psychic exchange enables human intelligence to enlarge its understandings and to integrate the total personality. In sum, then, Freud's study of the disturbed psyche necessarily led to corresponding pessimistic conclusions whereas Jung's study of the archetypes took into account both the negative and positive poles of psyche, leading to a greater comprehension of the dynamics of the sound mind. Jung's study, therefore, widens our awareness both of *Homo Sapiens'* handling of existential situations and of man's intuitive creativity in the arts.

The clue to man's deeper psychic capacities came to Jung when he discovered that a third of his patients were not suffering from clear cut neuroses but from ". . . the senselessness and emptiness of their lives."[22] This led him to acknowledge the individual possessed ". . . not only a present day, personal consciousness, but also a suprapersonal consciousness. . ."[23] This presence points to the archetypes, which embody experiences of a quasi-universal nature, containing the essence of human awareness or understanding. Hence archetypes are centers of psychic and existential meaning, which act as the hiatus between one's personal consciousness of life's problems and the suprapersonal consciousness of any racial group, between individual pathos and racial ethos. This interplay between personal and suprapersonal consciousness seems to derive from psychic energy which Jung conceives as a ". . . play of opposites in much the same way as physical energy involves a difference in potentials."[24]

JUNG'S ANALYTICAL THEORY

Jung complements Freud's causal exposition of psychic phenomena by a teleological interpretation. Jung regards behavior as conditioned by one's individual and racial history (causality) but also by one's goals and ambitions (teleology). Any given moment, one's life is influenced by the past *and* by expectations of the future. Indeed, such prospective orientation indicates the individual seeks out a particular destiny. It is Jung's view that man is endowed with teleological purpose which radically separates his theory from Freudian determinism.

For Jung, the personality undergoes creative development in its search for wholeness and completeness. Because of man's embryonic and phylogenic heritage and history, the human personality contains a built-in system of self-transformation, and this accounts in part for such intuitive and creative manifestations as myths, religions, and the arts. Put another way, the individual has inherited, along with parental intelligence and talents, a racial collective unconscious which enables the individual to assess experience with the wisdom of his race and to modify or elaborate that experience for his own purposes.

The structure of the psyche embraces a number of distinct but interacting systems as: the *ego*, one's personal unconscious and its *complexes*, the *collective* or *racial unconscious* and its *archetypes*, the *persona*, the *animus* and *anima*, and the so-called *shadow*. One might add that psychic interaction itself appears to be an archetypal process.

Let us define these terms in a preliminary way. The *ego* represents one's conscious mind, one's sense of identity through time, one's awareness of oneself as a personality. On the other hand, the *personal unconscious* adjoins the ego and stores experiences that one has consciously lived through. Within this personal unconscious exist *complexes* which represent clusters of feeling, thought, perception. and memories. An example would be the *mother complex*, i.e., all those personal and racial associations one imputes to one's own mother or to mothers in general. A complex focuses energies and notions so that it may be thought of as pursuing a life or destiny all its own.

It should be emphasized that Jung does not see such complexes as negative. For instance, in *The Archetypes of the Collective Unconscious*, Jung describes the mother complex or archetype, found in comparative religion, as manifesting both benign and malign characteristics. She may be associated with maternal solicitude and sympathy, with wisdom and spiritual exaltation, with the protective and sustaining. Or the mother complex may connote the secretive, hidden, the seductive, poisonness, the devouring, or anything as inescapable and terrifying as fate itself. She may be regarded as the source of life or linked with the grave and death.[25]

This example of the mother archetype admirably illustrates the breadth and depth of psyche largely ignored by Freud. Such archetypes well up from what Jung calls the *collective unconscious*, which contains the latent dispositions man has from his animal inheritance and from his ancestral heritage. This means man is born with certain patterns of perceiving, feeling, and thinking which individual experiences actualize. Such patterns Jung calls *archetypes*. An archetype is a pattern, process or form which focuses emotional energy and which draws on experiences shared by widely separated races in different climes and ages. Jung speaks of birth, death, rebirth, the divine child, the culture hero, the wise old man, demons, and God as archetypes present in dreams, myths, folktales, and religions.

Jung also singles out the *persona*, which is a mask the individual wears in response to social convention and to ethnic tradition. In contrast to one's private individuality, the persona is the public personality, and this persona grows out of the dominant archetype in one's nature.

In particular, one's archetype strives to unify the character into a totality or self. As center of the personality, it is the goal of one's life. Exemplified in such figures as Christ and Buddha, the *self* motivates the individual to seek out a destiny that unifies and integrates his life into a meaningful whole worthy of one's highest humanity. This archetype of the self is usually sought out in middle age after the personality has become fully developed and individuated.

This aspiration to selfhood is one consequence of the individual attempting to resolve the polar tendencies of his personality. Jung visualizes the personality as governed by antithetical attitudes: *extroversion*, which encourages the individual to come to grips with the external, objective world, and *introversion*, which inclines him to remain in the safety and secrecy of his inner, subjective world.

These polar tendencies most likely stem from our bisexual nature, for, according to Jung, everyone has both masculine and feminine characteristics. The feminine archetype in men is named the *anima*; the masculine archetype in woman is called the *animus*. Interacting, these archetypes mature the individual and engender his final identity in life. As the male and female themes in a symphony, the animus and anima together give the psyche its direction and meaning.

The human personality is also endowed with functions of thinking, feeling, sensing, and intuiting, which may act in an *inferior* way in dreams and fantasies or in a *superior* fashion when it con- sciously and intuitively transcends facts, feelings and notions to construct detailed models of reality.

Such efforts at synthesis point to the way that systems within the personality interact. Although a strong system may seek to compensate for a weak one, or two systems may directly oppose each other, two or more often seek to unite to form a synthesis. When this occurs, the personality effects a *progression* by adjusting the ego in a healthy way to the unconscious or to the environment. Or the personality undergoes *sublimation* such that instinctual energy is transformed and integrated into reasonable, noble, or spiritual undertakings. To be sure, an unsuccessful adjustment of ego can lead to *regression*, and the blockage of instinctual drives, *repression*, tends to disintegrate personality and cause irrational behavior.

Jung acknowledges, therefore, that the psyche is an arena of a struggle between rational and irrational forces, but he denies that such elements can only oppose each other to bring about neuroses and psychoses. To the contrary, certain psychic powers attract each other and ultimately unite so as to enable the individual to survive. Indeed, Jung names the prevalent tendency of psyche to union the *transcendental function* which operates to balance and synthesize contrary systems into an integrated self.

In other words, for Jung the maturing personality goes through two dominant phases in order to achieve true selfhood. A man is born with an undifferentiated organic-psychic wholeness along with his shadow, the animal side of his nature. As he grows and matures, certain aspects of personality unfold and develop. This means that the various systems of personality become completely differentiated. The way that the healthy, interested personality achieves the fullest degree of differentiation and development is called the *individuation process*. The second phase of personality maturation occurs in middle age when individuation has been achieved. At this moment the transcendent function of psyche begins to integrate all hitherto opposing trends of the diverse systems so that the personality may strive toward some ideal goal and attain completeness and selfhood.

Complexes

In *Complex/Archetype/Symbol in the Psychology of C.G. Jung* , Jolande Jacobi admirably explains the differences between Freud's and Jung's concept of the *complex*. To Freud, the complex is a manifestation of illness reflecting repression, which is the psyche's way of evading the conflict between man's primitive sexual urges and the restraints imposed on him by the morality of his society. Stemming strictly from one's private life, complexes are symptomatic of a diseased psyche.[26]

By contrast, to Jung the complex is a stimulus to greater effort. Because of Jung's fundamentally teleological view, the complex takes a positive and prospective direction, yet he sees the complex as having a dual nature. Complexes do derive from childhood, but they also arise during the spiritual crises of middle life. Furthermore, complexes stem from both one's personal life and the collective unconscious, and the complex is to be regarded as a healthy component of psyche. The reintegration of a complex into the total personality heals the psyche and releases positive energies. Jung stresses the need of the consciousness to understand, assimilate and integrate the complex.

Archetypes

Although Dr. Jacobi states that an exact definition of the archetype is not possible, she does a thorough job of examining its multifarious aspects. Originating in the archaic man still within us, archetypes arrange psychic elements into certain images so that certain structural dominants of psyche emerge as patterns of behavior.[27] Seen as latent possibilities of the psyche, archetypes find expression in all sorts of configurations, patterns, and happenings.[28] Archetypes are a factor which determine our modes of apprehension so that they may be viewed as living dispositions and ideas which influence our thoughts, feelings, and actions.[29] Inherited with the structure of the brain, archetypes are systems of readiness for action and may be considered as images of the instincts.[30] Moreover, archetypes have a transcendental function that prompts the unconscious to reach beyond consciousness. Hence although they are the primordial forms which make cognition possible,[31] they are affected by time and environment so that the individual in his lifetime can direct and foster the archetype through his unique and creative personality.

Symbol

To Jung, when the archetype is expressed in some form by the conscious mind, it becomes a symbol, and in fact, the symbol is the mode of the archetype's manifestation.[32] Obviously, then, Freud's use of the term *symbol* differs markedly from Jung's. What Freud calls symbols are actually *signs* or *symptoms* of subliminal processes. Freud's symbols are unipolar and causal whereas Jung regards symbols as bipolar, affecting a dialectic of psychic systems and reconciling opposites, such as the reconciliation of the masculine and feminine in the individual.[33] Freud thinks of sublimation as a unipolar transformation of libido where Jung thinks in terms of a bipolar transformation of libido, leading to a synthesis of conscious and unconscious.[34]

Also, Jung recognizes individual and universal symbols arising out of the psyche. They unfold their meanings because they are the result of a psychic process of development. For Jung, every symbol has an individual and a collective context of meaning.[35] In sum, the perceptible or represented archetype is a symbol.[36] An archetype can manifest itself on a lower biological plane, as Freud maintained, or at a higher spiritual place, as Jung averred. Complexes and symbols appear automatically in the healthy and the sick, but for the artist, they become part of his process of artistic creation.[37]

Implications of the Archetypes for Literary Study

In the *Introduction to the Essence of Mythology*, which discusses the archetype of the divine child, Jung gives us the key to the implications of the archetypes for literary study. To begin with, archetypes emerge as mental images in order to protect and deliver the psyche from danger.[38] Although primitive man may have distinguished himself by neophobia and an attachment to tradition,[39] the archetypes in mythology, religion, and poetry actually exhibit a creative tendency to synthesize experience, integrate personality, and synchronize energies with spiritual goals. The theme of the infant in myth and literature displays man's inherent intuition to create a superior self which can come to terms with both good and evil.

In his discussion of the divine child myth, Jung emphasizes how an archetype has a purpose as definite as the function of any organ in the body.[40] The function of the child archetype is to correct the peculiarities and extravagances of the conscience.[41] Although Jung is rendering the image of the divine child only, one is led to infer that the emergence of any archetype in myth, folktale, or literature directly or indirectly aids in the synthesis of the conscious and unconscious elements of the artist's and the reader's personality.[42] By reuniting contrasts, the child archetype, therefore, abets the process of individuation in both artist and reader.

In an analogy to man's organic and phylogenic nature, Jung sees the archetype as striving to realize a similar *entelechy* which represents the totality or wholeness sought out through individuation.[43] Despite the constraints of one's personal or ethnic consciousness, an archetype thrusts itself into one's cognizance. Acknowledgment of its presence affects one like a law of nature and becomes a means of maturation and self-transformation from a limited to a larger self and from an inferior to a superior awareness.

Archetypes as psychic residue or the genetic capacity of the individual, inherited from thousands of generations of survivors, represent a direct line from man's archaic origins to the present moment. The presence of archetypes in myth, folktales, and poetry is a clue to the significance of the racial experience embodied in literature. Such archetypes depict the existential situations and problems man has faced and solved, and where man has failed to resolve these crises, the archetypes show why, for their lesson everywhere is the need for man to draw on his ageless experience and in a sense to create form out of the inchoate.

Hence the archetypes are positive powers and patterns or generative forms and functions with which mankind is endowed by reason of the survival of the most creatively fit individuals and species. Even as instincts, archetypes are guides to survival. For this reason, the study of archetypes in literature should not be considered a mere academic preoccupation but be viewed as a vital part of man's education to the chances of survival.

Is the Artist Neurotic?

In contrasting the psychological and visionary modes of artistic creation, Jung made clear his opposition to Freud's psychoanalytical interpretation of the poet's psyche according to the artist's traumata, neuroses, and possibly psychoses. In my own view, Freud's choice of Leonardo da Vinci to illustrate the efficacy of his psychoanalytical method could not have been a worse choice for two reasons: (1) Freud demonstrated how tenuous and far-fetched his reasoning could go on the basis of the flimsiest evidence. Certainly no bona fide scientist would accept Freud's evidence of da Vinci's homosexuality as a proof of anything. (2) Da Vinci's whole inventive and experimental approach to a wide variety of fields of knowledge and art transcends any causal explanation of his imaginative mind or works. Da Vinci exemplifies the archetypal creative mind, which largely frees itself from the limitations of one's historical and sociological influences and even from one's own psychic past. In transforming the known and unknown to the new, the creative mind transcends the "law of causality."

Therefore, what Jung shows is that art is not repression due to some complex, but is release, and this release is not merely Freudian sublimation, transforming the instinctual into the socially acceptable. On the part of the artist, this release helps him to surpass the past and integrate his new self, which seeks to express the stages of the growing personality.

Freud's disciple, Dr. Ernest Jones, committed a similar error to his teacher in Freud's da Vinci essay by selecting to study Shakespeare's complexes via the tragedy *Hamlet*. Since Jones emulated Freud, one is tempted to say, "Like father, like son." Fortunately, as with Jung versus Freud or with Aristotle versus Plato, some spiritual sons enrich the knowledge of the world by surpassing the limitations of the spiritual father. These instances are further proof that a causal interpretation of human events in life or literature is fruitless.

The "Case History" Versus Literature

Personages in literature seldom exhibit any neurotic or psychotic traits, and therefore, they rarely represent "case histories" in the psychoanalytical sense of that expression. To be sure, 20th century authors have made use of Freudian theory to write vivid works. Examples of artists who have consciously explored Freudian themes are Sherwood Anderson, Eugene O'Neill, William Faulkner, and D.H. Lawrence. On the other hand, it can be argued that O'Neill, Faulkner and Lawrence actually delved into archetypal depths of psyche as well as in to Freudian neuroses and that the archetypal dimension is what actually makes their fictional works effective and unforgettable.

The fact that personages seldom manifest neurotic or psychotic traits should prompt the conscientious critic to exercise precaution when examining a literary work as an amateur psychologist or psychoanalyst. In other words, Occidental literature hardly offers statistical evidence that literary works largely portray "case histories" of mental patients or that authors are usually neurotics or psychotics working out their mental aberrations through fictions. Unlike the case history which depicts how a patient succumbs to his particular mental illness, the overwhelming majority of literary works show how the hero struggles to overcome evil, danger, or injustice. Put another way, the hero strives to reinstate goodness, justice, and peace in his world. To achieve this goal, the hero must solve his dilemma creatively, and this capacity to solve problems is manifestly archetypal. Throughout the ages, existential circumstances and events have tested, strengthened and developed this creative gift in man.

If it is prudent to exercise caution in psychoanalyzing an artist or a literary work, it is also wise to think twice before applying scientific determinism to literature. Let us take the case of 19th century naturalistic fiction in England (T. Hardy) and in France (the Goncourt brothers, de Maupassant, and Zola). As every literature student knows, literary naturalism showed man as a victim of heredity, environment and natural selection. To interpret such works according to the avowed theory of the naturalist authors seems a perfectly logical direction to take. After all, bad genes and an unwholesome milieu can largely account for individual tragedy. However, to the thoughtful reader these fictional figures also reveal other patterns of existence where, in order for the species to survive, the individual must learn to overcome his physiological weakness and the environmental perils around him. These other patterns, revealed in the grim lessons of survival, become part of man's archetypal experience. Thus naturalistic fiction, in fact, transcends its own theory when it serves much the same purpose as ancient myths and folktales — warning man against what would extinguish him. Wherever mankind is confronted with extinction, his instinct for survival requires brave deeds and creative thinking, and there we have archetypal situations and themes. Seen in this light, scientific determinism, whether as part of Freudian psychoanalysis or of literary naturalism, is simply an inadequate means of analyzing man's archetypal capacity for survival, and it is this capacity which literature largely depicts.

Causality versus Synchronicity

The fundamental disagreement between Jung and Freud reflects the disenchantment of 20th century scientific thought with 19th century determinism and its all-encompassing explanation of natural phenomena via the concept of causality. This mechanistic concept asserts that every effect has a cause, whether direct or indirect. Having its source in the physical sciences and Newtonian physics at that, the concepts could be effectively used to explain the laws governing motion and matter as distinct from those governing chemistry or living things. When behavioral scientists unconvincingly attempted to explain human choice as the result of inherited or environmental factors, the philosophy of determinism and the concept of causality discovered the limits of its applicability. In sum, to 20th century scientists, the analogy of causality drawn from the physical sciences simply proved itself an overextended simile which does not work when trying to account for matters of biology or of human thought and deed.

It is in this context that we can better understand Jung's own stand. In his "Foreword" to the Chinese literary work *I Ching or Book of the Changes*,[44] Jung maintains, "The axioms of causality are being shaken to their foundations. We know that what we term natural laws are merely statistical truths and thus must necessarily allow for exceptions."[45] Since causality is not an absolute but only ". . . a working hypothesis of how events evolve one out of another. . . ," Jung offers the term *synchronicity* which takes ". . . the coincidence of events in space and time as meaning something more than mere chance, namely, a peculiar interdependence of objective events among themselves as well as with the subjective (psychic) states of the observer. . ."[46] Thus in agreement with the millennia-old mind represented in *I Ching*, Jung considers coincidence to prevail over human events. In other words, the conditions and circumstances of an archetypal situation are not caused, and this state of affairs challenges man's ability to interpret correctly and acutely what his situation is, to accept it or to resolve it.

There may be an even more fundamental reason for the difference in viewpoint between Jung and Freud than the evolution of scientific thought between 19th century determinism and 20th century acausality. The differences between the depth psychologists seem to bear some similarity to the distinctions between two cultural currents in western civilization. In an essay entitled "Hebraism and Hellenism," Matthew Arnold perceptively described these historical influences.[47] Both Hebraism and Hellenism arose out of wants in human nature, and together they represent a law of human development. Indeed, both aim at man's salvation and perfection. On the one hand, Old Testament Hebraism stressed man's need to obey the will of God so that *strictness of conscience* became the uppermost virtue of the Hebraic mind. Consciousness of sin and abhoring and fleeing it was the Hebrew's lifetime duty. Thus self-conquest was the main striving of the Hebraic personality. By contrast, Greek Hellenism strove to see things as they really are, yet enjoyed an unimpeded play of thought. Sweetness and light may be said to be the attitude they sought to develop by seeing things in all their beauty. Hence Hellenism is most strikingly characterized by *spontaneity of consciousness*.[48]

To a certain extent Freud truly represented the ancient Hebraic mind in his emphasis on neuroses, psychoses, and complexes whereas Jung more clearly adhered to the outlook that man's myths, religions, and folklore reflected man's natural spontaneity of consciousness. In a very broad sense, the fearful, obedient, and awed attitude of archaic Hebraism versus the hopeful, disobedient, self-confident and creative attitude of Greek antiquity both seem to reflect archetypal tendencies in western man, and as such, these archetypes present a more convincing argument in favor of Jung's philosophy than it does of Freud's because Jung takes into account both the dark and the lighted side of man's collective unconscious and man's ethnic consciousness. Most of all, the Hellenic spontaneity of consciousness represents an argument against the causal interpretation of psyche and offers additional evidence that Jung's concept of synchronicity is a truer explanation of psychic phenomena and existential events.

Matthew Arnold's interpretation of Hebraic and Hellenic influence on the development of the western mind finds a corollary in Friedrich Nietzsche's version of the psychic forces which shaped

Occidental culture. In his *Birth of Tragedy* (1872), Nietzsche describes
the Apollonian and Dionysian impulses inherited from ancient Greece.
As absolute, nonrational powers, they work through a poet but
transcend his personal life or feelings.

To the ancient Greeks, Apollo was the god of medicine, the arts,
light and prophecy. For Nietzsche, Apollo symbolizes the poet's
intuition of form which enables the artist to create a symmetric,
beautiful, and understandable world. By contrast, Dionysus characterizes the poet's musical sense, which indicates his awareness of the
irrationality, pain, and suffering in existence. Dionysus' tale assured
his worshippers that death would be followed by resurrection. This
faith was part of the Eleusinian mysteries, and out of this form of
worship Greek drama was born.

Now it is obvious that faith in resurrection after death rejects the
causal interpretation of existence and asserts that the teleological
purpose of the universe ultimately transcends the natural law of earth.
Moreover, it is self-evident that the Christian belief in a life after death
also denies causality as an adequate explanation of human destiny.
Implicit in Christianity is a sense of life's synchronicity; that is, any
given moment in life may challenge us to decide our future in eternity.
Although no modern Christian would deny the influence of the
subconscious and of society on human decision, the decision is still
ours to make. Whatever the coincidence of circumstances, we often
are inspired to surpass the impasse of what seems a hopeless situation.

For Nietzsche, Aeschylus' tragedy best illustrated the interaction
of Apollonian and Dionysian forces. Although Socrates's irony and
skepticism taught us to separate reality from appearance, and although
modern rationalism taught men to speak of the "objective" and
"subjective" sides of their nature, Nietzsche regarded the Apollonian
and Dionysian impulses as perennial archetypal forces able at any time
to recreate great tragedy and to make man whole and great once more.

Thomas Mann supported the view that music is a materialization
of ageless Dionysian power in his literary works *Tristan, Death in
Venice*, and *Doktor Faustus*. Furthermore, Mann's consciousness of
the conflict and interaction of the Apollonian and Dionysian is clearly
manifest in *The Magic Mountain* where the spiritual dual between
Settembrini and Naphta represents the intellectual struggle of western
culture to find, in Jungian terms, a synthesis which would dialectically

resolve the archetypal opposition. More important, Mann makes clear that the Apollonian-Dionysian dialectic has no predictable outcome. Even though causality may influence human affairs, writers as Matthew Arnold, F. Nietzsche, and T. Mann point to a synchronicity of dialectical powers within and without man as being a greater influence in human affairs.

Jung's concept of synchronicity, therefore, shows striking affinities to major world views: the Taoist explanation of change in human life, ancient Greek spontaneity of consciousness influencing man's development along with Hebraic strictness of conscience, the interaction of man's Apollonian and Dionysian forces, and the Christian credo of the soul's survival after biological death. Taken altogether, these world views offer considerable cultural evidence that 19th century determinism with its concept of causality is inadequate wholly to explain the synchronicity of men caught up in actual events.

Further weight to Jung's central argument is the advent of 19th and 20th century existentialism. Developed through thinkers as Kierkegaard, Jaspers, and Heidegger and through fiction writers as Unumuno, Dostoyevsky, and Kafka, existentialism emerged in the 1940's as the doctrine that man is what he makes himself. Regarding life as dynamic and in a constant state of flux, the literary existentialists Jean P. Sartre and Simone de Beauvoir refused to consider man as predestined by society, biology, or God. Instead of the individual being determined by forces outside himself, he possessed the free will to decide his destiny and has, therefore, the responsibility to choose an authentic way to live. The existentialists believe in taking firm, positive action, called *engagement*, even though they at the same time acknowledge the presence of irrationality in human affairs. The fact that western man has come to think of himself as a rational being is the reason that, faced with the realization that existence is actually absurd, man feels in our age a keen subconscious and conscious anxiety.

At the center of atheistic existentialism is the conviction that *contingency* hovers over human destiny. In other words, the outcome of events is unpredictable because accident and uncertainty play such an important part in whatever occurs in life. The only thing that can be said with any certainty is that circumstances may make an event probable. In short, the sure predictability associated with causal explanations of the physical world simply proves impossible for human life in general. Obviously, this contingency bears marked similarities to Jung's definition of synchronicity.

To further examine the implications of Jung's concept in a very general way, let us consider the well-known figures of Don Juan, Romeo and Juliet, and Tristan and Isolde to see whether their destinies may be regarded as caused or whether synchronicity provides a better context by which to interpret their stories.

In Jung's *Archetypes of the Collective Unconscious*, he delineates the psychological aspects of the mother complex in the son. A boy may have quite opposite reactions to the fixation. He may become impotent, turn homosexual, or develop characteristics of Don Juanism, which means that he unconsciously seeks his mother in every woman he meets.[49] However, beyond these psychopathological limitations, a man with a mother complex may develop ". . . a finely differentiated Eros instead of . . . homosexuality," in which case he may become a supremely gifted teacher due to ". . . his almost feminine insight and tact." In addition, he may have a sense of history and keen receptivity to spiritual experiences.[50] Or in opposition to the negative side of Don Juanism, he may be bold and resolute, ". . . striving after the highest goals," willing to make sacrifices for the sake of justice, persevering, tough, and endowed with ". . .a curiosity that does not shrink from the riddles of the universe, . . ."[51]

From these possible destinies springing out of a single synchronic situation, we can draw a number of conclusions. Probably it will always remain a mystery as to why a son follows one direction rather than another. However, it should be quite clear that the mother did not *cause* the boy to become Don Juan rather than a homosexual or vice versa. In fact, if the boy had the intelligence or receptivity to tap a deeper archetype, he might become a supremely gifted teacher or a decoder of the riddles of the universe. In this way he would creatively overcome his complexes. To be sure, his temperament influenced him to take one direction and not another. Furthermore, multiple circumstances of his milieu were present to condition his choice. Yet ultimately Don Juan did choose the more virile rather than the more passive way to love and live. As teacher or researcher, the son would pursue a destiny freed from the debilitating influences of his "complex" and of the past. Thus synchronicity set the stage, causes were at work, but the son decided; and such decision meant that he made a creative choice in so far as his subsequent actions consciously avoided humiliation and self-destruction and sought out an archetypal destiny with intellectual rewards and spiritual fulfillment.

Literary examples also illustrate the difference between causality and synchronicity. In Shakespeare's *Romeo and Juliet*, the lovers are kept apart by the fact that their families are enemies. The social and ethnic circumstances should, therefore, have caused the youngsters to fear or even to hate each other out of loyalty to their families and out of respect to the blood spilt on each side. However, the fact remains that love, the most powerful and noblest form of all human emotions, simply overwhelmed all the "causes" against it. The story of Romeo and Juliet, the "star-crossed lovers" dramatizes how circumstances and the influence of sheer chance (the plague which separated them for a while) "fated" them to take their lives, for to them life without love was not life at all. Yet the example of their love finally freed the families from the ancient enmity, proving the efficacy of spiritual powers in human life and the capacity of men, faced with tragedy, to free themselves from the past by sensitive and sensible decision.

In *Romeo and Juliet* love is recognized as a higher self in human nature, in contrast to hatred "caused" by our bestial or selfish instincts. The recognition of a higher and nobler self, awakened by love, can only be associated with man's intuition of teleological purpose. For love, the ultimate archetypal wisdom, urges one to grow beyond one's lustful, self-centered being, to recognize the humanity and beauty in another person; love moves us to found a loving family, to be worthy fathers and mothers, to be faithful in all one does for the sake of our offspring and the future. In a Jungian context, love leads us to emulate God the Father and Sophia the Mother. Love awakens us to a higher Self.

The story of Tristan and Isolde is another literary example. As the emissary of his uncle to his uncle's betrothed, Isolde, Tristan is supposed to respect the relationship. Both the young persons owe a kind of loyalty to the uncle, for a marriage had been agreed to. Respect for one's solemn word, for society, law, order, and decency should have been sufficient "cause" to prevent any breach of promise, and yet the promise was broken. Whether the young couple yielded to lust, due to their drinking a magic potion as some medieval versions of the story imply, or whether they simply yielded to their mutual youthful attraction, the same archetypal event took place between them. They experienced an irresistible passion for one another.

Because the tale of Tristan and Isolde may be regarded as nothing more than a story of brute sexuality in chivalric disguise, an astute reader would point out that the tale exemplifies Freud's theory of the power of the libido. Of course, there is no small truth to that allegation. Yet why in virtually all love stories is the world nearly always on the side of the lovers against convention, taboos, social restrictions, family obedience, and the like? The reason is that love is the universally recognized source of human happiness. It not only reassures the human race of survival. True love requited, as portrayed in the medieval tale of Aucassin and Nicolette and numberless other stories down through the ages, is the revelation of free choice, two persons choosing one another for all life against all odds, for better or for worse. Love leading to a marriage of sincere minds and true hearts seems touched by a holy power. As creative choice beyond brute pleasures, such love cannot be considered a neurotic or psychotic complex waiting to destroy the individual. Rather, out of ageless human experience, the feeling of love strongly urges the individual to freely decide to pursue a nobler life. For this reason genuine love represents the highest archetypal destiny open to common mortals.

There are good reasons for critics and writers to be drawn to Jung's theory of psyche. A well known example is Thomas Mann. In his speech "Freud and the Future," delivered on the occasion of the celebration of Mann's 80th birthday in 1936, the novelist highlights his artistic transition from a basically Freudian view of human character to an appreciation of the mythical identities manifest in literature and scripture.

In retracing the evolution of his growing awareness of the archetypal in human existence, T. Mann refers to Arthur Schopenhauer's essay, "Transcendent Speculations on Apparent Design in the Fate of the Individual." The great idea contained in the essay was that our own will leads us inexorably to our own fate and that ". . . we are actually ourselves bringing about what seems to be happening to us."[52] Mann makes reference to another article, "On the Psychology of the Older School of Biography," which stresses how many human beings unconsciously live ". . . the destiny of a class or rank or calling." This article, says Mann, gives us ". . . the precise point at which the psychological interest passes over into the mythical."[53] Thus for Mann, myth is the timeless schema which provides us with insights into the higher, authentic, and eternal truths in life. As such, the mythical gives value to the present and acts as ". . . a fresh incarnation of the traditional upon earth." Life is a sacred repetition.[54]

Ortego y Gasset thought ancient man searched into the past for a pattern to live by. In ancient times a woman or a man sought significance through reliving a myth in flesh and blood as Cleopatra fulfilling her Aphrodite destiny onto death and Jesus following his ". . . lofty messianic sense of self."[55] Yet Mann believed mythical identification or "imitation" is psychologically possible at all times.[56]

Playfully tying in the celebration of his own birthday with celebration as part of a religious act, Mann speaks of how ancient feasts involved a dramatic performance or a retelling of the story of a god, such as the life and sufferings of Osiris. In other words, a feast took place ceremoniously according to a mythical prototype. To Mann the mystery play of the Christian Middle Ages with its scenes of heaven, earth, and the torments of hell also characterizes the mythical dimension as does Goethe's *Faust*.[57] Clearly archetypal in subject, theme, and form, such literature exemplifies Jung's interpretation of human experience.

Mann also speaks of the mythical identification one has with one's father, one's imitation of him, one's developing through such emulation a higher and more evolved character of one's own.[58] This shaping of the human being, this *Bildung*, is engendered through admiration and love, through the child's identification with the father image because of the profound affinities which exist between them. Ultimately, such emulation becomes *imitateo dei*.[59] Thus in myth lies concealed the seeds of our figure as individual and as humanity.[60]

Mann's observations urge us to look back over the history of the humanities, and that glance makes us realize that the thousands of geniuses who have made contributions to art, literature, and philosophy can hardly have been preponderantly neurotic or psychotic in Freud's sense of those terms. The mentally ill rarely produce coherent beauty. To corroborate their thesis, the Freudians might point to a handful of artists as Novalis, Baudelaire, and a few others who took narcotics, were confined to mental institutions, or committed suicide.

However, the hundreds of geniuses who did not yield to such self-destructive tendencies point, rather, to a healthy and virile force in the human personality which we can call the archetype of creativity. It is thanks to this archetype that man has created and developed societies, cultures, and civilizations.

Indeed, creativity seems to be the intuitive and intellectual manifestation of our embryonic and phylogenic heritage and history, and the mandalas of the arts focus our archetypal search for wholeness and meaning, where meaning signifies the birth of a higher stage of awareness and understanding. Implicit in this process is the self-transformation of both the individual and the race. Called forth from the collective unconscious and modified by ethnic consciousness, creativity decides which archetypes to actualize.

In general, world literature dramatizes those quasi-universal existential situations that human beings can do something about. Art and literature rarely depict situations where the possibility of human decision does not exist. Although life does face man with cataclysmic events and biological death, literature usually shows man at grips with his destiny, not as an unresourceful victim.

If we bear in mind that the races alive today are the survivors of the past, that indicates those races developed the capacity to survive the archetypal situations which threatened to extinguish the individual and the race. Not only did the physically fittest survive but also those with the greatest cunning, shrewdness, and creativity. In order to survive, men needed keen perception, some form of communication, inventiveness, and an effective means of accomplishing things to supplant the magic that did not work. That means that a man or race survived by learning, obeying, and improving the racial consciousness into which he was born.

Once we grasp the fact that man is not blindly impelled by the influences of the past, we come to a new understanding of human destiny. To be sure, life is full of confrontations demanding decision and action, but it is the unique synchronicity of each crisis which alerts and actuates an archetype to respond to the total situation, and each individual reacts differently according to time and place. Because learning promises survival, human intelligence represents man's archetypal capacity to learn and to think. This creative capacity is the key to the acausal interpretation of experience in life and literature.

We must learn how man learns; we must understand how man has learned to think. More than life itself, literature provides us with archetypal examples of how man has learned to survive by thinking creatively.

Literature shows this capacity for creativity in action, for literature largely dramatizes those situations in which the hero or victim personates the potentials we all carry within us. Hence when literature draws on man's collective unconscious and his ethnic consciousness, it portrays the pathos and ethos of *anthropos* himself confronted with problems which call forth his inherited creativity. The reason-for-being of literature seems to be to exercise this archetype.

CHAPTER 10
PAUL DIEL'S *PSYCHOLOGY OF MOTIVATION*:
SUBCONSCIOUS FATE VERSUS SUPRACONSCIOUS DESTINY

Freudian psychoanalysis has had its vogue in literary analysis and interpretation as has Jungian analytical psychology. If Freud awakened the literary student to the intricate association of ideas embedded in mind, experience, and story, Jung educated the specialist to the archetypal situations, characters, plots and symbols inherent in religion and literature.

If Freud focused on mental illness and humanity's sexual nature, Jung centered his studies on anthropology and the occult so as better to illustrate the universal symbols of mankind's collective unconscious. Jung concentrated on the ways psyche not only develops patterns of introversion and extroversion but also manifests individuation by which an individual works out a distinct personality or destiny.

Neither Freud nor Jung concerned himself with man's biological heritage or the evolution of our species. In other words, they quite left aside Charles Darwin's theory of evolution in the *Origin of species* (1859), a theory which has so profoundly influenced our biological understanding of human nature.

By contrast, Paul Diel's *Psychology of Motivation* investigates how our biological nature influences the individual mind and the destiny of our species. To be sure, this investigation should interest the student of literature who wishes to grasp the ultimate context and significance of the earthly life of human beings. He will discover the mental processes man has developed through human evolution, and these will make clearer why literature effectively evokes human experience in life and foreshadows characteristic human destinies.

To understand the scope and breadth of Diel's psychology, it is appropriate first to give a general summary of it.

The basic premise of Paul Diel's psychology is that soma and psyche form a biogenetic unity. As the human species itself evolved, soma and psyche developed concurrently. If there is present in psyche a function we may name *subconscious*, as defined by Freud, Paul Diel maintains that the pansexual interpretation of psyche ignores the true cause of mental illness, which occurs when human vanity calls forth senseless, exalted desires bound to be frustrated by the requirements of the real world. More importantly, the human psyche manifests a *supraconscious* as foreshadowed in ancient mythologies and in man's notions of divinity.

In such scriptures as the Old and New Testament, Diel contends that the eternal truths and intimations of immortality are mythical expressions of humanity's awakening awareness that man is endowed with a *supraconscious* and that human life has a biogenetic sense. For Paul Diel such myths represent the psychological pre-science of ancient peoples which can be developed into a true science when such myths are adequately interpreted in the context of contemporary depth psychology.

Hence Paul Diel's psychology depicts how the demons and powers of darkness in myth are psychic manifestations welling up from the subconscious whereas the gods and powers of light are signs of man's supraconscious. It is the intimation of this higher mental power which motivates man to subordinate and harmonize all his material, sexual, and spiritual desires to his essential desire, which is to find the sense and direction of human life.

This effort requires that the individual not only pursue self-mastery by overcoming the exalted, non-sensical desires of his vanity. Via sublimation and spiritualization, it also requires the individual to surpass his past self by obeying the evolutionary promptings that both soma and psyche incarnate. Such is man's true biogenetic destiny.

Throughout *Psychologie de la Motivation*,[1] Diel describes the intricate interplay of opposing psychic forces. The *subconscious* tends to disintegrate the personality whereas the *supraconscious* undertakes to transform, heal and integrate the personality into a definite identity with a purposeful destiny.

Diel's premise is that morality is immanent in life, and such morality is achieved in psychic equilibrium and harmony. (p.163) Diel defines true morality as *realizing* the sense of life. The subconscious and supraconscious become manifest in our lives by our actions and their consequences. Man's essential responsibility is to decide his destiny. (p. 164)

Despite confused motives, the individual can evolve durable, wholesome character traits. This harmonious self can be created by finding and pursuing the essential sense of life. Through sublimation and spiritualization, the individual is able to transform his motives and consequent life experiences into a meaningful destiny.

THE SUBCONSCIOUS

Diel distinguishes a number of characteristics which define the subconscious. It begins with committing the *vital sin*, which comes from exalting desires that are false and from failing to satisfy the vital need of the essential desire. (That vital need of the spirit is to realize the sense of life.) By this failure and the senseless pursuit of false desires, the individual's personality degenerates into noxious motives which become the sickness of the subconscious.

Diel also diagnoses the *exalted imagination* and its consequences. As the inverse to the mastery of excitations, the exaltation of imagination causes the deformation of the psyche. (pp.80-81) Moreover, such exaltation destroys clarity of thought and causes the destruction of the essential desire (to understand the meaning of life) by dispersing it "into multiple, senseless, parasitic desires." (p.81)

But what are these *multiple desires*? Created by the exalted imagination, they fail to procure natural pleasures. The multiplication of desires causes despair when the individual realizes how often his desires have deceived him. In fact, when the individual finds himself incapable of mastering his excitations, he experiences a kind of exalted suffering. To chase multiple desires is to fail to pursue life's essential goal. It is to fail to integrate oneself spiritually so as to realize the meaning of one's own life.

Diel also identifies the *banalized life* and its distressing consequences. Its foremost trait consists in the exclusive exultation of material desires. (p.89) The banalized individual covets material goods and the titillation of having succeeded better than others. He seeks to dominate others. This results in even the banality of his sexual experiences. (p 150) Most of all, he wants banal arrivism, i.e., material possessions , money, and social position. (The myth of Midas aptly illustrates this banalized state of mind.) (p.151) Ironically, the duped individual wants only to arrive, but never arrives. (p.l63)

The grave consequence is that the *banalized person* lives in a state of anguish before the opinion of others — living in fear of scandal and shame. The banal person loses all personality, all individuality. His life is directed by public opinion. Social success replaces the evolutionary sense of life. (p.l50)

In sum, by failing to pursue a path of psychic health and moral self-realization, we become victims of the subconscious. This failure can take place in at least six ways: (1) through our sense of guilt at failing ourselves; (2) through our misleading, exalted imagination; (3) through chasing senseless, multiple desires; (4) through the banalization of our natural desires; (5) through the vital sin of neglecting to seek out our deepest identity by realizing a worthwhile destiny; and finally, (6) through abandoning our pursuit of a fulfilling, meaningful life.

THE SIGNIFICANCE OF THE SUBCONSCIOUS

Diel defines the subconscious as exalted suffering.(p.51) Actually, the subconscious is the deformation of the conscious psyche. Such deformation is the consequence of vanity, the psyche's vital sin, of false motivations and of banalization, which all lead to neurosis and psychosis.

More precisely, vanity creates delusions about one's perfections, achievements, and unrealizable goals. (p.87) It chooses tasks beyond all possible realization. (pp.101-102) One loses the capacity to make significant decisions. (p.130) Defeated vanity leads to cynicism, a form of moral insanity. (p.128)

On the other hand, the vital sin contradicts the sense of life. (p.80) The vital sin is the loss of the evolutionary instinct to form for itself a supraconscious vision. (p.188) Satan is the personification of the vital sin. Together, vanity and the vital sin place one's whole life in danger of disintegration.

The cause of all human suffering is the revolt against our

sensible, inner guide and spirit. It believes in one's false motivations and turns life's experiences into a banal destiny. Moreover, guilt arises from the negation of the sense and spirit of life. In turn, the betrayed spirit becomes our innermost accuser. (p.192) The betrayal ultimately becomes our physical and moral disintegration.

THE SUPRACONSCIOUS

The Essential Desire

In contrast to the lifetime punishment we experience in chasing senseless, multiple desires, the pursuit of the essential desire rewards us. Through that pursuit, suffering can be sublimated and spiritualized. Rather than being misled by fatal choices, when we obey the voice of the *supraconscious*, we are able to make sound choices and realize a meaningful destiny. In contrast to brutish and hedonistic pleasures, which can lead to an individual's degeneration, the essential desire guides the evolved psyche toward a lifetime purpose, which challenges the individual's intelligence to seek out a moral meaning to his life.

As the expression of the essential desire, our evolved psychic capacities are due to the fact that man is endowed with biogenetic purposiveness, which recapitulates the evolutionary (teleological) direction of our species. (pp.40-41) Therefore, the function of the essential desire is to correctly judge, sublimate, and spiritualize our various temptations and desires. (p.72) The essential desire centers and unifies the conscious self into the conscience aware of its moral responsibilities. (p.182)

To be sure, environmental conditions resist the essential desire, which opposition seeks to impede its further evolution.(p.49) Yet suffering offers us a lesson for what is wrong with us and our direction in life. Our suffering awakens our need to discover and create meaning in our lives. Diel reminds us that our soma is at the service of our spirit, our soul, and our evolution as a species.

The great danger of the multiple desires is their tendency to trivialize and banalize our lives, eventually blinding us to the value of the essential desire, which has the foremost task to develop the supraconscious.

The authority of the essential desire is most clearly seen in its

power to concentrate the psychic forces. It is not only able to overcome contingencies and accidents. It gradually builds confidence in
one's capacity to master life. (pp.76-77)

Through the sound education of the essential desire, the individual is rewarded with life's essential success.

> The sentiment of having satisfied life and being satisfied
> with life is the *essential success*. Such success is independ-
> ent of exterior or accidental fate; it is the interior sense of
> destiny by which man masters fate . . . It is one's responsi-
> bility before life. (p.l62)

Essential success is more strikingly defined. "The ideal combat is not
to want to surpass others, but to surpass oneself in the evolutionary
direction." (p.87)

THE VITAL NEED

The function of man's higher intellect is to create a sensible plan
of life. At some point, the individual's conscious intellect becomes
aware that the psyche possesses a higher, supraconscious spirit
concerned with realizing the meaning of life. The vital need brings to
consciousness the fact that the psyche has, in its center, an essential
desire which judges life's experiences. (p.23)

THE SUBLIMATED
AND SPIRITUALIZED IMAGINATION

In contrast to the exalted imagination and multiple desires
characteristic of the subconscious, over time the supraconscious has
emerged and unfolded from a primeval mentality prey to superstitions,
fears and emotional excesses. Gradually superseding our irrational
anxieties and excitability, the psyche evolved a more rational respon-
siveness to human experience and developed a deeper insight into the
meaning of life.

Diel speaks of the sublimation and spiritualization of imagination. The general sense of *sublimation* is to convert an instinctual
desire or impulse from its primitive form to a socially acceptable

attitude. As a corollary concept, *spiritualization* means to purify an outlook or understanding from the corrupting influences of the world. Often, the term refers to sacred matters or religious values.

A broader, historical comprehension of the significance of these terms comes from a glance at ancient European philosophies and medieval moral concepts, which together are probably the cultural roots of Diel's psychology of motivation.

Formulated in terms of the individual, ancient Greek stoicism (Epictetus A.D.55-ca - 135 in Rome) described the wise man as being free from passion, unmoved by joy or grief, and obedient to natural laws. His goal was to be indifferent to pleasure or pain.

The similarities to Diel's psychology are self-evident. Stoicism advocates: (l) self-control; (2) freedom from passions; (3) indifference to pleasure and pain; and (4) obedience to natural laws. Similarly, Diel's psychology teaches: (1) self-mastery; (2) freedom from multiple desires; (3) the need to overcome life's contingencies and accidents; and (4) the commitment to the essential desire given us by our biological heritage.

In sum, both ancient stoicism and the psychology of motivation praise: self-discipline; freedom from excesses; fortitude against life's misfortunes, suffering and sorrow; and obedience to the higher laws of nature.

On the other hand, the ancient philosophy of Epicureanism has evident similarities to Diel's psychology. Epicureanism has been defined as the philosophy of Epicurus (341-270 B.C.) who believed in a moderated hedonism based on intellectual pleasures clearly superior to sensual and sybaritic delights. These superior pleasures include friendship, tranquility, and aesthetic contemplation.

Epicureanism admonishes us against chasing base, hedonistic diversions and recommends: emotional calm, aesthetic study, and intellectual rewards as superior to sensualism. In consonance, Diel cautions against the pursuit of senseless multiple desires, but commends tranquil joys and emotions, appreciation of the arts and literature, and the sublimation and spiritualization of desires. By these sensible practices, we concentrate life's élan vital, strengthen the essential desire and cultivate the supraconscious.

In sum, both Epicureanism and Diel's psychology caution us against trivializing or degrading our lives. On the other hand, both recommend and commend control of one's joys and emotions, the study of the aesthetic, and the refinement of our minds so as to cultivate our higher selves.

THE THEME OF HYBRIS AND
SŌPHROSYNĒ

These remarks on stoicism and Epicureanism make us aware of the influence of moral philosophies on literature. The awareness becomes more pronounced as we examine certain key concepts which have run through European literature for more than two thousand years. As we shall see, *hybris* and *sōphrosynē* are such moral concepts as are the well-known seven virtues and the seven deadly sins of the Middle Ages and beyond. In turn, the struggle between virtue and vice, *psychomachia*, in one form or another runs through literature to the present day.

Hybris

The term *hybris* (hubris) meant "excessive pride" or "insolence" in one's conduct, inevitably calling for retribution. Aeschylus's trilogy the *Oresteia* (458 B.C.) is the gruesome story of a fatal sequence of acts of retribution through the descendants of the House of Atreus.

The blood feud began after a bitter quarrel between Atreus and his brother Thyestes. As an act of revenge, Atreus killed his brother's children and fed their flesh to him at a banquet. In turn, the son of Atreus, King Agamemnon was betrayed and murdered by his wife, Queen Clytemnestra for having sacrificed their daughter Iphigenia to gain fair winds for the Greek fleet setting out for the war with Troy. Urged on by his sister Electra, Orestes avenges his father by murdering his own mother Clytemnestra and her lover Aegisthus. Orestes is hounded by the Furies for his matricide. Finally, the goddess Athena frees him and ends the curse.

In such manner, the original *hybris* infected the descendants of the House of Atreus. Its fatal consequences — crime for crime, body for body — revealed the awesome power of fate.

From this early example, we draw the conclusion that *hybris* is an act of transgression against a moral law due to arrogance, extreme vanity or passion. Often *hybris* is accompanied by *hamartia*, blindness to the consequences of one's action or blindness to one's effect on others.

Hybris, in modified form, is also characteristic of tragedy over the millennia. A superior person with a "tragic flaw" becomes inextricably involved in a situation from which there is no escape. Despite his fatal predicament, the hero fights to free himself and refuses simply to submit to his fate. Faced with moral disintegration or death, he achieves a moral victory in his coming to terms with his own destiny. (Shakespeare, Racine, Goethe)

Sōphrosynē (Temperance)

The true significance of *hybris* emerges when contrasted to *sōphrosynē* (temperance) as used not only by the ancient Greeks but also by Europeans throughout their history.[2]

In contrast to hybris, *sōphrosynē* urges the avoidance of immoderate or irrational behavior. Professor Helen North points out how the lyric poet Pindar reflects ". . . on man's fatal tendency to indulge in excessive hopes and ambitions, to refuse to limit his thought to what befits his moral nature . . ." ". . . the tragic hero . . ..is often conspicuously deficient in *sōphrosynē* (self-knowledge, self-restraint, and moderation)." The hero ignores the limits of self-assertion and is overcome by catastrophe. Aeschylan tragedy opposes justice, piety, freedom and masculinity (*sōphrosynē*) to emotionalism, immoderate behavior, and other forms of excess (*hybris*). (p.366)

On the other hand, in Sophoclean tragedy, the failure of *sōphrosynē* marks heroes as Ajax, Antigone, Oedipus, and Electra. The failure is a blindness ". . . to something essential in himself or his situation." Thus Sophocles teaches that it is self-knowledge that enables a man to face reality, delusion, and to understand his destiny. (p.367)

By contrast, "Euripides consistently related *sōphrosynē* to the conflict between the rational and the irrational. For him, its basic meaning is 'self-restraint'." In *Hyppolytus* and the *Bacchae*, the hero is at once *sophron* ("of sound mind") and hybristic, fanatically virtuous and yet blind to the wholeness of life. (p.367)

The connections between *hybris* and *sōphrosynē* and Diel's own set of psychological polarities should be obvious to the reader.

Professor North further elaborates the concept. In *Republic*, Book IV, Plato describes the four cardinal virtues wisdom, justice, courage and temperance. For him, *sōphrosynē* means control of the appetite for food, drink and sexual indulgence. In the *Gorgias* (503-08) he saw "that *cosmos* in the universe, justice in the state, health in the body, and *sōphrosynē* in the soul are completely analogous, all of them manifestations of order and harmony." (p.368)

In Aristotle's theory of the Mean, moral virtue is a mean located between extremes of excess and defect, a sensible measure and control of our biological pleasures.

In ancient Rome there was some resemblance between chastity, moderation, modesty and *sōphrosynē*. Cicero equated *sōphrosynē* with *temperantia*, close to our temperance.

Among the early Christians, the concept of *sōphrosynē* was welcomed as kindred to their ideas of purity, chastity, sobriety, and self-denial. (p.370) They identified Joseph, Susanna, and Judith as *sōphrosynē* types, and they interpreted Biblical texts "as injunctions to practice this virtue." (p.371)

THE SEVEN VIRTUES VERSUS THE SEVEN DEADLY SINS

Professor North also traces how the cardinal virtues of antiquity and the virtues of the Christian faith found expression in the iconography of religious art and architecture over the centuries. Gradually the virtues and vices were visualized in mortal combat, known as *psychomachia*. "By the twelfth century, the three Pauline virtues (faith, hope and charity) are added to the Platonic quartet (wisdom, justice, courage and temperance); and the resulting seven virtues are linked with other sevens: vices or deadly sins, Sacraments, and the seven petitions of the Lord's Prayer." (p. 372) "By the thirteenth century the tradition of *psychomachia* had transformed to the clear triumph of virtues over the vices, illustrated by their being trodden underfoot. (pp.372-3)

The fact that the symbols of the vices and virtues dominated European thinking till the 18th century shows the enormous influence the heritage has had in shaping European literature.

ECSTASY IN LIFE

In discussing Diel's psychology of motivation, we have learned the individual is responsible for discovering and obeying the essential desire of life. It is also the individual's duty to educate the psyche. Only through a lifetime of sublimating and spiritualizing psyche can the individual realize the significance of the supraconscience. It alone has the power to shape a destiny worthy of human intelligence, talents, and character.

The experience of ecstasy is directly related to this lifetime commitment. Ecstasy comes from being in control of one's life and in seeking a worthwhile destiny.

Quite obviously the experience of ecstasy is distinct from the exalted imagination. Indeed, *hybris*, sexual passion, and vanity are easily mistaken for the real thing, but self-indulgence and self-adulation have no part in ecstasy.

Paul Diel contrasts ecstasy to banalization. Ecstasy is "to experience a state of high spirits in being alive." It is "an intense satisfaction," which comes from not giving in to transient pleasures of little worth. Rather, ecstasy comes from the certitude that one can overcome doubts, anxieties, and fears through sublimation. Moreover, ecstasy is the "sublime courage before life," the courage to deal boldly with the accidents of life. In short, ecstasy comes from the sense one can master life.

The ecstatic joy in life arises from setting the vital force in full action. It is experienced when the essential desire functions freely and directs our lives. It comes from knowing one has satisfied life and has been satisfied by life. It comes from having fulfilled one's responsibility to life. (p.162)

It is of interest to note the affinities between Diel's ecstasy and the ancient Greek expression *"Eureka!*," exclaimed by Archimedes on discovering a method for determining the purity of gold. Thus the term expressed joy and triumph upon making a discovery.

Ecstasy also has affinities with the term *epiphany*, which originally expressed awe at the appearance of the divine being and, later, wonder at the sudden manifestation of the essential desire or meaning of something. Today epiphany is used to announce an intuitive grasp of reality unveiled by the unexpected. In literature, it is a revealing scene, moment, or discovery.

Diel himself describes two forms of ecstasy. These are not begotten from any sensuous, sensual, or sexual experience. For the enlightened human being in search of the sense of life, the experience of moral ecstasy takes place when he has discovered his essential interest in life and, by pursuing it, actualizes and realizes his true, superior self.

The second form of ecstasy is that arising directly out of our search for the meaning of our single destiny. The "ecstasy of significance" is experienced when we discover the meaning of life's events which educate our personal psyche. When such ecstasy leads us to grasp the meaning of our particular destiny, it is a further stage in our self-realization. When we grasp the significance of human destiny *per se*, we experience total enlightenment, a great spiritual conversion.

In understanding either form of ecstasy, it leaves an imprint or signature on the psyche or soul. For one moment at least, we realize our highest self as human beings.

In sum, in the context of Diels' psychology of motivation, ecstasy means experiencing joy in the lifetime search for truth and in the realization that one's life has become a meaningful destiny.

THE SUPRACONSCIOUS AND
THE SUPRACONSCIENCE

The Supraconscious Versus the Practical Intellect

To understand how the supraconscious evolves into the supraconscience, we need to distinguish man's practical intellect from his speculative spirit.

A parallel exists between the pragmatic mind and the supraconscious. "The practical intellect knows how to eliminate unrealizable desires, therefore to diminish the number of desires."

(pp.66-67) Dreams are replaced by the realization of projects. (p.67) The practical mind eliminates all else except what it wants. "The practical spirit, reason, attempts to control projects which (might) prevent its own from being realized." (p.67)

Much like reason, the speculative spirit tends to visualize the essential and lawful reality of nature. Though the speculative spirit does not envision practical goals, it does satisfy the essential desire by its search for spiritual knowledge and truth. Because of the psyche's deeper need to find the meaning of life, the speculative spirit is primarily concerned with discovering the laws of the interior world so as to guide the developing reason. "Contrary to utilitarian logic, spirit is not logical; it is analogical and intuitive." (p.68)

Diel further compares the reality envisioned by rationalism with the reality visualized by our biogenetic psyche when he juxtaposes civilization and culture. "Civilization creates itself. Civilization is the intellectual transformation of the exterior world into a habitable, organized world." By contrast, "Culture is . . .the organization of the interior world." (p.71)

As with reason's suppression of all useless distractions to guarantee the completion of practical projects, so too the awakened supraconscious dominates the dangerous multiplication of desires. Furthermore, whether the individual determines the outcome of his life subconsciously or supraconciously, that outcome expresses the degree to which his essential self has realized itself, i.e., has assumed responsibility for the individual's destiny. (p.58)

Early in *Psychologie de la Motivation*, Diel provides a concise definition of the supraconscious.

> Definitive satisfaction comes only through the harmonious realization of meaningful desires. The realization of the sense of life is due to a mental function higher than the intellect because the sense of life creates the most sensible plan for life. This ideal of life becomes the individual's supraconscious goal. Thus "the intellectual consciousness finds itself subordinated to the supraconscious spirit, a spirit conscious of life's sense and the means of realizing this sense." (p.23)

Diel further clarifies the relation between our biogenetic evolution, the essential desire of life, and the emergence of the supraconscious. "The essential desire, the elan vital, obliges all life to evolve, to realize its meaning." (p.23) "The essential desire is the essential cause of every sublimating and evolutionary transformation of the psyche." (p.28) The essential desire evolves through the supraconscious to the supraconscience.

THE SUPRACONSCIENCE
AND DEATH

Diel's psychology also confronts the sense of death in life. "Man aspires to find the accord between reality and his spiritualized desires and ideas." This aspiration becomes an imperative, a goal, an ideal. Yet if "through spiritual effort, through science, man can conquer the sadness of life due to accidental causes, he has found it impossible to vanquish the tragedy in life — death. It is necessary to accept death." (p.77)

True, death is the ultimate reality. Nevertheless, the fact of death is what initiates the mature person's search for the meaning of life.

Evolution has been nature's way of confronting the death of the individual. In the fact of death, if we were to listen to the *subconscious* self, we would wallow in anguish, anxiety, panic and despair out of self-pity and fear. However, the evolutionary thrust has over time become our *supraconscience*, which teaches the individual psyche to control itself, to master its fears, to confront death with courage, even with superhuman fearlessness.

The reality of death kindled in humankind the evolution of the *supraconscience*. Not only does this evolved stage of psyche enable us to add up the joyous experiences of life but also to concentrate our energies to create meaning. In contrast to the senseless multiplication of desires spawned by the *subconscious*, the *supraconscience* multiplies our insights into the meanings of life's various experiences. If the last truth of life seems to be our mortality, the *supraconscience* proclaims that death has no final victory over us. It has taught us how to transcend the ephemeral, the enigmatic and senseless. Across the generations of mankind, the *supraconscience* has given us the literatures of the world to ponder.

THE SUPRACONSCIENCE
AND MORALITY

Diel makes clear the moral significance of the supraconscience. The essential desire provides the drive which unifies the conscious self under its moral aspect: the *conscience*. The essential conscience has foreknowledge of the inherent sense of life. To the extent the essential desire animates the essential conscience, the psyche's introspective vision creates the *supraconscience*. (p.85)

Moreover, "Morality is a living principle in man animating humanity." It urges him to realize his essential interest. "Morality is the essential force" immanent in life, which develops "our aptitude to experience life's most intense joy." The purpose of morality is to satisfy our (biogenetically evolved) superior self. (p.29)

We can satisfy our sense of both the superior self and the moral principle of life. The spirit of the supraconscious is to live in harmony with the total self. By harmonizing and integrating our life energies, we help to actualize the *supraconscience* in ourselves. Pleasure comes from the concentration of our forces which gradually become permanent, intense and sublime. (pp.76-77)

UNIVERSAL THEMES
IN LITERATURE

Psyche and Destiny as Disintegration and Integration

Generally speaking, Diel's psychology of motivation has absorbed and transformed two universal themes running through European literature. These universal themes are now seen to define biological and psychological laws of human destiny. As such, these teach us ageless moral lessons.

Beyond the obvious fact that life itself is a continual fluctuation of pleasure and pang, delight and distress, of living and dying, our mortality challenges us to come to grips with the meaning of life. Similarly, through the history of literature are manifest themes of degeneration and generation, of moral disintegration and moral integration.

The ancient Greeks came to terms with human destiny. In their tragedies, the hero who suffered from *hybris* and *hamartia* came to a tragic end. The moral taint of *hybris* spelled disintegration. By contrast, the theme of ancient literature was the need for *sōphrosynē* or temperance in our thoughts and actions. The sound body needed the sound mind.

Similarly, the ancient philosophers, like Epictetus, taught that the individual needed to learn to face adversity, human suffering, and sorrow with self-control. Thus stoicism counseled intelligent resistance to pain and death and suggested that mental strength could resist the disintegration of one's character.

On the other hand, Epicurus urged the need to integrate one's life by meaningful pursuits and pleasures. In aesthetic contemplation, the higher intellect learned to absorb the balance, harmony, symmetry and unity of the beautiful object or literary work. In such manner did the individual discover his own sense of *sōphrosynē*. Thus aesthetic pursuits fostered intellectual and moral integration.

In Diel's psychology, we saw how multiple desires lead to psychic disintegration and how the essential desire guides us to psychic integration. We saw how banalization disintegrates the deeper sense of life and how true, moral ecstasy integrates life to realize a superior destiny.

By recalling the battle of the seven virtues against the seven deadly sins, we remembered how *psychomachia* not only illustrates a theme central to literature over a thousand years. We also realized that the struggle between good and evil, in multiple guises and disguises, pervades the thought of literature across the ages. As such, evil led to the disintegration of psyche and soul; good led to the ultimate integration of heart and mind.

In this context, we are to understand and appreciate Paul Diel's discussion of the subconscious and the supraconscious ubiquitous in universal man and omnipresent in world literature.

CONCLUSION

The reader may see fit to apply Diel's psychology of motivation to his own specialized field of literature. In view of the commonly held vision of *psychomachia* in Judaism, Christianity, and Islam, of the antagonism between evil and good and between human vices and virtues, Diel's psychology offers a fundamental understanding of mortal man, which is able to elucidate the plot, character, themes, and symbolism in many literary works.

Furthermore, Diel's concepts of the exalted imagination, multiple desires, the banal life, and the vital sin not only are evidence of the *subconscious* but also are archetypal manifestations of moral disintegration in literature.

On the other hand, Diel describes the *supraconscious* as arising from man's essential desire to find the meaning of human destiny and the *supraconscience* as the individual's realization of his own higher morality and humanity. Whereas the superhuman in epic narrative and the Faustian theme in drama may be said to manifest degrees of the *supraconscious*, nevertheless, lyric and mystical poetry, indeed, all sublime literature revealing noble and great thoughts appear to qualify as instances of the *supraconscience* in both secular and religious literature.

It would seem, then, that Diel's psychology of motivation, based on humanity's biological and cultural heritage, offers a conception of human nature valid for analyzing and interpreting timeless themes in world literature. The reader is invited to make use of it in his own studies.

BIBLIOGRAPHY OF PAUL DIEL'S WORKS

les principes de l'éducation et de la reéducation. Paris: Petite Bibliothèque Payot, 1961. (PBP 276).

le symbolisme dans la mythologie grecque. Paris. Petite Bibliothèque Payot, 1966. (PBP 87).

Psychologie de la Motivation. Théorie et application thérapeutique. 3ᵉ éd. revue, Paris: Petite Bibliothèque Payot, 1969. (PBP 165).

La Divinité Le symbole et sa signification. Paris: Petite Bibliothèque Payot, 1971. (PBP 184).

le symbolisme dans la bible. l'universalité du langage symbolique et sa signification psychologique. Paris: Petite Bibliothèque Payot, 1975. (PBP 246).

La Peur et l'Angoisse. Phénomène central de la vie et son évolution. Paris: Petite Bibliothèque Payot: no date (PBP 116).

PART FIVE:
THE MYSTICAL DIMENSION
IN LITERATURE

INTRODUCTION TO
PART FIVE

In general, very few 20th century theorists would have thought that secular, imaginative literature should be studied for its mystical dimensions. One reason for this attitude was the association of mysticism with the "occult sciences" based on popular superstition and hocus-pocus reasoning. Other "critical thinkers" were cynical of the value of studying mysticism *per se* because, for the past three centuries, science and philosophy had devalued any insights that might emerge from mystical experience. Since mysticism dealt with the ineffable, how could literary criticism provide intelligible interpretations, even if found in secular literatures? Rather, the academic role of criticism was thought to be either to emulate the sciences and rationalisms of the age or to pursue the study of literature as analytically, hermeneutically and conventionally as possible.

Yet by the end of the 20th century, it was already obvious that the traditional language of literary theory had become largely obsolescent, especially as academe lost contact with humankind's emotional intelligence.

On the other hand, during the last three centuries (18th-20th), literary theorists made an intelligent effort at incorporating the new knowledge of modern science and philosophy. It would appear they were intellectually awed by the advances of the sciences and they admired the incisiveness and comprehensiveness of the philosophers (Newton, Kant, Hegel, Comte, Spencer, Haeckel, Dewey, Whitehead, Russell, et al.). Twentieth century theorists (the Chicago critics) renewed veneration and study of Aristotle's *Poetics* and *Ethics*. But perhaps the psychological motivation behind this attention to such ancillary studies was a self-conscious uneasiness that literature was losing its esteem and respect as humanistic knowledge in an age with an increasingly pragmatic and utilitarian outlook on life.

However, any patient probe into science or philosophy eventually discloses fearsome conflicts among the scientists and philosophers. At times, their opinions and theories vary to such a degree that their viewpoints and arguments become antinomies as contradictory as truth versus fantasy or logic versus illogic.

Obviously literati would find it difficult to side with this scientific theory or that philosophical argument, if and when they understood the principle behind it. Basically, the same difficulty manifests itself in theoretical disputes about literature and in contradictory interpretations of the meanings of literature. In addition, by basing their studies on popular sciences or philosophies, there was always the danger of imposing a paradigm on a literary work which had little rational or sentient relationship to it. Moreover, theories come and go.

What appeared pertinent and useful in one decade was regarded as impertinent or useless to the next. What was praised in an earlier quarter of a century was ridiculed in a later one. Unfortunately, at times it seemed quite foolhardy for a student, scholar or teacher to suggest a new method of study or to hazard an educated evaluation of any literary work because the next generation, in all its pristine wisdom, would find their predecessors quite wanting in sensitivity, insight or basic intelligence.

In turn, some in the next generation seemed to want to prove themselves prophets or already patriarchs of their literary age by heaping caustic satire or demeaning sarcasm on the lesser mortals that went before them. However, it is self-evident that a measure of modesty about one's own "incomparable" intellect or knowledge is in order as a healthful antidote to self-adulation and self-delusion. Members of academe are often in need of a dose of *sōphrosynē*

In any event, the "late twentieth century" gradually became aware of obsolescent terminology and questionable concepts because they were based on the dualistic epistemology inherited from the past. Even in the analogical use of biological and psychological concepts, it became clear to literary theorists that the factuality of science was inadequate to account for the quality or intensity of an individual's lifetime experiences as portrayed in literature.

On the other hand, later 20th century psychology guided some scholars and critics to a deeper appreciation of the *sound* psyche. I refer not to the research measuring the electrical impulses of regions of the brain to check, as it were, how far we are like the robots Descartes envisioned in the 17th century. Nor do I refer to the study of our subconscious demonology inherited from traditional religion, which demons we now call neuroses and psychoses.

Breaking away from S. Freud's own obsession with mental illnesses, C.G. Jung studied the archetypal situations, human types, and life patterns in various world cultures. His analytical psychology taught us to search for the universal motifs and meanings in human experience.

Existential psychology (V. Frankl et al.) was significantly based on the life-and-death terror in concentration camps. Through the media, the world witnessed the horror of man's murder of man. The holocaust moved us to profound compassion for the victims. Their fates made us ask what staying alive really means. Such experiences motivated us to seek the deeper meaning of existence.

The humanist psychology of Abraham Maslow et al. also moved us away from the worst of Freudian psychoanalysis by encouraging the study of the positive potentials of psyche and by underscoring the achievements of humanity. More, Maslow studied the peak experiences that men and woman reach through exceptional accomplishments.

These examples alone convince us that any significant study of literature should go beyond exercises in critical thinking. The range of human experience in world cultures requires us to perceive the physical, emotional and spiritual dimensions in human nature. For this reason, literary study calls for concentrating on what literature expresses and evokes by way of memorable experiences, resilient humanity, and wisdom.

Anyone who earnestly dedicates his life to know the everlasting value of literature grasps the fact that readers need more than an academic rendition of it. Moreover, discussing literature means more than sharing our poetic euphoria with sympathetic listeners. Unforgettable literature draws up our deepest feelings to teach us its insights into life's varied meanings.

Thus in times of stress and discouragement, we read literature to find enchantment, elation, and hope. At other times, we read to learn how to overcome life's rigors, vicissitudes, reversals, and afflictions. In ages when society's domination is too severe to bear, literature provides the individual with lessons in moral courage. At all times, down-to-earth stories of heros, who are dauntless and decisive, heroines who are ardent and faithful, stir our admiration for their human nobility. Even the earthly parables and sayings of an unknown wiseman or the unsentimental fables of an Aesop teach us greater understanding of our humanity than any pedantic interpretation of literature or all the disputes in literary theory about immaterial matters.

At its best, literature offers what the great imaginative and moral teachers of humanity give — examples and exempla — living pictures with simple, earthly, moral lessons, which reveal to us how to live more sensibly and wisely.

As much of human history, the 20th century displayed how the shadows and "demons" of the past (our prejudices, hatred, violence, wars) still haunt our daily lives and memories. The daily genocide in the media fill the individual with fear and horror. Based on this nightmarish picture of mankind's excesses, immorality, cruelty and bestiality, one would conclude that humanity is totally depraved.

Yet the individual knows there are good people in the world too, upright, honest, selfless. Some devote their lives to give hope to the hopeless or help to the helpless. There are those who dedicate their lives to tending the sick, the wounded, the dying. There are teachers, veterans, and heroes unknown to the world. There are mothers and fathers who surrendered their own happiness for their sons' and daughters.' Those who gave and sacrificed accept their fate to be forgotten.

Alone in a room, the individual also knows that one day he will die, no matter how good, moral or worthy his character was lifelong. It is in such hours that he remembers literature with intimations of some great mystical meaning.

He remembers a medieval poem in which the young Dante struggled to decipher the riddle of why death ended the life of his beloved Beatrice. There was the story of the fisherman Santiago bewildered at having to kill a majestic marlin in order to find the spiritual truth of his own life. There was the novel about the scholar Roquentin, who discovered that what he believed to be knowledge meant nothing — not only because existence itself was without meaning but also because human beings spent their whole lives in totally mindless ways. Yet out of his existential despair, life revealed to him one durable, authentic verity.

That individual alone in a room remembers them as if they were mystics in search of a destiny.

However, that solitary soul is not so alone as he fears, for 20th century anthropology found that, worldwide and throughout history, individuals everywhere have yearned for a spiritual experience to give their lives meaning.

Such anthropological studies were I.M. Lewis's *Ecstatic Religion* (1971)[1] and Mircea Eliade's *Shamanism. Archaic Techniques of Ecstasy.* (1974)[2] Their comprehensive investigations provide abundant evidence that mystical ecstasy is experienced in the lives of people throughout the world. This fact should make clear that the sublime, as spiritual encounter, is also present in literature from the world's various cultures. Moreover, Bruno Borchert's *Mysticism. Its History and Challenges* (1994)[3] offers a copious list of renown mystics in world literature and philosophy, which list should enlighten the most hard-headed skeptic that mysticism is a reality on a par with any system of reason, mathematics, or science produced in Europe or America in the past four centuries.

Furthermore, Paul Diel's psychological interpretation of Darwin's theory of evolution made us realize we likely do have a biogenetic destiny. Additionally, Diel studied the psychological inferences possible in Greek mythology, the Bible, and the Divinity. Indeed, humanity's perception of the divine in nature, in sacred Scripture, and in ourselves probably fosters the evolution of a racial Conscience.

To open-ended minds of the twenty-first century, it should become obvious that we need a balanced, holistic understanding of life in order to interpret literature aptly. That means we should acknowledge that the magnificent mysteries of existence offer us the possibility of understanding life's mystical meanings and through it the spiritual regeneration of humanity.

Hence in the past, when individuals underwent a supernatural experience of the Supreme Being, it might actually have been a sign of man's evolving Conscience. Such mystical intimations were perhaps the foreshadowings of humanity's future wisdom. Be that as it may, mystics have had experiences in which the soul of man, for brief moments, achieved a Oneness with the highest conceivable power in the universe.

In biogenetic terms, that sense of wholeness may derive from the omnipresence of the natural processes *morphogenesis* and *symbiosis* which have created, integrated, and evolved all life forms on earth. This 20th century insight into nature counterbalances the popular phrases "the struggle for survival" and the "law of predation," which define the Darwinian understanding of life.

Put another way, the experience of the mystic may have evolved from prehistoric man's sense of communion with nature. A sense of wonder shared by all mankind, life was worshiped, and man felt a deep passion to discover its secret significance. Thus throughout the ages, men and women with the mystical calling pursued their search for a superior truth to live by.

The mystical intuition may also sense that, throughout nature, there is omnipresent a teleological purpose, for all forms of life have the purpose to survive. But beyond that instinct for self-preservation, there is the even deeper instinct of the preservation of the species. Nevertheless, the deepest inference we may draw from nature comes from plant life. The inborn power of the humblest seed can transform it to become the mightiest living tree on earth, the sequoia of California.

It may be that this entelechal power in nature is also found in evolving humanity. It may account for the evolution of our Supraconscious nurtured over eons of time by our successive understandings of Divinity. If this be so, mysticism may reveal the psychic zenith of life's purpose for man. The mystical dimensions in literature may testify to the possibility that the human race itself carries within, tiny but real, the psychic seed of a superior, humane destiny.

CHAPTER 11
DANTE'S *VITA NUOVA* AS RIDDLE:
A MEDIEVAL MEDITATION
ON THE NUMINOUS

INTRODUCTION

Dante Alighieri (1265-1321) wrote *Vita Nuova*[1] (The New Life) at the age of twenty-seven. Two years before, his beloved Beatrice had died, and his grief led him to love her beautiful spirit as only a mystic can love another. Lifelong his love for her transformed him from an early master of lyric poetry to become Italy's greatest poet when he completed *The Divine Comedy* just prior to his death in 1321. This masterpiece (*La Commedia*) describes Dante's progress from personal grief and horror of damnation in hell to bliss for heaven's pardon of one's earthly failings. Thus his works are magnificent translations of Europe's mentality during the Middle Ages.

The *Vita Nuova* describes young Dante's search for the direction and meaning of his existence. This quest required him to face life's ultimate riddle — death. By contrasting present and past, Dante's creating the *Vita Nuova* led him to discover his deepest self, and this discovery prepared him to pursue his life's purpose.

Already as a youth, Dante recognized in existence the enigmas of matter, form, and reason. As a Christian, he saw man's being as an earthly trinity of vital, animal and natural spirits emanating from the holy Trinity — God. Thus, gradually, mystical numbers seemed to hold the key to explaining the mysteries of human destiny.

Moreover, to him the fact that love appeared the center of a circle equidistant from all points of the circumference of the universe seemed a geometric form enclosing a universal truth. In reality, since ancient times, the circle had been a symbol of the Deity, and for Christians the love emanating from the center came from Christ as Savior. Similarly, in the *Vita Nuova*, Beatrice became the pivot of the universe, the very center of Dante's new life.

Beatrice's death matured his understanding of the meaning of love. In her death, he visualizes her soul ascending to heaven. He envisions her receiving the gift of Divine Love, and this illumination led him to feel the transforming and transsubstantiating power of love. The Miracle at the heart of existence had transfigured her, and for him that transfiguration resolved the riddle of death in life. Thus her death was the Resurrection of the poet's own life. Her own saintly life awakened him to a mystical quest to solve the mysteries of existence.

Dante believed that the patterns of the universe influence our earthly lives. As part of his mystical education in his new life, he becomes aware of a symbolic concordance between the acts and experiences of his personal life and his salvation, between his terrestrial and his divine destiny. He aspires to Beatific Vision and Union with God.

In his dreams, ancient myths taught him the need for personal atonement. Moreover, they confirmed his faith in a personal immortality. In Mithraism and Gnosticism, he found further evidence for his belief in the doctrine of redemption through a personal savior — as Beatrice and Christ. Thus the wisdom learned from the past, wed to the real and mystical experiences of his present life, guided him in his lifelong quest for meaning. Indeed, they inspired him to strive for spiritual and moral perfection.

Thus Dante, the poet, became a great mystic seeking out the eschatological significance of human destiny. Through his devotion and dedication to one woman, he created for himself a new destiny.

* * *

Dante's canzone "Ladies, refined and sensitive" in Chapter XIX is addressed to ladies in love who themselves are refined and sensitive. Dante's ostensible purpose is to ease his mind. In speaking of his loved one, he experiences such sweet feeling that his discourse would turn his hearers all to lovers if his courage did not fail him.

In heaven an angel prays to God to bring his beloved's soul there, and the saints desire her company to complete the divine realm, but God permits her to remain on earth for Dante's sake so that when the poet descends into hell, he may tell the damned he has beheld the hope of heaven.

On earth, too, his beloved is much admired. Indeed, her magnificent soul has the power to thwart evil thoughts and vile hearts and to change them to good. Through her, people speak with God.

The beauty of her body is such that the highest nature and the most gracious purity is achieved in her. Indeed, she is the model of all beauty. Her eyes, as initiators of love, reach into the beholder's heart to enkindle it with love, and her mouth (which smiled upon him and greeted him) evokes such a supreme desire for love that he cannot gaze at her too long.

Finally, the poet admonishes his song, as his true, ingenuous child of love, to be kind to whomever it meets and to show itself to men and women sensitive to love, for they will lead the song to his beloved and speak well of him there.

The tone of this canzone comes as a relief from the pervasive self-pity of the first movement (Chaps. I-XVI), in which the poet explored the psychological effects of love à la Cavalcanti. In the second movement, according to translator M. Musa, Dante emulates Guinicelli who showed the poet the way to depict the angelic and miraculous qualities of his lady.

This conscious poetic exploration, however, serves only as a leading Thesean thread through the arabesque texture of the *Vita Nuova*, which may be likened to a labyrinthian riddle of Byzantine complexity. Because the work is unified by Dante's retrospective insight into the direction and meaning of his life, he is able to foreshadow events and divulge the secrets which ultimately led to his mystical vision. Through this revelation, he discovered his true subject and theme, his personal rhetoric (contrasting the *now* and *then*), his prophetic voice, and his teleological purpose.

The elaborate explanation of the parts of the canzone shows the legacy of Hellenic reason and of medieval Scholasticism in Dante, just as the canzone itself unveils the mysticism at the heart of Dante's mythological and religious attitudes. Yet the canzone and its explanation are also a microcosm of the *Vita Nuova*, for they together represent a riddle and the key to its solution.

Put another way, the reason the *Vita Nuova* should be so studied is that it expresses Dante's mystical view of existence. Held together by supernatural forces, the Ptolemaic universe and existence itself are united and sustained by the concentric Power of the Holy Trinity. So too is *Vita Nuova* integrated by the centripetal power of Beatrice at its center. In essence, these relationships encompass the mystical vision revealed to Dante through his anguish at the death of Beatrice.

There is abundant evidence to justify the interpretation of *Vita Nuova* as riddle. To begin with, the poem itself incorporates a series of riddles represented by the canzone. With explanations as keys to their poetical and allegorical meanings, each canzone seems to conceal and reveal an insight into the overall pattern of the work. At the level of courtly convention, Dante disguised his true love for Beatrice by feigning admiration for another woman. At the artistic level, there is the poet's search to unravel the riddle of the most apt poetic method to relate his experience. (p.30) Another is the riddle of mystical numbers to which he repeatedly refers. Then there is the riddle of words and names. "Names are the consequence of things." (p.21) In sum, there is the enigma of the ultimate poetic form, that of numinous numbers, the mystery of words and their meanings, and the riddle of human reasoning.

Yet the most sophisticated puzzles occur where spirit begins. For instance, the implicit riddle of man is that three spirits are united in him in an earthly trinity — his vital, animal and natural spirits. Each human is a microcosm of the Trinity itself. Moreover, Dante is puzzled by his conflicting thoughts which hinder his peace of mind. (p.21) More intriguing are the riddles of certain images and dreams, like the vision during the fourth hour of the night (p.l) when a lordly figure brought him Beatrice scantily clothed in a crimson gown. Through the power of the entity's art, it made her eat the poet's heart. After a short time, the princely being enfolded her and took her to heaven.

In a later dream, the Lord of Love comes to him to bring Dante a moment of reassurance. Then there appears Beatrice's much loved friend Joan (*Primavera*) followed by Beatrice herself. (We recall that the feminine name Joan has its masculine counterpart in the name John.) It was St. John who preceded Christ, the True Light, to declare "I am the voice of one crying in the wilderness." (pp.51-52) So in Dante's dream when Joan goes before Beatrice, his beloved has reached an apotheosis in the depths of his being.

Other riddles focus on Love, called at one time "a maze" (p.22),

another time "a pilgrim in rags," and still another time, Love poses
Dante a riddle. He describes himself as being the center of a circle
equidistant from all points of a circumference. It takes some reflection
to realize that just as the Trinity is the hub of the medieval universe so
is Dante's love for Beatrice the center of the *Vita Nuova* and his actual
New Life. Put another way, Beatrice, Love and Christ are united in
one perfect, ineffable, and complete Trinity, which has guided Dante
to his destiny.

But we have yet to understand how Dante himself faced death. It
is, after all, the riddle of riddles on earth. As seen in Beatrice's
weeping for her father, death can bring great grief to the mourner. And
yet Jesus (Lord of Glory) did not refuse death for Himself . (p.40)
Then Dante realizes Beatrice "will surely have to die." and that "You
too shall die." The realization fills him with anguish. The answer to
this Riddle comes in his waking vision of the soul of Beatrice, as a
white cloud, accompanied heavenward by a host of angels. Thus his
physical awakening is transfigured by his own soul witnessing the
actual Ascension of his beloved.

This numinous experience casts much light on the deeper
mystical meaning of Beatrice's life. It is after his epiphany that Dante
is able to perceive Beatrice's uncanny powers. He sees her humility as
a miracle in commonplace reality. (p.56) He now understands how her
spiritual beauty works magic on others so that they also want to move
in love, faith and grace as she does.

At the very beginning of the Second Movement of the *Vita
Nuova*, he realizes that love is a potential force, a power that may be
brought to bear in life. This realization results in his conversion from
the passive suffering of the First Movement. This power exists in both
matter and form. It can transfuse and even transsubstantiate. It
transformed Beatrice's life, and it transfigured her in death. The power
is the beatitude of love. In contrast to his own self-pity, Dante came to
realize why Beatrice is honored in heaven.

In sonnet XXI, the power of love in his lady's eyes quells the
anger and pride of those who see her. Those who catch sight of her
feel blessed. Even her gentle smile seems a miracle too rich and too
strange to behold. When the medieval period became the Renaissance,
da Vinci saw in the inscrutable smile of *La Gioconda* the many facets
of womankind as: the sister, the mother, the *puttana*, the nurse, the

nun. Dante saw in Beatrice an emanation of Divine Love. If before he experienced his epiphany Dante saw life, death and existence as riddle, her Ascension explained all.

To Dante, time itself is a riddle because Arab, Syrian and Christian live by different cycles of time. (p.60) Another riddle is how the nine heavens at birth influence our lives, for at Beatrice's birth, all nine were in perfect alignment. (p.61) Such vast patterns of time and space seem to explain her life and her spiritual affinity to the Father, the Son and the Holy Ghost. To Dante the miracle of the ineffable Trinity is that it radiates Divine Love, which in turn creates Form out of matter, Spirit out of flesh, Life out of death, Cosmos out of chaos, Meaning out of mystery.

In the above, complex context, we may begin to define Dante's mysticism. From his *Divine Comedy*, we know he placed the mystic Joachim (author of *The Everlasting Gospel*) in paradise. Hence the poet admired the mystic and probably emulated his holy ambition.

A mystic seeks to cleanse his soul , to wash away selfish individuality and the delusions of reason. A medieval mystic hoped to attain a Beatific Vision of the eternal and divine and perhaps thereby achieve union with God. But for Dante the poet must first come to terms with the apparent riddles of the world.

Evidently Dante believed in some mystical concordance between experiences and acts in his private life and his salvation. (To be sure, this belief echoes Augustine's theory of a symbolic concordance between events of the Old Testament and the New.) Hence for Dante, certain *figarae* (as Beatrice, Joan and the Lord of Love) appeared as signs of some inviolable, numinous reality.

To the medieval mind, suprasensory apparitions existed and the mystics among them believed the soul could break free from its corporeal prison to fly away to the world of the supernatural. Since the Church admitted the claim of mystics to a direct approach to God, Dante's own fasting, abstinence, and psychological self-punishment as a man and his self-discipline as a poet is comprehensible, even laudable. Yet it took Beatrice's death to purify him of his adolescent confusion, to free him of his overweening self-pity.

At this point it is time to consider the *Vita Nuova* for its defects and weaknesses, lest the reader suppose that Dante became a flawless artist through one great leap of imagination or a stunning mystical insight that illuminated his entire work.

In the beginning of *Vita Nuova*, Dante displays a number of faults due to his emotional and artistic immaturity. The young poet is annoying by his literary artifices and his fanciful deification of love in the manner of the troubadors. At times, his number mysticism (3's, 9's) may seem artificial, and his long-winded scholarly dissertations can be tiresome. Yet thoughtful reflection shows that these affectations are largely transcended as he gradually matures. Nevertheless, we often sense that he is exploring his feelings less for their depth, breadth, and meaning than to exercise his poetic faculty. One wonders frequently if his "grand passion" is geniune or merely an insincere ritual so as to practice his craft as the ancients who used a muse for inspiration and guidance.

Furthermore, at times Dante seems to lack sincere feeling for Beatrice as when he auto-erotically displays his adolescent heartache. Sometimes he seems to be trying to impress others with his puberty. Much of the time, courtly love affectations and poetic poses are all we can see. Occasionally the *Vita Nuova* seems hysteric rather than historic, traumatic rather than dramatic, purgative rather than poetic. One cannot help recalling Hamlet's letter to Ophelia, which he breaks off with "O dear Ophelia, I am ill at these numbers; I have not art to reckon my groans." (Act II, Scene II, lines 118-121), and by this recollection of Hamlet's sincerity, which prevents him from metrical reckoning, to see Dante's self-conscious "artistry" as insincere and even pretentious. In other words, the *Vita Nuova* appears at first both a failure as a love poem and as the new testament implied by its title.

However, such negative judgements are shortsighted and impatient, and of all poets Dante requires depth of insight and much patience.

To appreciate him for what he synthesizes within himself and for what he expresses that is new, we must turn briefly to deeper sources of inspiration than found in his contemporary poets or even in ancient literary models, for Dante towers over his age, even in this limited work, by reason of his mystical awareness of the mysteries of existence.

The *Vita Nuova* has an eschatological substructure in at least four ways: by its presentation of Beatrice as a sign and promise of ultimate redemption and by Dante's last vision of the redeemed Beatrice lifted up to eternal paradise. (She is both redeemed and redeemer.) In addition, the substructure is revealed by the theme of the new-life-to-be after death and by Dante's fulfillment of his poetic calling through the grace of "Saint" Beatrice.

Consciously or unconsciously, the *Vita Nuova* embodies the experiences of two significant pagan myths, which mirror the essential credo of Christianity and its central ritual — the Mass. Both this earlier work and the later *Divine Comedy* reflect the Orphic cult — the death and resurrection of Dionysus, and the Eleusinian cult — the abduction of Persephone by Pluto, god of the underworld and the dead. (In the latter cult , redemption is made possible through Demeter, the Great Earth Mother.)

Dante's lord of Love has the aura of a Plutonian figure and Beatrice that of Persephone. In Dante's *Paradise*, the role of the Great Earth Mother is played by the Virgin Mary — as in the love story of Beatrice and Dante. In any event, both cults envision atonment, salvation in after-life, ecstatic union with the divine, and hope for personal immortality — all found in the *Vita Nuova.*

Moreover, in ancient Rome, both Mithraism and Gnosticism vied with Christianity for predominance. Living in an age that absorbed and refined religious beliefs, Dante evidently found inspiration in "pagan" religions as well as in Christianity. Both Mithraism and Gnosticism held the doctrine of redemption through a personal savior like Christ (Mithra and Hermes Trismegistus).

Dante's sense that his individual salvation was at stake may well have been inspired by Gnosticism. Gnostics disbelieved truth was to be discovered by reason. Rather, they believed that recondite, spiritual knowledge was revealed directly by God, a belief shared by Dante, if we take his poetic visions seriously. Furthermore, Gnostics taught esoteric knowledge that only the initiated could understand. Similarly, Dante's sacramental devotion to Beatrice led him to mystical insights expressed in hermetic language measured by sacred numbers.

Mithraism may also have had a certain influence on *Vita Nuova.* Aside from the common belief shared by Christianity and Mithraism that the truly faithful will participate in the final resurrection, Beatrice's affect on those around her was very much like the numinous presence felt in Orpheus, Jesus, and in Mithra. The followers of the god Mithra believed he could silence and subdue all living creatures, tame and wild, by his presence. In *Vita Nuova* Dante declares that such was the power of Beatrice's love and grace that all drew near her to feel her saintly warmth and beauty.

There is a further connection. In a dream, the lord of Love had Beatrice eat the poet's heart and, thereafter, the lord enfolded her in his arms to take her to heaven. Although at first the experience may remind us of the Christian Mass where the faithful partake of the Eucharist, yet Mithra too reputedly ate a sacramental meal with the sun and thereafter ascended to heaven.

On the other hand, Manichaeism believed that spiritual substances like fire, light and the souls of men were created by God. The enduring influence of this belief on Christianity, Judaism, and Islam was complemented by the view that human nature is basically evil. The moral consequence was that the truly faithful must refrain from sensual pleasures and avoid gratification of the sexual desires. Dante himself sought ardently to abstain from venial sin. Although a compassionate young lady offered to relieve his silent suffering, Dante rejected her as a substitute for the unattainable Beatrice.

Coincidence? Or do these subtle connections tell us something about the *Vita Nuova* that illustrates the true breadth and depth of its implications and meanings? In the simplest terms, Dante oriented himself not only in the four cardinal directions of the earth but beyond them. His poetic gift reached back across time to all known sources of the holy and to religions which embraced a moral purpose that searched for the meaning of life and death. He looked beyond Christianity to try to discover what it may have failed to perceive. Not only did he seek poetically to embrace as universal an understanding as was possible in his age. He was seeking to transcend the irrefutable fact of death which appeared to make life itself meaningless.

Perhaps the most compelling influence on Dante was that of St. Augustine and the Church Fathers. In particular, it was the standard of perfection they expected of the chosen few who would withdraw from the world to lead saintly lives as monks and nuns. Despite his political aspirations at one time, Dante's dedication to his poetic mission made him withdraw from the troubled and incomprehensible world around him. By his meticulous artistry and by his life-long search for meaning, he strove to attain his own spiritual and moral perfection. Dante was one of the great mystics — for whom love and one woman were salvation from the sad riddle of an all too real world.

CHAPTER 12
FOUR DIMENSIONS OF SIGNIFICATION
IN *THE OLD MAN AND THE SEA*

INTRODUCTION

The reader may be somewhat startled to find Ernest Hemingway (1898-1961) listed under authors whose literary works reveal a mystical dimension. Most readers of Hemingway's short stories and novels remember his lean prose and muscular style. They recall too the "male chauvinism," the cynicism and disillusionment of his characters who seem to squander their lives in drinking, brawling, and whoring. Yet his protagonists also pursue masculine life styles: fishing, hunting, fighting for what seemed just causes, even when in the end these proved delusions. Their toughness and courage were centered around an honest core in their characters.

At the same time, as the men of his generation who understood the immense waste of life in the brutal wars of the 20th century, Hemingway seemed to consider so-called civilization as hollow, unfeeling, senseless, not really worth dying for. The expatriates in Europe in *The Sun Also Rises* (1926) and the sense of the absurdity of war in *Farewell to Arms* (1940) typified the Hemingway who became convinced that life was fundamentally tragic.

Then in 1952 when *The Old Man and the Sea* was published, Hemingway revealed a deeper understanding of the manly life. In the characterization of the fisherman Santiago, we witness the fully matured talent of Hemingway both as a writer and as an elder made wise by raw life. Indeed, the four dimensions of Chapter 12 attempt to show how Hemingway may have come to terms with life's mystery: (1) as mandala of meaning in the emptiness of the sea of life; (2) as a solitary pilgrimage; (3) as a labyrinth of signs and numbers with some sort of mystical significance; and finally (4) as his last tribute to the

truest camaraderie of all — symbolized by Santiago and the boy
Manolin — the pure platonic friendship between a spiritual father and
son.

A. INTO THE MYSTERY OF THE MANDALA: A JUNGIAN VIEW OF HEMINGWAY'S THE OLD MAN AND THE SEA

It is remarkable how Carl G. Jung's psychoanalytical theory of
archetypes of the collective unconscious illuminates depths of human
experience hitherto unsuspected. A case in point is Hemingway's *The
Old Man and the Sea*. Although a plot outline of the novel restates
what happens to the hero Santiago, it fails to plumb the depths of
meaning of the experience. The plot is as follows.

> To find a great fish after eighty-four days of bad luck,
> Santiago went alone in a skiff as far out as the Gulf Stream.
> Once the old man found the fish and hooked it, he had to pit
> his endurance and suffering against the fish's pain and
> agony for days and nights. Finally, Santiago was able to kill
> it, but on the way back to port, sharks attacked and de-
> stroyed his catch. Back on shore, the other fishermen said
> it was the largest marlin anyone had ever seen. It lay in the
> garbage waiting to drift out with the tide.

A thoughtful reader will see in the tale an ironic contrast between
what a man sets out to do and what fate may decree for him. A second
reader will conclude that in life the predators triumph, the good are
defeated, and the beautiful destroyed. Obviously life is ironic.

However, the implications of Santiago's story go deeper than any
noetic irony, for as the fishing lines, the allusions in the tale reach
down into the murky mystery of existence itself. Indeed, the story
suggests an evil duality rules the world and that at every moment a
malignant power endangers the heartbeat of life.

The key to the enigma is in the dual name given the sea. For the
young fishermen, who used motorboats to catch sharks, the sea was
the masculine *el mar*, but for the old man, she was *la mar*. (pp.29-30)[1]
As archetype welling up from man's collective unconscious, such

duality of vision reflects a stage of mankind's consciousness. According to Carl Jung,". . . the majority of cosmogonic gods are of a bisexual nature,"[2] and he adds that this syzygy way of looking at nature is found in mythology, comparative religion, literature, and psychology.[3] Not only do deities come as male-female pairs but also opposite traits often are united in the same figure, which accounts for the moral ambivalence of the gods.

In this conjunction, Santiago's attitude toward the sea is of particular interest, for ". . . the old man always thought of her as feminine and as something that gave or withheld great favors, and if she did wild and wicked things it was because she could not help them." (p.30) It is clear he looks upon her as a passionate or benign woman, as a mistress or as a mother.

It is a commonplace that the sea is regarded as the mother of earthly life, yet Jung's description of the mother archetype deepens our understanding of Santiago's insight into the true nature of the sea, and by inference, into existence itself.

For Jung, the archetype manifests two opposite sides. On the positive side the mother represents ". . . maternal solicitude and sympathy, the magic authority of the female; the wisdom and spiritual exaltation that transcend reason, any helpful instinct or impulse; all that is benign, all that cherishes or sustains, that fosters growth and fertility."[4] By contrast, the negative side connotes "anything secret, hidden, dark; the abyss, the world of the dead, anything that devours, seduces, and poisons, that is terrifying and inescapable like fate."[5]

Hence Santiago's awareness of the duality in the sea provides an important clue to the mystery at the center of his story — the unfathomable presence of death in life. Or as the ancients saw existence — the power of Fate over men's lives.

Jung points out how the goddesses of fate (Moira, Graeae, Norns) also had ambivalent natures.[6] They were symbols of evil as ". . . the witch, dragon (or any devouring or entwining animal, such as a large fish or a serpent), the grave, the sarcophagus, deep water, death, nightmares . . ." and the like.[7]

It is as just such a figure that Santiago looks upon the Portuguese man-of-war, which floats by his skiff, with its deadly filaments trailing behind. He calls it "*Agua mala*. You whore." (p.35) Here again the bivalence of a name points to duality.

Such archetypal images pose the ageless question — why do evil
and death lurk at the center of existence?

At this point a dominant psychic image suggests itself — the
mandala. According to Jung, the term is derived from Sanskrit and
means "circle." As a psychopathic phenomenon, it appears in the
dreams, expressions, and artifacts of schizophrenics. In other words,
the mandala manifests the inner conflicts a mental patient may
undergo. On the other hand, in Tibetan Buddhism ". . . the figure . . .
assists meditation and concentration," and as such the mandala is the
archetype of wholeness.[8] Hence depth psychology has discovered that
the same image may manifest quite opposite preoccupations of the
mind. Or the same image reflects two different stages of consciousness
— one inferior because it has not resolved inner conflicts, the other
superior because it becomes the means to a higher stage of consciousness which integrates the apparent duality of understandings into some
form of supreme synthesis. It is in both senses that we may regard *The
Old Man and the Sea* as a mandala — given shape by the sea, the
world, the universe, and even the cosmos, but in the center of which
exist malign powers, cruelty, and predatory death.[9]

If the schizophrenic has succumbed to the paradoxes in self and
in existence, Santiago most certainly has not. In contrast to the
delusions and hallucinations of the schizophrenic or the imaginary
persecution of the paranoiac, Santiago recognizes and combats real
predators in nature.

Predatory realities abound in the novel. Hawks seek out and kill
the fragile sea swallows. An hour after Santiago won the battle with
the great marlin and tied it along his skiff, the first shark hit his catch.
Its huge jaws had eight rows of teeth slanted inwards, shaped like a
man's fingers when crisped like claws. The old man finished it off by
ramming his harpoon into its brain.(pp.100-102) Although Santiago
had had to kill it in self-defense, he understood that ". . . everything
kills everything in some way. Fishing kills me exactly as it keeps me
alive." (p.106) Later *galanos*' attacks devour most of his catch, and
despite his determination "I'11 fight them until I die," his last weapons
are torn out of his hands.(p.115) In the end, the sharks defeat him and
by midnight he knew the fight was over. (p.118)

Obviously the predatory realities restate man's perpetual
problem: Why is there death and how does one act in the face of it? If

existence is a miraculous mandala due to the presence of life, how does one explain the mystery of death at its center? It is this ambivalence of nature and this paradox of life that Santiago's archetypal destiny seeks to resolve.

The archetypal aura to his daily life is made clear early in the novel. When the old man pushes the boat into the water before dawn (pp.27-28), we enter another dimension of experience. As he rows away from the island, the gliding of the boat through the phosphorescent water has something mythical about it. The world grows remote in time and place. The coast dwindles to a long, green line and gradually Santiago is alone on the dark blue water, floating as it were at the edge of the world. His mind is fixed on only one thing, "My big fish must be somewhere." (p.35) And Santiago is clear that fishing has a special meaning for him. It is "That which I was born for." (p.40) Such an expression typifies archetypal thinking. At the same time, it is evident he does not ply his trade mechanically or mindlessly. Nor is his way of life merely a manifestation of stoicism and undeniable courage. What he does is in the nature of a spiritual calling.

In contrast to the predators and hunters, what Santiago does and the way he feels about the creatures of nature reveal the significance of this calling. A hunter tracks spoor and stalks game whereas a fisherman cannot even see the fish and must attract it to the bait. The fisherman must have the touch and know the right moment to hook the fish, and according to its power and instinct, he must let it fight itself to exhaustion before reeling it in. At any time, because of ignorance or impatience, the fisherman may lose his catch.

The sport is reminiscent of the evil women of ancient times who lured men to their death. One recalls Circe enchanting the men and turning them into swine and the Fates who held a man's life by a thread and could cut it at will. So curiously, to fish is the luring, feminine way of survival. What makes Santiago's act masculine, of course, is the size of the prey he is after.

As a man intimate with nature, Santiago feels the omnipresence of her secrets, and to him the smallest signs of the sea portend meanings. But his purpose to catch the great fish reveals him to be a man of spirit as well. Indeed, profane and sacred themes run through Santiago's life.

The profane is clearly linked to the pervasive irony of his story.

There is not only the irony of his apparent defeat nor the irony that predators appear to triumph in the end. Back on the shore the exhausted Santiago slept face downward on the newspapers with his arms outstretched and the scorched palms of his hands up. (p.122) Does this not personify Christ on the Cross facing contemporary civilization, the violence, murder and terror that daily appear in the newspapers? The gesture in imitation of Christ seems to ask the world why he sacrificed Himself. Or does the gesture ask why modern man daily desecrates the sacred in life? These affinities between Santiago's defeat and Christ's crucifixion point to the terrible irony of any noble sacrifice for ungrateful mankind. Finally, there is the irony of ignorance as displayed when the woman tourist does not recognize the marlin for what it was. Such ignorance stresses the contrast between the majesty of nature and the garbage of man's civilization. But Santiago knows the difference and the meaning of each realm.

For this reason, Santiago has chosen between the sacred and the profane. The clue to that choice is the difference between the rich listening to their radios and the old man's colloquy with nature and with his own natural soul. His choice was either to live by courage and the great laws of life or to live as the sharks for the sake of hunger, to live in what the daily newspapers tell us is reality. He chose between the patient plan of the giant cycles of nature and rejected the impatience of contemporary civilization and its money grubbers. He chose between the clear use of intelligence, which is the power man has equal to nature, and the luck of superstition. Thus even though he acknowledges the reality of profane death, he still seeks to perfect the human soul. For Santiago, fishing is a spiritual exercise not unlike those suggested in Ignatius Loyola's *Exercitia spiritualla*. Santiago's need is a daily baptism of intelligence resisting pain and of courage confronting death. And each great catch is for him a trial of passion finally triumphed over by compassion.

Passion and compassion are traits of the great mother archetype, and Santiago's identification with *la mar*, whatever way she may be, provides the salient reason for Santiago's choice of his destiny. According to Carl Jung, an essential characteristic of the mother archetype is that beyond maternal solicitude and sympathy, beyond fostering growth and fertility, the mother presides over ". . . magic transformations and rebirth . . ."[10] Santiago's intimacy with the sea has had such a transforming influence upon his character and life.

The vastness and silence of the sea summon him to his destiny. Somewhere in her mysterious depths is the great reward for patience, devotion and love. In her he must seek the great marlin and his destiny.

That destiny is in contrast to his life ashore. For that life on land is all those things he no longer dreams about: the fights, the women, the storms. It is everything too that had humbled him: his poverty, the death of his wife, the daily defeats, all those inconclusive gestures and deeds that lead nowhere, all the trivial desires and delusions a man must learn to let die along the way.

His life has been less than his destiny. More than plying a trade, Santiago understands what it means to be a fisherman in the vast recurrences of nature. Destiny is the meaning he has given his life. Destiny is not the man's career, but his comprehension of life. Destiny is the fulfillment of one's essential nature, pulling out of oneself one's essence, giving one's life discipline, skill and ultimate direction.

What makes him different from other men is that he obeys the great laws of time in which beautiful things must ripen.[11] In the novel we are aware of the alteration of time: of work with rest, of sleeping with waking, of darkness with light, of moon and stars with sun. There is the flux from strength to infirmity and back again as Santiago fights the pain in his cramped hand. There is the ascent of expectation when the old man catches the fish and the surge of anxiety as he beats off the sharks. There is the descent into sickening dejection when at midnight he sees the battle is lost. There is the pulsation of pain a man resists until it disappears into unconsciousness. All these fluctuations disclose how sensation may be transmuted into experience and how experience can transubstantiate time into meanings.

Human sensation and experience lead us to the mandala of time, the "protective circle" around the center of chaos, as Jung said.[12] As the old man's pulling the fish to him in contracting coils of space and time seems a ritual in honor of death, fate may be likened to a whirlpool sucking men into the absolute, dark finality from which there is no escape. If this is so, why do religions use the circle or mandala as symbol of God's perfect being?

The reason may be that the circular or cyclical is an archetype of death and resurrection, as described in Mircea Eliade's *The Myth of the Eternal Return* (1969).[13] A new birth implies suffering and passion, and God's vanquishing the forces of darkness and chaos will bring about the renewal of the world.

The style of *The Old Man and the Sea* seems to support the cyclical archetype promising a new life. If Santiago's dreams and memories appear merely to eddy back to the symbolic centers of his life, the archaic simplicity of Hemingway's style echoes the grandeur of ancient epic and the rhythm of the Old Testament. Certain passages have the intonation of Genesis while others are like the Ecclesiastes reiterating the cyclical nature of all things that begin and end. In the novel still other phrases, centered on the great fish, echo the New Testament.

To be sure, the story depicts the migration of the birds, which points to the great rhythms of nature, reminding us of the death and rebirth of the year. If to the ancients, the gods of vegetation died in the winter only to return to life in the spring, our era still sees this renewal as the manifestation of the birth, death, and resurrection of Christ. If killing is the axiom of animal life, the cycles of nature show that creation is a higher law than destruction. In Jung's explanation that the mandala is ultimately female, we see the mother archetype triumph over the rapacious male principle. The cyclical continuation of life in the face of so much death proves conclusively that there is one dominant law of existence. The higher power in the universe is female.

It is now that the meaning of the sea as mother archetype becomes clear. If woman has her Stygian depths, her maternal side requires the male to attain wisdom and spiritual worthiness. In a sense this is Santiago's response to the lessons of the sea, for she has taught him to see through the mindless, malevolent forces in nature. To attain this state of awareness, he has had to be alone with her. As Jung observes, it is only in utter solitude that the higher consciousness awakens.[14]

It is the maternal sea which has prepared Santiago for the encounter with the marlin. Throughout the battle with the fish, Santiago feels at one with the marlin, symbol of Christ. From the moment the fish tugs at his line when Santiago visualizes it 600 feet below nibbling at the bait, the fisherman imagines what the fish thinks, feels and has experienced. We sense how the caution and shrewdness of the fish match the old man's skill and intelligence. (pp.41-42)

Santiago pities the fish he has hooked and wonders if it is old too. Its strange ways make him wonder if it is as desperate as he is.(pp.48-49) When the old man notices his hand is bleeding, he thinks that something hurt the fish too. (p.56) Gradually through the day and night, the fish becomes his true friend. The old man senses too how the punishment of the hook and the hunger of the fish are nothing compared to the marlin's not knowing what it is up against. (p.76) And so, united in their struggle for survival, the man, feeling for the fish with his own flesh, has respect and reverence for the great being out of the sea.

Here too Jung's archetypal view leads us to a deeper understanding. As Jung suggests, ". . . the man who is inwardly great will know that the long expected friend of his soul, the immortal one, has now really come . . . to make his life flow into the greater life . . ." Jung concludes, "Christ himself is the perfect symbol of the hidden immortal within the mortal man."[15]

In his battle with the marlin, Santiago is the middle point of the creature's ellipse around him. Santiago is at the center of the mandala of the cycle of life and death. Alone on the sea, the old man is the focal point of the immense circle of the ocean and of the hemisphere itself. It is as if he is the radiating point of the quaternity of the four directions of the world, the four winds, the four Gospels, a star, a cross. Circle and quaternity coexist as symbols of the deity. Even the particles of phosphorous radiating from his skiff lend the dark sea a kind of luminescent halo.

In a profound sense, then, Santiago is in the mysterious heart of the mandala just as Christ is the focus of Romanesque and Gothic tympana where three sacred animals and the angel, representing the four evangelists, surround Him. On the sea in his skiff, Santiago appears as the point of intersection of an infinite cross within the protective circle of the sea.

Jung also provides us with the clue to the ultimate meaning of Santiago's story. The depth psychologist tells us, "The *sarkikos* (carnal man) remains eternally under the law (of death); the *pneumatikos* (spiritual man) alone is capable of being reborn into freedom."[16]

It must be clear that Santiago is such a *pneumatikos*, for each day out at sea he experienced a sacrament of initiation and of purification, each day was a baptism of his spirit in the great soul of the sea. Such *renovatio* was for the purpose of healing and strengthening his own soul against the civilization he lived in, as his cruciform body on the bed of newspapers symbolized. It may be that Santiago is a silhouette of the Savior, and yet if so, what is the fish? Rather, it would seem the old man is God pulling up the Christ-like soul, the large souls among us — those with beauty, power and inner nobility, letting the lesser beings go. As Jung affirms, He raises up ". . . the *corpus glorificationis*, the subtle soul in the state of incorruptibility."[17]

What was Santiago's true destiny then? His real calling was to reveal the inviolable might and sacred magnificence in profane nature. His mission was to show men the immortal spirit within mortal life.

The story of this simple fisherman confronts our civilized irresolution with an act of bravery. An old man would allay our fears that life is absurd because the universe appears tyrannized by death. If humanity seems to have run out of luck and out of time, as apparently it had for Santiago, the single man need not accept the verdict of Fate. Santiago tells each of us that we must daily fish for the hidden sense to the deceptively meaningless days of our lives — if we are to find the higher consciousness of faith which can transmute suffering and even death to some everlasting truth for mankind.

B. SANTIAGO AS PILGRIM:
AN ANTHROPOLOGICAL VIEW

It is not difficult to infer that Santiago is a Christian figure. While his story undeniably supports such an interpretation, this ethnocentric reading tends to omit those dimensions of his character and destiny which go beyond the purely Christian. For this reason, the purpose of this section is to use an anthropological approach which will show how Santiago represents an archetype transcending the confines of any given religion or culture.[18]

Associations with the hero's name lead one immediately to the story setting — the Caribbean Sea. Santiago City is the capital of Oriente Province in south-east Cuba. This geographical clue leads us to speculate on those inferences to the name Santiago beyond its obvious translation into Saint James.

Santiago de Cuba was formerly named Oriente, and this name is plainly cognate to the English word Orient. The Spanish word refers to the eastern coast of the island, and its English counterpart, in the context of the story, implies the eastern sky and the sunrise. As a matter of fact, Santiago begins his day of fishing at dawn, and he rows his skiff westward so that he must face the rising sun, which glares upon the flat sea and would blind him if he did not keep his eyes fixed on the water next to the skiff and on his lines.[19] (p. 32)

Santiago's name also evokes association with the word *orientation*, which noun signifies one's awareness of personal, spacial, and temporal relations. In the Gulf Stream, Santiago orients himself according to the signs of the sea, the seasons, and other natural cycles. For instance, he knows the great fish come in September and October as do the hurricanes (p. 37). Is this not a figurative way of saying that in life the September and October years are fraught with danger for a man, and yet those same years, representing the time of a man's greatest skill and wisdom, enable him to find the great meaning to his destiny? Santiago is also aware of the "homing instinct" of the seabirds, which at the same time reflects migratory patterns. Perhaps this may be regarded as a figurative allusion to Santiago's own pilgrim instinct. The deeper intimations flowing beneath the surface story of *The Old Man and the Sea*, as the currents themselves flow beneath his skiff, will confirm the hypothesis that Santiago's destiny is that of a pilgrim.

The designation *Orient* suggests a further meaning to the word *orientation*. Architecturally speaking, it means the alignment of a church upon the east-west axis, so that the altar (where the Eucharist takes place) is at the eastern end.[20] On the other hand, it should not be forgotten that at the west end of the church, on the facade which faces the setting sun, the tympanum over the main entrance traditionally portrays a Last Judgment scene. In this context, Santiago's rowing westward seems to be in the direction of death or the eschatological end of man and the world, although Santiago faces the east in the direction of life. One can even draw an age-old inference from this simple act. The impossibility of looking directly into the sunlight is like the ancient mystical notion that one cannot look directly into the face of God without being blinded by His magnificence and splendor. God's speaking to Moses through the intermediary of the burning bush is a Biblical example of this belief. Perhaps for this spiritual reason, Santiago cannot look into the glare of the real sun in the morning. Or perhaps as a pilgrim, he is blinded by the nearness of God.

Such an interpretation would be fitting as a mystic translation of his journey. Beyond the immediate Judaic-Christian connotations to the geography of the story, the infinitive *to orient* means to determine one's position on the earth and to adjust oneself to recognize truths. In a larger sense, Santiago's story is precisely such a recognition, for daily the facts of life and death force him to come to terms with his own meaning in existence.

Furthermore, the old man's name clearly suggests a renowned place of pilgrimage in Northwest Spain, Santiago de Compostela. That he feels he was born to be a fisherman (p. 50) and that he senses his destiny is linked with seeking out the remote sanctuary of the great fish lends his life the aura of an actual pilgrimage.

Proof that this assertion is not merely a lapse into pseudo-religious rhetoric comes from the evidence provided by seasoned anthropologists.[21] Their description of the traditional traits of pilgrimages brings considerable weight to the claim that Santiago's way of life has distinct pilgrim characteristics.

As far back as anthropology can go, there have always been cults of nature and sanctuaries which have been the object of arduous journeys. Ancient religions revered sacred places as forests, caves, rivers, bodies of water, and even fissures in the earth. Natural phenomena gave rise to religious practices in which divination had an important role. Prophecies were made upon observing the flight of birds, flashes of lightning, or the entrails of sacrificed victims. Corporeal relics were venerated such as the head, heart and even sexual organs. In the Christian era, as is well known, the bones of a saint were sent to the four corners of Christendom to become the saintly relic upon which to build a church.

A moment's reflection shows how such anthropological facts help clarify that Santiago's story should be regarded as a pilgrimage. First of all, fishing takes place in nature, that is, on the sea, the source of life. He himself divines the meaning of the flights of birds, much as a naturalist would do, but also with a mystic's compassion. The novel ends with the fish as a victim, a carcass of bones, whose sacrifice to the sharks takes on a darkly ironic meaning when the tourists (who represent a travesty on true pilgrims) misidentify the marlin as a shark. To be sure, such ignorance is a bitter commentary on modern civilization at the same time that it points to the authenticity of Santiago's natural and ritualistic way of life. The other fishermen, the initiated, recognize what Santiago has done. If Santiago performed no overt religious act that might ordinarily be associated with a pilgrimage, the fight with the fish and its great size imply he has taken part in a supernatural event.

There are other characteristics of pilgrimages which seem to provide further evidence that Santiago's experience at sea is such an undertaking. The pagans of Greco-Latin antiquity had cults in the woods, by sources, rivers, and fountains. Brahmans go to rivers, Buddhists to mountains (cf. Hemingway's "Snows of Kilimanjaro"). Christians went to grottos, islands, and lakes. Such places often are associated with depths, the feminine, and the source of life just as is the ocean in *The Old Man and the Sea*. Furthermore, centres of devotion are usually remote from civilization and far from the main routes of communication. Distances traveled to these holy places confirm the idea that a pilgrimage often obliges the pilgrim to undergo physical discomfort or pain to arrive there. Certainly the place Santiago has chosen meets these qualifications for a real pilgrimage.

Very often a physical trial is associated with the difficulty of the road, which trial enhances the merit attained by the voyage, the *Peregrinatio religionis ergo* of Erasmus. The distance traveled for a holy purpose is entwined with a certain stoicism, which typifies Christian and Moslem pilgrims alike. Indeed, the true pilgrim departs heroically alone on his voyage to the sanctuary and endures much in order to be worthy of the experience of the Holy Presence. Obviously Santiago's voyage out into the remoteness of the sea, where the great currents crossed and where the greatest depths were reached, in order to seek out his great fish, strongly indicates that he is a lone pilgrim in search of the great truth for his soul to live by. Like other pilgrims, Santiago is exposed to death, to physical privations, hazardous routes and the difficulty of the way chosen.

If the pilgrimage has its pains, it also has its rewards. The Moslem who reaches the Mecca is absolved of his sins. Back in his village, the Moslem acquires *hadji* or nobility. For Brahmans, the ritual bath in the sacred river opens paradise to them. For most pilgrims, heavenly benedictions descend upon their lives. Santiago experiences a similar reward in catching the fish and beginning his return to the port — until the sharks attack.

The ironic twist of fate in this attack is not the only factor which separates Santiago's experience from that of other pilgrims. Unlike pilgrimages undertaken to expiate some mortal sin, Santiago is not required to endure humiliation or to flagellate himself publicly, as is the case even today in some Moslem countries. Nor as with Buddhists, Brahmans, or Moslems, is it necessary for Santiago to live in misery or to beg for a living, although like them he willingly exposes himself to the harshness of nature. Nor does Santiago practice any kind of masochism or self-mortification. (In humility and hope, Christians in the Middle Ages went great distances on their knees to pray at a sacred place. Or again Buddhists measured the distance to a sanctuary with their bodies by lying down, getting up and lying down over and over again. Nor does Santiago employ some easy device as the famous prayer wheel used by the Tibetan Lamas to spin prayers up to heaven.) On the other hand, Santiago's prayer "Hail Mary" and his solemn promise to go on a pilgrimage to the Virgin of Cobre (p. 65) echoes the ritualistic phrasing of pilgrims of other religions.

Ancient animistic custom often made a tree, such as a mighty oak, the object of pilgrimages. Worship is associated with the tree under which Gautama Buddha meditated for five years, and Western scholars do not hesitate to identify the Cross as the "Tree of life" on which Christ achieved his apotheosis. In rural Europe the custom of hammering nails into trees still persists, and this act has transparent symbolic associations with the crucifixion of Christ. Similarly Manolin recalls when Santiago killed a fish in the boat, the old man's clubbing it was "like chopping a tree down and the sweet blood smell all over me" (p. 12). Such associations provide at least peripheral evidence that Santiago's life is a pilgrimage, whether conscious or not.

Obviously the ancient veneration of water and the associations of many saints with water (as Saint James, the fisherman) apply to the old man's story. Furthermore, pilgrims bathe in life-giving waters, and Santiago's dipping his wounded hand into the sea to be healed is a practical, curative and spiritual gesture.

Another ritual associated with the pilgrimage is that of circumambulation. In many religions pilgrims often circle three times around a sanctuary or object of veneration. The ancient Celts did it in the direction of the sun; the Brahmans consider circular ways around sanctuaries to be purifying; the Buddhists require pilgrims to circle around lakes and mountains; and Moslems circle the kabba seven times at Mecca. Should one see in Santiago's drawing the fish to him in ever-tightening circles more than a practical necessity? Perhaps not, and yet since Santiago's way of life has many other acts kindred to pilgrimage rituals, the similarity is striking.

Anthropologists believe circumambulation is in homage to the sun. Santiago too is aware of the cyclical patterns of the sun, of the seasons, of the cycle of life and death as evinced in the struggle for survival. Santiago's mystical encounter with the majestic marlin in the dying part of the year seems to bear witness to a similar form of reverence.

The pilgrim often makes a deeply felt promise like Santiago's vow to catch the great fish. The object of a pilgrimage is spiritual communion. Often a sacrifice is made (as the lambs, cows, goats, and camels at Mecca) after which the flesh is given to the poor. If Santiago's killing the fish may be regarded as such a sacrifice, it is to the beauty and power of life in the marlin, and his act is clearly a re-enactment of the Eucharist. Ironically, in the story, the sharks get the meat, not the meek and the poor.

A Christian can undertake a pilgrimage, as can the faithful of other religions, if he has undergone spiritual purification. Sexual abstinence is a frequent practice so that the experience may be moral. Not only is Santiago's life clean in this respect, but his calling the man-of-war a whore implies a pure attitude on his part. Without stain of any kind, Santiago is worthy of the holy voyage he has undertaken.

If pilgrimages are sustained acts of faith by men and women who seek to give their lives a spiritual meaning, Santiago's soul must surely find salvation from the meaninglessness of other men's lives. The mystic love he bears the creatures of nature, his readiness to endure suffering and to risk his life prepare him for the encounter with the great marlin. He is worthy of communion with the mystery of life and death, and such worthiness promises the true pilgrim a deathless destiny.

C: A NUMEROLOGICAL INTERPRETATION

Introduction

As early as the sixth century B.C., the Pythagoreans held the belief that numbers held some mystical message. Pythagorus himself believed in the eternal recurrence of nature, in the harmony of the spheres, and in metempsychosis (the passing of the soul at death into another body, human or animal). To be sure, the belief in metempsychosis demonstrated an awareness of some symbiotic conjunction between man and animal. Also implied was the sense that all earthly life is symbiotically or ecologically one, governed by the seasons and the cyclical nature of the universe.

Similarly, the medieval and modern system of Jewish mysticism developed a cipher method for interpreting scripture. The awareness of esoteric meanings camouflaged in exoteric passages was characteristic. Indeed, the study of scripture revealed strange and remarkable coincidences. When the Hebrew alphabet was translated into numbers, as in the Kabbalah, miraculous messages appeared before the cabbalist's eyes. Such exercises in ingenuity pointed to a different perception of reality and a different dimension of "reasoning" than that perceived in the physical sciences or practiced in the procedures characteristic of arithmetic and mathematics

In the Pythagorean or cabbalistic conception of numbers, there seemed a symbiotic intuition at work that there existed a logic-defying intricacy between numbers, nature's phenomena, and man's inherent reasoning. This deeper perception of reality seemed to emerge from the reassurance that numbers create order out of chaos and sense out of the circumstantial. Numbers replace disorder with some kind of superior order.[22]

However, unlike the practical use of numbers in arithmetic and mathematics, in the Kabbalah, numbers go beyond being integers to become symbols of religious meanings as if they somehow sum up the significance of life and existence.

Similarly, the numerologist's mystical perception of numbers dwells on patterns of recondite connections between abstraction and substance. This search for the invisible finds a parallel in 20th century biology. Biologists are now fully convinced that body and mind are one. Moreover, this sensory-somatic-sentient-noetic entity, known as man, now studies the comparable symbiotic nature of all life forms, both microscopic and macroscopic. Such a unified vision implies that symbiotic order rules the animate world and human nature itself.

Thus, even if the conclusions of Pythagoreans, cabbalists, and numerologists remain questionable, they, nevertheless, seem intuitively on to something. The numerologist seeks out the hidden connections between quantity and quality, between number and the numinous.[23] Through such orientation, mystics study how abstract knowledge, rooted in number and quantity, might relate to or conjoin with experience of the sacred. Somehow such mystics believe mankind has an eschatological destiny. What they seek then is the final meaning of existence by transmuting the cryptic into a deciphered message from God.

∗ ∗ ∗

The opening paragraph of the novel makes much of time and numbers. The old man has had eighty-four days of bad luck, which are divided into two periods: the first forty days fishing with the boy, and the forty-four days since the boy's parents no longer permit the boy to fish with Santiago because the old man was said to be jinxed. The eighty-four days can be divided into forty before and after plus four extra days.

Ever since Pythagoras believed that numbers held the secret to the world and that numerical ratios, as the intervals in the musical scale, were the keys to relationships in the universe, numbers have fascinated Western man. Pythagoras's explanation that the movement of the celestial spheres produced a heavenly harmony or music added a mythical or mystical aura to this fascination.

Undoubtedly, Hemingway's use of numbers in his novel had the immediate artistic intention of arousing reader response to the old man's bad luck and of awakening admiration for Santiago's tenacity. Yet why precisely eighty-four days and the story itself taking place on the eighty-fifth day?

The number forty calls forth Biblical connotations. Even the reader with the most rudimentary recollection of the Old Testament must recall the forty years that the ancient Hebrews underwent trials and tribulations until they reached the Promised Land. Similarly, one would recall in the New Testament the forty days Jesus fasted in the wilderness, during which the devil tempted Jesus to make bread from stones to feed himself. In any event, the number forty usually represented in ancient times a long period rather than an exact number of days or years. Obviously then the number forty brings to mind both Moses and Jesus. In the novel, Santiago too is seeking the fulfilment of a promise (to himself) and willingly undergoes hardship and humiliation to find the place where his promise may be fulfilled. He too rejects the temptation of bread, the money begotten from an easy catch closer to the shore, in order that his life might find a higher purpose.

If so, what significance have the four days? In the context of the story, the number reminds us of the four cardinal directions of the world, the four winds, the four corners of the earth, the four celestial angles (sunrise, sunset, zenith and nadir), and the four seasons of the year and of life. However, since the number forty has so directly led us to Biblical associations, the number four awakens other possible allusions. There are four rivers around Eden, four branches of the Cross, the four great prophets of the Old Testament, four sacred figures (the angel, bull, lion, and eagle) associated with the four evangelists, the four parts of the New Tetament (the Gospels, the Epistles, the Acts, and the Apocalypse), and the four basic materials of the sacrament — wine, oil, water and bread.[24] In the hermeneutics of the Bible, there are thought to be four meanings to Scripture: (1) the literal or historical sense, (2) the allegorical, (3) the moral, and (4) the anagogical or mystical sense. Bear in mind that anagoge is the mystical or spiritual interpretation of words and numbers, especially of the Old and New Testament.[25]

As obvious as such numerical associations may be to the scholar, there is yet another way of studying the implications of the number eighty-four because that number results from multiplying seven and twelve. Astrologically speaking, the successive positions of the seven planets of the solar system, timing the rotation of the twelve signs of the zodiac, could account for Santiago's bad luck. On the other hand, seven and twelve are probably the most renowned mystic numbers in Christian numerology.

For instance, there are the seven deadly sins (pride, envy or malice, wrath, lust, gluttony, avarice, and sloth). Appearing as allegorical figures in many theological, artistic and literary works of the Christian Middle Ages, they often provide the sevenfold system of organizing such works. It is clear that Santiago is guilty of none of these sins. Then there are the seven virtues — the four cardinal virtues of pagan antiquity (justice, temperance, courage and wisdom) plus three Christian or theological virtues (faith, hope, and charity). Careful reflection will show the reader that Santiago indeed possesses both the pagan and Christian virtues.

The seven words spoken by Christ on the Cross, translated as "My God, Why have You Forsaken Me?" seem to express the state of civilization Santiago saw when the carcass of the fish (symbol of Christ) lay in the garbage and the tourists did not even recognize what the fish was. There are seven holy sacraments (baptism, penance, the Eucharist, confirmation. ordination, matrimony, and Extreme Unction). There are seven ecclesiastical orders. In the Apocalypse were seven series of visions, and in the first four visions appear seven churches, seven seals, seven trumpets, seven chalices, and a seven headed beast. During the Annunciation the angel spoke seven words to the Virgin; and the gifts of the Holy Spirit are said to be seven. According to the Gospel of John, Jesus manifested the power of God (the Logos) by seven miraculous events: (1) turning water into wine at the marriage feast in Cana, (2) healing the nobleman's son who was on the point of death, (3) healing the man at the sheep gate pool, (4) walking on water, (5) feeding the 5,000, (6) healing the man born blind, and (7) raising Lazarus. Thus the number seven is the symbol of eternal life and of seven sacramental ways of initiation to that life.

The number twelve has Judaic and Christian associations as well.[26] In the Old Testament, Jehovah distributed the twelve tribes into four groups according to the four cardinal directions of the world. Jacob had twelve sons by four wives, and twelve minor prophets are subordinated to Isaiah, Jeremiah, Ezekiel, and Daniel. The twelve patriarchs are matched by the twelve Apostles in the New Testament, one of whom was Saint James or Santiago. Of even greater significance, if we accept the fish as traditional symbol of Christ, is the fact that the Mass has twelve parts. As evidenced by the relics of his deceased wife and Santiago's references to the "Lord's Prayer" and "Hail Mary," he was completely aware of Christian ritual and values.

Knowing the Mass by heart, the twelve phases and their spiritual meaning must have been central to his everyday thought whether consciously or not.

Because Santiago's fishing will be shown to have the aura of a holy, archetypal ritual, it is worthwhile to allude briefly here to the twelve specific stages of the Mass. First comes the *Introduction* or preparation of the faithful for confession; second is the *Introit* or opening act of worship with the entrance of the Choir singing the litany "Gloria Patri"; third, the *Epistle* is given during which a psalm is intoned and a collection for the poor is made; fourth, the Gospel of the day with a sermon is given; fifth, the *Apostles' Creed* or the Christian confession of faith is offered, during which three dogmas are directed to each cardinal direction of the world; sixth, the *Offetory*, during which the bread and the wine are consecrated, is enacted and alms collected; seventh, the *Preface* is offered, the prayer of thanksgiving ending with the *Sanctus* that introduces the canon of the Mass; eighth, the *Elevation*, the raising of the Eucharist elements for adoration; ninth, the *Pater Noster* of Lord's Prayer; tenth, the *Fraction*, the act of breaking the bread in the Eucharist, with the *Agnus Dei*, prayer "O Lamb of God"; eleventh, the *Communion*, the Eucharist and a chant (antiphon) after the distribution of the Eucharist elements; and twelfth. the *Benediction* or act of blessing at the close of the worship.

While these symbolic suggestions of numbers have their undeniable interest, the reader may well question if this series of numerical analogies actually helps explicate the novel. As tenuous as the mythical and mystical associations seem to be at first sight, they are symbols mirroring the collective unconscious of Santiago or the conscience of Hemingway, which provide an Ariadne thread out of the dark labyrinth of death to light, life and freedom.

If for the moment we accept at face value the need to decipher the meaning of numbers in any given text with mythical or religious connotations, as numerologists would contend, then we can further explore the hints such numbers augur.

In the ancient interpretation of the zodiac, each cardinal number had a meaning. For instance. the number seven was associated with Hermes/Mercury, which name is linked to Hermes Trismegistus, the Greek name for the Egyptian god Thoth, regarded as the founder of alchemy, astrology and other occult sciences. (The word *hermeneutics* ultimately derives from Hermes and the deciphering of his cryptic writings.) On the other hand, the number twelve in the ancient zodiac referred to the moon, the chaste Artemis, guardian of childbirth. Now, if the number seven implies the need to decipher mysterious symbolic allusions and if the number twelve originally had something to do with childbirth, we are led to a startling discovery as to their possible implications in the story.

According to the zodiac, the number three is that of Neptune, who is father of the currents and rhythms of the ocean, and he, therefore, has some connection with Santiago's mythical story. To be sure, three also symbolizes the Holy Trinity. If we divide eighty-four days by three, the result is twenty-eight days, which marks the period of a woman's ovulation. If we divide this twenty-eight day period by four, the number of the Gospels, we get the number seven, which according to John, denoted the number of miracles proving the Presence of God in the life of Jesus. Also, the seven words spoken by Christ on the Cross seemed to indicate death was near at hand for Jesus, but according to ecclesiastical history, those words were the prelude to the advent of the Resurrection. Similarly, the seven words spoken to the Virgin by the angel announced the birth of the Saviour. Hence it would seem the sacred numbers three, four, seven and twelve indicate a ratio of mystic meanings implicit in the story of a fisherman.

If asked what justifies these mythical and mystical numerological implications to the novel, I contend that both explicit and implicit evidence provide such a justification.

Santiago makes explicit statements of a religious character. One of his recurrent phrases to the boy is "have faith." Although he states he is not religious (p. 64),[27] he promises to say ten Our Fathers and ten Hail Marys that he should catch the fish, and he promises to make a pilgrimage to the Virgin of Cobre. (P. 65) He confirms what might otherwise be considered merely a passing exclamation by saying with finality, "That's a promise."

Later during the battle with the fish, Santiago states he will say a hundred Our Fathers and a hundred Hail Marys (p. 87), and this exaggeration might have humorous overtones if at the crucial stage of the struggle, he did not in all earnestness state that it is a sin not to hope (pp. 104-5), for he here reflects the official Church stance which regards despair a grave sin because Christ brought hope to mankind.

In addition to this explicit evidence justifying a numerological interpretation of the novel, a great deal of implicit evidence is on hand as well. For instance, there is the fact that Santiago's story is so closely identified with symbols and creatures traditionally Christian: the heart, birds, the fish and fishing. To cite only a few of the most striking instances, in Santiago's hut there hangs a picture of the Sacred Heart of Jesus and of the Virgin of Cobre, which were relics of his dead wife (p. 16). Later Santiago states he had no mysticism, but then he senses his identity with turtles that have a heart, feet and hands as his own, and he feels compassion for the turtle because heartless men cut out its heart, which will beat for hours after the turtle is cut up and butchered (p. 37). The link between Christ's crucifixion, the Sacred Heart, and the turtle's heart forms an obvious symbolic equation.

Santiago's calling the stars his friends may at first seem an earthy observation of any man who sails on the sea, and yet the phrase "I am glad we do not have to kill the stars," as he must the fish (p. 75), creates a transparent association between the possible death of a celestial body and the fish, traditional sign of Christ. (One could even argue that Santiago's namesake, Saint James, brother of Jesus, implies a mystical relationship between the old man and the stars).

Although seabirds do not appear in Christian iconography, in the novel they bear a message of compassion and of hope. When Santiago watches the small delicate terns, who seek food but almost never find it, he feels pity for their small sad voices over the sea (p. 29). They are bearers of nature's signs, and the omens they bring the fisherman are that some birds have no chance (p. 34) and that predator birds will soon come to kill them (p. 55). Thus at one level they typify the struggle of life and death in nature, and yet the survival of the fragile tern as a species seems a numerological presage, for the word *tern*, meaning three, implies the ternary and perhaps ultimately the Trinity. Since birds since ancient history have been viewed as augurs of heaven, this ultimate implication may be true.

To be sure, a number of other instances illustrate the religious implications to this contest in nature. For example, the man-of-war dangling its long deadly filaments may be a sign of entangling death, yet the tiny fish that swam between them were immune to its poison (p. 35). More than a sample of symbiosis, the fish (again as tiny symbol of Christ) seem to say that the Christian is immune to death. Then the turtle returns, as image of the (Sacred) heart, to devour the man-of-war (p. 36).

Such symbolic clues lead us to understand Santiago's archetypal story as involving a deeper significance than Darwin's theory of the struggle for survival in nature. Indeed, the novel is a modern Christian exemplum. Santiago's going out on the ocean early beyond all other men lends his actions either a heroic or mystical dimension. The old man's identification with the fish as his brother (p. 64) and Santiago's vow to kill him "In all his greatness and glory," (p. 66) already orient our intimation as to the religious relationship between them. Further-more, Santiago finds that both he and the fish are strange in their endurance and in their capacity for suffering. (At this point it seems that fishing is some kind of a ritual of life and death for Santiago.)

When he had caught the fish and tied it alongside his skiff, the fish's eye looks as detached as the eye of a saint's statue in procession. Then the old man recalls how at the end of the struggle the fish had come out of the water and hung motionless in the sky before it fell. Santiago was sure there was some great strangeness in that moment. In the context of both traditional Christian associations with the fish and Santiago's own mystic feeling toward the great marlin, that moment imaged forth Christ on the Cross. Thus Santiago's story conveys an esoteric message to those initiated into the secrets of nature and into the mystery of existence itself.

The key to those secrets and to that mystery is divulged, at least in part, by the mythical and mystical numbers we have been examin-ing. If three, four, seven and twelve are of special significance in Christian numerology, what figurative implications can they have in the story? If we accept the heart as the center of Christianity and as an important symbol in the novel, we recollect that three hearts are mentioned: that of Santiago, that of the turtle (analog to Christ because its heart still beats on long after the creature has been chopped to pieces), and the picture of the Sacred Heart next to that of the Virgin of Cobre .[28] If we add the three symbols of the heart to the four gospels, we get the number seven, which alludes to the dying words of Christ on the Cross, to the angelic words announced to Mary, and to the seven sacraments which guarantee salvation to the faithful. If we divide the number twelve, which is the zodiac sign of Pisces, the fish, by the four cardinal directions of terrestrial and celestial phenomena, we come back to the number three. Or if we divide the twelve stages of the Mass, deep in the memory of Santiago, by the four Gospels, we come to the Holy Trinity.

The number twelve has another association. On a clock, in a calendar year, or as the final number of the astrological cycle, twelve designates the end of the old but indicates also the beginning of the new. Furthermore, the number twelve, associated with Artemis, guardian of the unborn, is a promise of a new beginning or of a new life. If we divide that twelve into the eighty-fifth day of the actual story, we get seven with the number one left over.

This fact leads us to ask what one represents. In the ancient zodiac one meant unity. In Christian doctrine, the trinity is the union in one Godhead of three persons: Father, Son and Holy Ghost. When we recall that the Virgin gave birth to the one and only Son of God in the twelfth month of the year (at the winter solstice, December 22, which is the beginning of the earth's new solar cycle) and that she first learned of her destiny through the seven words of the angel, we come to understand the meaning of the eighty-fifth day. Beyond the mystical closure of the forty years of Moses' wandering and the forty days of Jesus in the wilderness and of the four Gospels, the next day for Santiago represents a new beginning. Indeed, *one* is not only the beginning of all numbers, it is also the start of life, springing from the fundamental unity at the heart of all apparent dualism. One unites differences and diversity — sexually, metaphorically, symbolically — because in spite of the law of competition and the struggle of survival, love sustains life through death. Therefore, the chaste Artemis, guardian of the life to be, and the chaste Virgin, who gave birth to the Messiah, deliver living creatures and mankind from death.

Somehow numerology does provide a key to deciphering the hermeneutics of Santiago's story. In the total context of sea, space and time, through Fate and Providence, Santiago was bound to encounter the Greatness and the Glory he had sought on that eighty-fifth day so that at last he could come to grips with his own high destiny.

Through his experience Santiago fathomed the unrevealed truth. Even though the repeated shark attacks on the marlin seem to prove the power of death, and even though in the end there is nothing left but the skeleton of what once had power and beauty, the ironic conclusion to the novel actually serves the purpose of recalling for the reader everything that the uninitiated would miss and will never find in their lives.

Despite defeat, Santiago has learned the truth about existence. The ultimate cipher to Hemingway's hermeneutics in *The Old Man and the Sea* is given when Santiago said his prayers to Mary, "Blessed are thou among women and blessed is the fruit of thy womb, Jesus," adding, ". . . pray for us sinners now and at the hour of death." This maternal image mirrors Santiago's naming the sea *la mar* (unlike the men with the motorboats who called it the masculine *el mar*.)

For Santiago the sea is like woman, whose moods are governed by the moon. (p 30) (cf Artemis) As a male child with his mother, he is a part of her and of nature. His very love of the birds, the porpoises. and the fish proves how much he is one with creation. For this reason, his identity with the fish and the deep respect he feels for all living creatures enable his spirit to survive the shark jaws of death. For this reason, he never feels alone at sea. (p 61)

It is the rhythm of the sea which makes him aware of the rhythm of all existence. While fishing, Santiago is a part of the great natural cycles — the migration of the birds, the flowing of ocean currents, and the blowing of the winds. At one level, we may say Santiago partakes of the earth's share in the great solar and sidereal cycles, and at another level, Santiago is part of the astrological cycles said to influence the destinies of men. Yet Santiago's mystical oneness with life and his worship of woman, as the sea and the Virgin, reveal the truth of his life. And his ability to endure great physical and mental suffering reveal that fishing, for Santiago, is a ritual re-enactment of spiritual rebirth which transcends physical death. The central mythical and mystical numbers unsealed from Santiago's conscience reveal the eschatological truth that love is stronger than death. For this reason, Santiago's daily sacrament proved him worthy of the Great Essene.

D. THE NOVEL AS TESTAMENT

There may be consummate fools who do not understand what fishermen do, but the latter will not mistake the timeless meaning of their action, for the symbol of their craft is many centuries older than the still unfaded story of the Grail.

> C.G. Jung, *The Archetypes and the Collective Unconscious*, Bollingen Series XX, p.24

Santiago's fishing eighty-four days without a catch is more than mischance. Despite skill and courage, strength and fleeting success, the old fisherman finally loses his catch to rapacious sharks. As observed earlier, his story reveals an ironic contrast at the very heart of existence — between what a man may set out to do and what fate may decree for him.

If the surface story depicts the struggle for survival and the power of Fate over the individual life, the deeper tale testifies to the fact that existence embraces greater and more intricate truths. Consequently, the epic struggle of one man against nature incarnates a more complex, infinite dimension. In the old man's earthy understandings, there is divulged one of the most meaningful visions of human destiny modern man has attained.

Santiago obeys a powerful instinct that requires him to face his fate. His life demands the kind of battle which ends either in destruction or survival. Indeed, he represents the fact that the isolated individual must learn the meaning of death in life.

When the old man pushes the skiff into the sea, he does so as part of an ageless ritual. When he rows away from the disappearing island, it is as if he and the boat glide into a mysterious realm. Stroke by stroke, the world grows remote in time and place as in legend.

A speck on a limitless sea, Santiago drops thick fishing lines into the deepest reaches of the sea. The succulent bait he uses shows how he is to test the hunger and intelligence of the deep sea being by his own shrewdness and tricks as an old fisherman. Santiago's mind is set on one thing. "My big fish must be somewhere."[29] (p.35) He feels he was born to do this task. (p.40) Yet his self-doubts make us wonder if he still has enough strength, clear memory, and skill to raise the leviathan singlehanded from the dark depths of a fathomless sea.

On this eighty-fifth day he has set his mind against his bad luck. He admonished himself ". . . fish the day well." (p.41) Later, when the fish takes the bait and heavily jerks the line, the first pivot point of the story has been reached: from here on the two are linked in a fight to the death. He must try to endure.

To this moment, the ill-luck of eighty-four days seems to weigh down the days of his life that is coming to its end. Dwarfed on a limitless ocean, his physical and moral strength are called into question. Yet the old man pits his tiny will and subtle skills against time.

Lonely without the boy Manolin to fish with him, he fights his sense of aging and desolation. Will the great fish be too much for one old man alone?

His right hand is cut and bleeding from a quick pull of the fish. His hand cramps like a claw. In speaking to his hand as if it had betrayed him, the fisherman reminds us of man's affinity to all that is flesh. Each man is in and part of that nature.

Santiago resists his pain, and in spite of the marlin's power, he vows, "I'll stay with you until I am dead." (p.52) Even as he improvises ways to make it jump and fill its pouches with air so it cannot go deep to die (p.53), he is resolved to show the fish what sort of man he is. (p 64) He lashes two oars across the stern to slow down the pull of the marlin.(p.73) By exploiting its pain and keen hunger, he will let the fish pull the skiff until, in exhaustion, it is ready to die.

Unable to free itself from the hook, at sunrise on the third day, the fish begins its inward ellipse (p.86), and the old man draws in line to make the circle tighter and tighter. (p.87) The symbolic meaning of this slow spiral toward death becomes clearer as the intricate, infinite vision of the story unfolds.

In the ensuing hours, the two are one in their resistance and their ebbing strength. Whatever advantage the fisherman gains, he is threatened with losing all because he himself is weakening. Both are afflicted, but if Santiago can control his own pain, the creature's will drive it mad. (p.88) Santiago's stoicism shows that in being superior to anguish, a man is not an animal.

As the marlin is drawn to the skiff in a narrowing vortex, the fisherman is faint from fatigue and sleepless nights."You are killing me, fish." (p.92) Finally, when he is able to bring the marlin alongside the boat, he plunges his harpoon into its heart.(p.94) He lashes the dead giant to the side.

Santiago's victory is short lived. Sharks bring a kind of fateful retribution. Although he beats them off, they break his weapons and tear them out of his hands. (p 115) Finally, he admits defeat.

Had he come out too far? In a sense Santiago is a tragic figure, who, despite largeness of soul, brings about his own defeat through excessive pride. In the end, the Fates seem to mock this simple man. It is as if they merely toyed with his courage and will to find some great moment in life.

However, the fisherman's story transcends the meaning of any single life because what happens to a man of courage happens to all of us. For three days he enacted the destiny of the entire human race. As Santiago, each of us wages a battle for himself — and without realizing it — for humanity. His sealed fate becomes our fate too.

Yet is he fated? To accept such a surface interpretation is to be misled. Indeed, there is a danger to seeing human experience from any limited point of view, for it may constrict our perception to a fraction of the true or ultimate meaning; or worse, it may lead the beholder to miss life's infinite significance.

By solely examining the surface narration of *The Old Man and the Sea*, the reader would be led to the bleak conclusion that dark injustice eclipses human fate. Such a judgement would be tantamount to fearing the shadows cast across our lives without acknowledging the light that is far beyond all penumbra. A simplistic interpretation of Santiago's life would ignore the charity, hope and faith implicit in his story.

Santiago seems a simple man whose sole interests are baseball and fishing. Yet the boy's recognition of the inner man helps us gain a truer insight into Santiago's resolute nature. Manolin's thoughtful love shows the child's trust and respect for the old man. When Santiago wishes the boy were there to help him bring in the big fish, the man confirms the deeper relationship between them. If Santiago's life reveals him to be a man of faith, the boy as faith-seeker senses what the old man has yet to teach him.

Nevertheless, it is the antagonists who are closest to one another: the marlin and the man. From the moment the fish tugs at his line 600 feet below to nibble at the bait, the fisherman wonders if it remembers being hooked once before. (pp.41-42) With that thought, the two become one identity, for we see how the caution and experience of the fish resist Santiago's cunning and skill. Yet the fisherman has deep compassion for the creature he outwits in the end.

Through the days and nights, he has come to realize the fish was his friend as indeed all the creatures in the sea are our true brothers. (p.75) He knew the punishment of the hook and the hunger of the fish were nothing compared to the marlin's not understanding what it was up against. (p.75) The old man's flesh knew what the fish felt, and he suffered for its great spirit.

Yet one moment illumines the ultimate act. With Santiago's last strength he harpoons the long silver shape where its heart is. The startled spirit rises above the old man with the last of its power to fall dead beside him in the water. If Santiago's intelligence and deceit prevail over the fish, its lack of malevolence, its innocence of the man's evil intent, somehow make it superior to him.

The scene of the struggle took place between sky and sea. As *la mar*, as woman, the sea conceals what is most secret and sacred to her, so a man never knows what he will arouse or draw up from her depths. Yet he feels at one with her also. Indeed, Santiago is at one with creation as is seen in his love of the birds, the porpoises and the great fish. Hence even though his battle with the fish portrays the Darwinian law of "survival of the fittest," Santiago knows, nevertheless, that all living creatures are part of one Identity transcending nature.

The narrative alone can yield only certain truths about the story. To go deeper, to go as deep as Santiago's lines in the depths of the sea, we need to explore the images and figures which augur further meanings.

It is metaphor and time which unravel the paradox of existence. While at sea, Santiago is part of the great cycles of nature — the flow of the currents, the blowing of the winds in the month of the hurricanes, the migration of the birds. There he is part of vast cycles of time. Similarly, metaphor recycles past, present, and future into recurrent meanings. The old man likens the deep creased scars in his hands to old erosions in a fishless desert. (p.10) In his experience, there is only one source for such an image: the wasteland where Moses and Christ walked. Santiago's own wilderness is the sea.

In the metaphorical context of Santiago's story, the most common objects take on a new aura. The coiled fishing lines in the boat recall the fish circling the boat to approach its death. The gaff and the harpoon remind us of the old man's cramped hand and numerous references to a bird's claw. Around the mast, the sail was furled like a flag in permanent defeat. (p.9) Yet when the old man carries the mast on his shoulder (p.l5), we recollect the Biblical counterpart of Christ bearing the cross to Golgotha.

Metaphor also provides the clue to Santiago's mature credo. When the boy tells him to remember it is September and to keep warm, the old man replies it is the month of the great fish and adds cryptically, "Anyone can be a fisherman in May."(p.18) He means that anyone can accomplish what he wants when he is young. To do the same thing in the September of one's life takes more. He feels a man's great works can only come when experience, knowledge, and courage direct his searching spirit.

The true complexity of the novel's figurative meaning appears when we realize there is a central metaphor which radiates throughout, as it were, emanating from the mystery of existence. C.G. Jung's analytical psychology helps fathom the way ancient humanity envisioned enigmatic nature. At the core, duality reigned. This dualistic vision is most effectively described in terms of the mother.

Nature as Mother archetype shows "material solicitude and sympathy . . . all that is benign," but she may also represent ". . . anything that devours, seduces, . . . that is terrifying and inescapable as death."[30] Even so is the sea. Santiago hates this ambivalence in nature.

Yet beyond this malignant duality is the spiritual oneness of nature. Although "Santiago had no mysticism about turtles," he sees its heart, hands and feet are like ours. He thinks "Most people are heartless about turtles because a turtle's heart will beat for hours after he has been cut up and butchered." (p.37) Not only is this an image of the life force within the creature and in Santiago himself, but obviously it highlights the Christian import of the story. Santiago thought people were unworthy to eat the marlin, implying they were not worthy of the Eucharist — of partaking of the substance of God.

(Similarly, the boat may be the symbol of the Church being towed in the depths by Christ since the *nave* of a church means boat.) Hence in the marlin we have a metaphor for the cannibalization of Christ and in the turtle a symbol of His heart beating on through the centuries after His death.

Metaphor and irony play as light and shadow across the story to make visible the intricate patterns of Santiago's experience. Though the empty sea seems to isolate him from life and hope, a flight of ducks against the blue sky reassures him a man is never alone. Later, the deep silence reminds him of his dreams of porpoises mating and of young lions playing on the beach. (p. 81)

Even predatory images take on a more spiritual importance as when the old man sighted two sharks coming to attack the remains of the marlin. His outcry "Ay!" was the kind of noise a man might make ". . . feeling the nail go through his hands and into the wood." (p.107) Santiago is obviously imagining what Christ felt on the cross. In a like manner, when the old man harpoons the fish (p.94), the reader can feel the spear being shoved into the heart of the crucified Christ. The fisherman's cry shows his deep empathy for Jesus. He too knows the desolate face of death. In spite of the danger of his own extinction, Santiago performs a daily sacrament to the meaning of life.

As an archetypal fisherman, Santiago studies the birds for signs of sea creatures in the waters below. To him the secrets of nature are omnipresent, and the smallest things portend meanings. Even his own body offers spiritual signification, for how else interpret the self-scorn when his hand cramps? Why so much anger at his own body and no trace of self-pity? Surely not to prove his bravery to himself. Rather, the incident again points up his affinity to Christ. Jesus, unlike the Apostles who denied him because they were afraid to die with Him, did not yield to the fear of the agony of the mortal body. Jesus' own flesh did not betray Him. And so Santiago fought that subtlest of all treacheries. He has learned that if the flesh can perish, it can also recover. Both the cramp and the old man's scars show the healing power within life, and such regeneration and restoration within nature seem to assure us the promise of salvation is real.

The intermingling of the worldly and the holy is depicted among the ironies of the story. When neither the woman tourist nor her male companion recognizes the marlin for what it is, their ignorance not only shows that citified man has lost that wisdom which understands and respects the living. The gist of modern civilization, seen in the garbage, is contrasted to the skeleton still majestic in death and mark of the noble spirit in nature. Since the fish is also the symbol of Christ, their incomprehension attests to how Christianity today is stripped of its former meaning.

This interpretation is borne out by the incident of the old man sleeping face downward on the newspapers with his hands out-stretched and the palms of hands up. (p.l22) The news in the papers is like a hostile world jeering the sacrifice of the Man on the Cross. And Santiago confirms his defeat when he tells Manolin about the sharks, "They beat me. They truly beat me." (p.124) Implied in the juxtaposition of these episodes is that men daily profane the sacred — life itself.

But not so Santiago. Rather than exist as the sharks for the sake of fulfilling hunger or believe the predatory reality reported by the newspapers, he chooses to live by wiser laws. If fishing for Santiago is a spiritual exercise, it is not only by confronting death and mastering pain that the old man seeks to perfect his soul. He has learned something from the giant cycles of nature. They have taught him what life is.

It is not all those things he no longer thinks about: the fights, the women, the storms. It is not even everything that humbled him: his poverty, the death of his wife, the daily defeats. Nor is it all those inconclusive gestures and deeds that lead nowhere, all the trivial desires and delusions that a man learns to let die along the way.

What makes him different from other men is that he has come to terms with the great laws of time which bring things into being.[31] They have taught him which things depend on him and which do not. They have taught him the patience shown in his profound humility and in his capacity to endure.

Time seems to have the duality of existence itself. As a power that atrophies and destroys life, it appears circular and malign. Happiness that is past can never be recaptured, although the memory of its loss brings fresh remorse and despair. Thus time is circular when pain reappears or the living return to non-existence. A Freudian might see time in terms of the traumata about which our psychic lives turn. A Jungian might interpret time as a mandala, "a protective circle" around a center of chaos. This circularity of time recalls the old man's pulling the fish to him in contracting coils of space. The act appears a ritual of death. Yet religions traditionally use the circle as a symbol of God's perfect being.

This death-in-life paradox is further expressed in the style of the novel. If Santiago's story has the archaic simplicity of ancient epic or the Old Testament, some of his observations have the intonation of Genesis while others sound like the Ecclesiastes, thus reiterating the sense of the beginning and end of things. However, transcending this circularity of style are the passages which presage a destiny to be fulfilled. Stemming from the New Testament, these passages show Santiago to be millennia-remembering man burdened with the memory of Christ.

The old man is pursuing a destiny, and all that this means is clarified by C.G. Jung. "Higher consciousness, or knowledge going beyond our present-day consciousnessness, is equivalent to being *all alone in the world*. This loneliness expresses the conflict between the bearer or symbol of higher consciousness and his surroundings."[32] This definition of awareness not only contrasts Santiago to his fellow fishermen but also differentiates him from the mindless, malevolent forces in nature. Moreover, he knows he must live in this new state of being alone. Jung emphasizes, "Identity does not make consciousness possible; it is only separation, detachment, and agonizing confrontation through opposition that produces consciousness and insight."[33] This is the significance of Santiago's solitary struggle with the fish.

His isolation is seen in other ways. He stands alone at the center of the marlin's ellipse about him. He is also the focal point of the immense circle of ocean and earth. At night in the darkest hours, the particles of phosphorous form a ghostly halo about the skiff.

Jung also brings out the importance of the mandala image. As archetypes of wholeness, they ". . . often represent very bold attempts to see and put together apparently irreconcilable opposites and bridge over apparently hopeless splits."[34] Just so the old man has tried to reconcile his knowledge of the predatory laws of existence with his cognizance of the underlying identity of all species. His share in their symbiotic and ecological fate has brought him the deep humility he has. All his life long he has sought to conciliate the laws of death with the laws of life.

This understanding suggests that for the old man fishing is a submergence of spirit, a baptism. Every day at sea he performs a sacrament of initiation, of rebirth and purification. When he seeks out the great fish, he is committing his soul to the Omnipresent. Santiago instinctively feels the need of this daily *renovatio*,[35] this healing and strengthening of the soul. He is pursuing his ultimate destiny.

The story of this lowly fisher confronts our irresolution and doubts. An old man would allay our fears that life is absurd because the universe appears tyrannized by death. If humanity has run out of luck and out of time, the single man need not accept that fateful verdict. Santiago tells him that all of us must seek the hidden sense to the deceptively meaningless days of our lives. The old fisherman has taught Manolin that man has in truth a higher destiny and that only the unquenchable soul can make its dream come true. Thus the old man's faith, hope and charity become part of the boy and of us.

The paradox of existence is now seen as its Yin and Yang. We now understand why man need not despair. Although twists of fate may ridicule men, there is, nevertheless, a vast, durable cosmos prevailing over the chaotic and transitory. The Occidental mind still believes in destiny, and Santiago's transcendental vision offers us the timeless karmic faith of the Oriental.[36] Indeed, in compensation for the perpetual disappearance of the single life, the old man and the boy — as end point and beginning — join together to reassure us of the eternal power of love.

CHAPTER 13
THE MYSTICAL DIMENSION
IN J.P. SARTRE'S *NAUSEA*

INTRODUCTION

J.P. Sartre (1905-1980) was a French philosopher, dramatist and novelist, who fathered an atheistic form of existentialism. His novel *Nausea* (1938) was a significant contribution to European literature because it portrayed the 20th century anxiety that man existed in an unfathomable universe where God was declared dead.

Sartre's premise that God no longer existed meant that our childhood faith in an eternal, benign and loving God was gone. Skepticism and cynicism ruled much of 20th century Europe so the intellectual and the common man often no longer believed in the church, disregarded its moral guidance, and seriously doubted life had any deeper meaning than the satisfaction of the senses and our biological needs.

Even the faithful must have wondered where God was in a century filled with mutual distrust and hatred among nations, with racial madness, with the butchery of wars and widespread suffering. Even the economies of entire continents were afflicted by a Depression that lasted years, leaving vast populations unemployed and humiliated to be out of work and parents in despair at being unable to feed their children. Plagues of influenza, tuberculosis, and scarlet fever killed adult and child indiscriminately. Fear of human extinction was real and justified. There was little to give the multitudes reassurance that their mundane lives had a deeper spiritual meaning or even that life had any sense. There seemed no proof that God intercedes in the affairs of mankind to mitigate human anxiety, sorrow or extermination. What moral law could man live by?

It was in this existential context that Sartrean atheism became the necessary intellectual basis for living life authentically. In a way, it was a manly atheism in its determination to live without illusions or delusions. The authentic atheist was prepared to pay the consequences for his decisions and acts. No more lies, hypocrisy, or sanctified, meaningless morality.

Nor did Sartre himself remain entrenched in the few remaining, academic certainties of his time. Yet in the novel *Nausea*, his atheistic tough-mindedness underwent a significant transformation when he came to sympathize with the victims of civilization. The novel condemned society's dehumanization of the outcast, the mentally sick, the perverted, and the downtrodden. It portrayed the lost, the helpless, and the dying.

Yet this humane attitude toward the alienated, the estranged, and the sinful as well as his compassion for the pariah, the castaway, and the moral leper seemed to echo a voice from the distant past.

We barely hear the faint whisper of the words of Jesus across two millennia of forgotten time. Unexpectedly, the atheist's hardened thoughts yield to the gentler wisdom of the human heart. The change serves to explain the atheist's anger at the perception that God is responsible for everything that occurs on earth when, in fact, it is we who are mainly responsible for what happens to humanity. Sartre's existential nausea is his distress and disgust at so much dishonesty, senseless anguish, and ignored suffering in the world. He is pained by mankind's mutual hatred, blame, damnation and fratricide. In sum, *Nausea* urges the reader to forgive as Christ Himself would have done.

Yet there is more in *Nausea*. There is more than genuine empathy and pity for the dehumanized and the victimized, for the insane and forgotten. The novel is a call to arms — not to commit acts of destruction, assassination, or terrorism against faceless leaders of institutions, states, or nations. Sartre's existentialism calls for *engagement* against one great enemy — the world's evil — the abuse of helpless humanity, the destructive nihilism of misled idealists, and the despair of the masses of debased humanity. Sartre wants a pledge from us, an emotional commitment, an act of creation to undertake to heal what can be healed; to resurrect our faith in human dignity; to pursue tough-minded, moral honesty; and yet to listen with the heart to those in need.

Is that what is meant in his essay *Existentialism is a Humanism*

(1946)? Is this Christ-like compassion the mystical dimension in *Nausea*? If so, where is the rapture experienced by the mystic?

If there is any mystical ecstasy beyond the pain and suffering of humankind, it is the ecstasy of the Crucifixion when God seemed to have abandoned humanity along with Christ on the Cross.

It is the novel's symbolism that enables us to enter the inner sanctum of its meanings. For the symbolism reveals why the protagonist rejects rationalism and scientism. As intellectualist examples of civilization, they know nothing about the essential truths of life. Roquentin dismisses the historian's "facts" as spurious interpretations of the past. He declines to accept the biographer's lies. Roquentin shuts out the empty promise of an eternal reward for blind faith and obedience.

By contrast, Roquentin responds to a plaintive American song sung by a Negress and written by a Jew — pariahs of society. The song teaches him a profound lesson. It tells him if life has any significance, it is understood when the song is over. This insight implies that life, like the song, has a teleological purpose. Through creativity, one can eke out an essence from existence, and one can create meaning without God. For Sartre, man's destiny is not predetermined. Man is free, but must be committed to responsibility for his own decisions.

So the alienation of the protagonist, 20th century man, does not result in disintegration or in fatalism. Rather, Sartre urges us to commit ourselves to a moral Cause, for in such commitment and through creating an art or a life, there is redemption from the absurdities of existence. Man is what he makes himself, and he alone is responsible for his destiny.

The *engagement* counseled by Sartrean existentialism is that we, as existents, should courageously resist the evil in the world and refute death for the sake of life. The way to defy the nihilism and overcome the hopelessness in the world is through creativity and Christ-like compassion for all humanity — whatever their origins, their station in life, or their estrangement from us.

Sartre's *Nausea* urges us to face the fact we are alone in the universe, lost in infinite time, doubting if we have any actual destiny to fulfill. Yet somehow we know we are here for some reason. It is by our decisive acts we learn who we are, what we value, and what we will do with the time we have on earth.

* * *

Anyone familiar with Jean Paul Sartre's atheistic position will be confounded by the title of this explication. However, if a mystic can be regarded as one who seeks hidden, secret or esoteric meanings in human experience, the record of Sartre's hero in the novel *The Nausea* may be considered the "confession" of a mystic, Furthermore, if mysticism is the spiritual or real way by which men have historically sought to transcend the demands of reason, then Roquentin's story depicts a mystical transcendence of rationalism. Since Sartre's hero must gradually reject Cartesian and scientific ratiocination in order to attain a viable and durable truth, Roquentin's existential preoccupation with symbols serves as the key to the mystical symbolism of his experience.

The present explication will, therefore, proceed in the following manner. First, Sartre's literary affinities with French symbolists will be examined. Second, beyond this sensuous and synesthetic stage of symbolism, *The Nausea* will be shown to manifest eight distinct patterns of existential symbols which resolve themselves into four spheres of significance. The third part of the explication will not only describe Sartre's affinities with Pascal and with Dante, but it will also show how Eric Auerbach's concept of *figura* admirably illuminates Sartre's mystical view of both peripheral and central personages. Fourth and last, the explication will show how the characters and situations prophesy symbolic destinies.

LITERARY AFFINITIES
WITH FRENCH SYMBOLISM

The Nausea is a symbolic novel both by internal and external evidence. In the beginning of the novel, we learn that Roquentin, the narrator, has experienced an inexplicable anxiety due to some mysterious change in the nature of things. He senses a mutation in himself and in the world around him. He reacts to coincidences, to things decaying and people dying, to his own physical fragility, to human suffering, to the Absurd, to the pseudo-purposes of bourgeois life, to the contingency governing Existence, and finally, to the meaning of a simple melody. By recording the incidents and phenomena, the perceptions and transformations, he will seek to understand the images of his metaphysical anguish — his nausea. Through the matrix of symbols and metamorphoses emerging out of Roquentin's search, the reader will discover where the senseless ends and the meaningful begins.

This "symbolism which seeks" is associated with the self-expressive poets sometimes called symbolists. Even if Sartre had not been directly inspired by such poets as Baudelaire, Verlaine, Rimbaud, and Mallarmé, he shows eclectic affinities with them. Much like Baudelaire, Antoine Roquentin wanders through a "forest of symbols," looking for correspondences; the spleen in "Quand le Ciel Bas et Lourd . . ." is like Roquentin's nausea. When Baudelaire asks, "What is a poet — if not a translator, a decoder . . . of the universal analogy?"[1] We recollect that Antoine perceives an underlying unity beneath the images, metaphors, and symbols of experience which express his *Weltschmerz* and intimate the sense of the world. A compendium of correspondences, the novel divulges its dominant meaning through the nausea.

The novel calls to mind the *Art Poetique* in which Verlaine would have the poet seek inspiration in music rather than in sculpture or painting. It may be a singular coincidence, but Roquentin disdains both sculpture and painting to extol music. In fact, the jazz melody in the cafe becomes the symbol of Roquentin's new, authentic way of life because, even though its sounds decompose, the melody remains the same, young and firm, a witness without pity.[2] The music has nothing in excess (*de trop*). It *is* (p. 246). It inspires him to create a work of art as durable and as absolute. Moreover, Verlaine's idea is "Only the nuance . . . , the hazy and floating, are the means of art because the object of poetry is not the clear idea, the precise sentiment, but the swell of the heart, the chiaroscuro of sensations, the indecisiveness of the states of the soul."[3] In the same way, *The Nausea* gives expression to the modulations of heart, mind, and soul which are translated by the inflection of the imagery.

Roquentin as narrator in *The Nausea* bears marked resemblances to Rimbaud in his *Season in Hell*, 1873. Van Tieghem tells us that the poet's inventions "would have the monstrous power to change life, that is, to create not only a new aspect of things, but a new world."[4] This, indeed, is what Sartre seeks to achieve in his work. Van Tieghem adds: "the reform of poetry implied a reform of the sensibility, of vision. The Poet must become the clairvoyant 'by a long, immense and irrational disordering of all the senses.'" What better definition of Roquentin's own obsession with the nausea? The approach of a crisis of nerves, the hallucinatory visions of Rimbaud's *illuminations* are Roquentin's own.

Finally, Sartre's intellectual purpose seems to have significant parallels to the poetic of Mallarmé in his *Divigations* of 1896. Van Tieghem explains Mallarmé's poetics as follows: "Poetry must therefore be neither descriptive nor narrative, but suggestive." For Mallarmé "the object is only designated by an allusive image; the subject-matter of the poem is an idea, that is, an abstract, intellectual or emotive notion."[5] Clearly, Sartre's novel primarily expresses an abstract idea in the narrator's anxiety before man's existential situation. Furthermore, *Nausea* is like a poem in being unified by a dominant mood.

These affinities of the novel to French symbolism provide external evidence that it is symbolic. However, there is also internal corroboration.

Norman Friedman reminds us in the *Encyclopedia of Poetry and Poetics* that one may determine in three ways when an image is truly symbolic: (1) the connection between the image and thing symbolized may be made explicit; (2) it may be made into something by virtue of the speaker's reaction to it; and (3) the pressure of implicit association may be so great as to demand a symbolic interpretation.[6] It is clear from Roquentin's explicit statements and from his powerful reactions to images that they have a symbolic significance for him. Moreover, the pressure of the relentless anxiety upon his whole being demands a symbolic interpretation of the signs and symptoms of that anguish.

PATTERNS OF
EXISTENTIAL SYMBOLS

An examination of the images and metaphors in *The Nausea* discovers that Roquentin's metaphysical anguish translates things, places, persons, situations and events into symbols which measure the four dimensions of existence. As clusters of schemata of meaning, they ultimately reveal existence to have four spheres of significance: (1) Nothingness (*le néant*) versus Plenitude (*de trop*); (2) The Fixed and Immutable versus Change and Metamorphosis; (3) Appearance versus Reality; and (4) Existence versus Essence. (To assist the reader to visualize these groupings, he is invited to refer to the schemata of symbols given below.)

EIGHT PATTERNS OF EXISTENTIAL SYMBOLS
SCHEMATA OF SYMBOLS

Nothingness (Isolation and Loneliness	*Plénitude (de trop)*
1. the stone	1. the king of hearts
2. street names	2. the library
3. the street lamp	3. the museum and all its paintings
4. the torn billboard signs	4. the chestnut tree and the root
5. the wall without doors or windows	
6. the solitary sound of the siren on the wind	
7. the scream of Lucie in the night	
8. the Negress's voice and the song itself.	
9. Bouville itself next to the sea and in the middle of nature	

C.	**Fixed or Immutable**	D.	**Change and Metamorphosis** (Decay, Decomposition, Death Versus Creativity)
1.	the song and the record	1.	the paper in street becomes a beast
2.	the king of hearts	2.	his face and flesh become vegetable, sub-ape, a polyp
3.	Boulevard Noir	3.	rust in workshop and rotten boards
4.	*Musée de Bouville*	4.	bench like a dead donkey
5.	*Dictée*	5.	people dying
		6.	ruins everywhere
		7.	Roquentin stabbing his hand
		8.	the song causes his nausea to disappear
		9.	hand and arm move as a majestic theme of music
		10.	the melody teaches him to suffer in measure

E.	**Appearance**	D.	**Reality**
1.	the sea — its mirror surface	1.	its black reality full of beasts
2.	cities and places seem different	2.	they all resemble each other

3.	days, months, and years seem orderly	3.	they are all the same
4.	explanation of history, the world of "facts"	4.	the new cannot be explained by the old, the effect by the cause
5.	making love	5.	the juices, mucous, the smell — the biological reality
6.	scientific explanations	6.	related to the root — function does not explain anything
7.	colours, flavors, odors, and definitions seem true	7.	we cannot define with genre + *differentiae* (colours, etc. are never true)
8.	a world of natural order (cause and effect)	8.	the world is one of contingency

G.	*Existence*	H.	*Essence*
1.	at museum, Roquentin sees self as stone, plant, microbe	1.	jazz introduction = an inflexible order
2.	world of things and people, chestnut tree and root exist beyond explanations	2.	the fragile durée of the music
3.	Roquentin senses self by organic sensations	3.	something has happened
4.	existence is the realities: the organic, the dying	4.	like the melody one must suffer in measure
5.	the swarming *de trop* of nature	5.	the Negress and Jew are saved

6.	absurdity of existence	6.	to have moments of life as a life one recalls
7.	contingency is absolute	7.	existence is the privileged moment; something has need of him to be born
		8.	he is his thought
		9.	self-transcendance = to make life essence

Schema A: The signs and symbols which depict *Nothingness* gravitate around objects or sounds that express the isolation of loneliness of all things in existence. Hence the stone Roquentin picked up and threw away because its dirty side filled him with a mild revulsion. The street names "Black" and "Fear" also evoke repulsion. The street lamp, the torn billboard signs, the wall without doors or windows also call forth a sense of solitude or of no escape. The solitary sound of the siren brought with the wind, the agonized scream of Lucie in the night, the Negress's voice and the song itself "Some of these days, You'll miss me, honey," all bespeak a sense of loss or of bereavement. And the city of Bouville itself, next to the dark sea and in the middle of nature, portrays loneliness. Lost in existence, man recognizes his finite fragility. As symbols of death, these things recall to man his nothingness.

Schema B: The signs and symbols that display *Plénitude* are fewer than those which describe man's existential isolation. The king of hearts represents so many gestures now disappeared. The library with its many books displays the mass of man's "knowledge." The museum of paintings reflects the bourgeoisie and their host of projects and ambitions. The chestnut tree and its mighty root sunk into the earth seems to Roquentin like the mindless, super-abundant self-reproduction of nature.

Schema C: Images and symbols also exhibit the *Fixed and Immutable*. The song's inflexible order gives birth to the notes but prevents them from existing for themselves. In the card playing, the king of hearts follows a rigorous chain of events which is as irreversible as the song itself. The Boulevard Noir is as inhuman as a mineral or a triangle. In the library there are the books describing the constant forms of the animal species and the conservation of energy in the universe. In the museum, the paintings are like a claim to immortality by the same bourgeois who seek the guarantee of heaven through their religion, but Roquentin knows ironically there is only absolute death. When Roquentin cannot pick up the piece of notebook paper entitled *Dictée*, he realizes he is not free, and the nausea attacks him. In all these symbols, then, are revealed the unalterable or irrevocable; and they chain Roquentin to his rock as if he were Prometheus.

Schema D: In contrast to the fixed and immutable is the imagery of *Change and Metamorphosis*. There is the piece of paper in the street which seemed to become a living beast. When he looks at his homely face in the mirror, Roquentin sees in his features something sub-human, sub-ape, something vegetable, something like a polyp. Then again he notices the sunlight, like a judgment without indulgence, brightening the rust and rotten boards in a workshop. Another time Roquentin notices a bench which seems a dead and swollen donkey, its legs in the air. And Roquentin detects people who are dying: the cashier at the café who is rotting inside, Lucie's husband who has tuberculosis, and Doctor Rogé with his own fatal disease. Then all that Roquentin remembers from his extensive travels over the world is that the places he visited now seem ruins just as his memories have become dead leaves, become words. Thus there are many signs and symbols of decay, decomposition. destruction, and death.

Yet there are keys to creativity also, to metamorphosis in the direction of life, beauty, and meaning. The song the Negress sings causes Roquentin's nausea to disappear. He feels his body stiffen and resist. The melody shows him the way to measure his anguish just as, at last, it will lead him to make of his dissolving life a melody — young. firm, and abiding,

Schemata E and F: Other signs betoken Roquentin s apperception of *Appearance versus Reality*. The sea which appears as a mirror surface is in dark reality filled with beasts. All the places and cities seem so different at first, but finally, they all resemble one another. Days, months, and years seem an orderly procession, but they are all the same — today as yesterday. "Making love" is a euphemism, for Roquentin visualizes the juices, the mucous, the smell, the biological reality beneath it all. History, pretending to be a world of fact, is not true, for the new cannot be explained by the old, the effect by the cause. Anything can happen anytime. And the root of the tree in the public garden makes him realize that function does not explain anything; hence the explanations of science are useless. Colors, flavors, odors, and definitions seem true, but we cannot really define genera by them, for colors, odors, flavors are never true. Finally, the world of natural order which seems governed by cause and effect is an illusion, for there is only existence.

Schema G: Other clues point to Roquentin's insight into *Existence*. At the museum he sees himself as having existed as a stone, a plant, a microbe — hence a part of the All. He senses himself by a muted, organic sensation. Existence is all those realities he detected beneath the appearance of things. It is the organic — deteriorating, dying. As the reality of the root is beyond any accounting, existence itself is beyond all knowledge, beyond all explanations. Everything in nature is an excess, and he himself is *de trop* in the universe. Existence is absurd, absolute, and contingent. And what is man in such a universe? Roquentin knows he is like the stone, the plant, the microbe in the cosmos — and nothing more.

Schema H: Other indexes and clues bring Roquentin to discover the *Essence* in Existence. The notes introducing the "rag" time rhythm of the jazz melody give birth to an inflexible order, which in turn destroys them by not permitting them to exist for themselves. Roquentin must accept the moments of his life just as he does the death of the musical notes. The melody makes him realize there is another kind of happiness in the *durée* of the music. Although everything can break the fragile music, nothing can interrupt it, for the melody is a necessity.

   The music makes Roquentin realize that something has taken place, "I knew it! . . . something has happened," and his nausea dissipates and disappears; he is in the music, his gestures become part of a majestic theme. The melody leads him to understand all at once that the Negress who sings the song and the Jew who composed it are saved. They have washed themselves clean of the sin of existence. Roquentin then wants to see the moments of his life organize themselves as the past one recalls. He wants to live in the direction of his destiny. Existence has become the privileged situation which can be transformed, not into Anny's perfect moments, but into a meaningful life. Roquentin then comprehends that something needs him to be born. He knows he cannot stop thinking because he is his thought. He exists because he thinks, and he will justify his existence, by thinking. He will create a work of art which will make men ashamed of existing mindlessly.

This brief review of existential symbols discloses the experience Roquentin has gone through. If the images of nothingness, as an absolute, call forth his awareness of death, the isolation and loneliness of things and places arouses his anxiety and compassion. If *plenitude* makes him aware of the fact of nature's superabundance, at the same time it fills him with nausea. Although the things and places symbolizing the *fixed and immutable* divulge an adamantine order to existence, they recall man's own perishable nature. In the symbols of *change and metamorphosis*, he feels horror of things decaying, dying, and decomposing, yet change and metamorphosis open the way to creativity which, in its turn, promises an abiding order. In the items of *appearance versus reality* appearance *seems* sure and safe whereas reality reveals the chaos beneath the appearance of orderliness. In the emblems of existence, Roquentin finds the cosmos itself is absurd and contingent with man lost in that "All." Consequently, the symbols of existence evoke anxiety. Through the insignia of essence, Roquentin becomes determined to measure his suffering and to transform his dissolving life into a permanent purpose. As the music has a fragile duration (*durée*), life itself is a privileged moment, but a moment only. To endure is to think. To be worthy of life, one must seek out a thought-filled destiny.

FIGURAL REPRESENTATION OR THE
QUEST OF A MYSTIC

Roquentin's search for the correspondences of an essential reality, revealed through the signs and symbols of existence, is comparable to the quest of the mystics. The connection of *Nausea* to Pascal's *Thoughts* is that both depict the existential situation of man. What Roquentin describes is the frightening grief and senselessness of men's lives, of men's agonies — as absolute and continual as the infinite spaces of Pascal. What Roquentin feels is how lonely men are, each ignorant of the other, each surrounded by an eternal silence of terrifying meaninglessness. Both Pascal and Sartre depict man's position in an existence unaware of him and which man cannot ever really comprehend. Sartre's own artistic intent is to arouse the reader's nausea not only by brutally expressing the relentlessness of Existence but also by showing that human life is hell when lived mindlessly. (Indeed, Sartre seems to note modes of hell in *La Mort dans l'Ame, Les Mouches, Huis Clos, La Diable et le Bon Dieu* and *L'Être et le Néant*.)[7] The intention in *Nausea* is similar to *Thoughts* where Pascal represents an existence that can crush man because man is the weakest creature in nature, where man himself is a paradox, a chimera, a monster, a prodigy, a worm — the glory and the shame of the universe. For Pascal's purpose is to show that without God human life ends as a cruel and absurd hell.

While this archetypal theme unites Pascal and Sartre, the kinship between Sartre and Dante may not be so apparent. Yet the artistic intention of the medieval Italian and the twentieth century atheistic existentialist is remarkably similar. If any pattern emerges from Dante's "Inferno" it is the hopelessness of destinies devoid of purpose and meaning, for what otherwise do the repeated, senseless gestures of the sinners in hell show? They have missed the whole aim of earthly life revealed to medieval man by God; to love man, to practice the commiseration of Christ, and to offer the mercy of Mary. What unites the "Inferno" and *The Nausea* is their main purpose: to evoke a specific emotion — whether the dread of death, the horror of hell, or the terror of final self-destruction. Their secondary intention is to come to terms with existence and to point a way for man.

Time provides the ultimate form and mystical meaning of Sartre's symbolic novel in the same way that time in religious literature unites past, present and future through the representation of *figurae* as described by Erich Auerbach.[8] "Figural interpretation . . . establishes a connection between two events or persons in such a way that the first signifies not only itself but also the second, while the second involves and fulfils the first."[9]

This description calls to mind Norman Friedman's point that a poem is "symbolic" when it resembles larger ritualistic patterns as purgation, scapegoating, and the artist-archetype. In this pattern the artist is seen as the hero and his art as a sacrificial ritual. He dies to this life in order to be reborn in his art as redeemer.[10] It is obvious that Roquentin becomes such an archetype when he decides to lead the authentic, creative life.

In his discussion of the *Song of Roland*, Auerbach remarks:

> This impressiveness of gestures and attitudes is obviously the purpose of the technique . . . when it divides the course of events into a mosaic of parceled pictures. The scenic moment with its gesture is given such power that it assumes the stature of a moral model. The various phases of the story of the hero or the traitor or the saint are concretized to such an extent that the pictured scenes . . . closely approach the character of symbols or figures.[11]

Nausea also is such a mosaic of gestures, symbols, and figures as I shall show in my examination of the figurae of the novel.

The Nausea and Dante's "Inferno" are comparable in their dominant mood, in their preoccupation with man's existential situation, in their sense of eternal justice and their mode of presenting that justice. Dante's figures have the characteristics of concrete historical reality at the same time that they are symbolic or allegorical personifications. The individual souls of the dead find their proper punishment, penance or reward.[12] Hence the overwhelming realism of Dante's hell is due to the fact that the figure and its fulfilment are one, that the figurae are phenomena and historical events at the same time. In Sartre's *Nausea* the figures of Lucie, of Rollebon, the Autodidacte, the bourgeois, the cashier at the café, the doctor Rogé, the simpleton M. Achille, *le bonhomme à la pèlerine*, the young couple, Anny, the

Negress who sang the song, the Jew who composed it, and Roquentin himself are true figurae — people of everyday reality transfigured by the destinies they have fulfilled or are to fulfil.

Auerbach's description of the damned reinforces the parallel between Dante and Sartre: ". . . they are but exempla of the winning or losing of eternal bliss. But the passions, torments, and joys have survived; they find expression in the situations, gestures, and utterances of the dead."[13] When Auerbach describes the inferno as "the portrayal of a collective punishment,"[14] we visualize Roquentin's journey through the nausea into a realm where merciless Existence damns men forever to a state of dying.

Dante's theosophic scheme of things is defined by Auerbach as follows: "The connection between occurrences is not regarded as primarily a chronological or causal development but as a oneness within the divine plan, of which all occurrences are parts and reflection."[15] Herein lies the important difference between Dante's medieval existentialism and Sartre's atheistic vision, for in the universe of the nausea there is no divine plan. *Nausea* is a rhyme without reason, a cosmos without a purpose, an Existence without Exegesis.

Nevertheless, the novel's spiritual unity is achieved through the kind of figural representation to which I have been alluding. All the characters in *Nausea* are figurae because they describe the conditions of existence and of mortal humanity. Some represent the senselessness of human life. Others foreshadow the fate of those unable to master the anguish of dying. Others will surrender to the contingencies of existence. One will create a durable work of art with a timeless meaning.

The reason for having compared the figural world of medieval literature to *Nausea* was to underline the preternatural powers in both. What medieval figurae divulge is a Presence within reality, an Essence sustaining and directing human existence. In the novel, time is the medium through which men may convert existence into essence, and Sartre's characters become figural representations of that possible conversion.

The figurae seem to group themselves into two types around the four main characters: Rollebon, the Autodidacte, Anny, and Roquentin. Early in the novel (p. 20) Roquentin recalls when he was eight years old there was the old man who terrified the children because they felt he was alone and because they thought he must have the ideas of a crab. This solitary type reminds one of Roquentin who has made the children snigger because he had not skipped the stone across the water but had seemed bewildered. Hence the old man seems a specter image of Roquentin himself and what he might become in the eyes of others.

Another early figura is the cleanup woman Lucie. Working where Roquentin lives, Lucie is incapable of consoling herself when she thinks her husband is drinking himself to death (p. 23). (Roquentin is sure the man has tuberculosis.) She cannot free herself from her anguish — "she is tied in a knot" (p. 24). Hence Roquentin sees her imprisoned in her situation. One night Roquentin happened to witness Lucie being abandoned by her lover. When Roquentin heard her scream in the dark, he refused to help her in her solitary tragedy (p. 45). He will decline to act again to stop the man in her garden from exposing himself or to prevent the Corsican from catching the Autodidacte making a homosexual pass at a boy in the library.

Another figura is a *vieux toqué* who is on the verge of having a mental crisis (p. 99). Treated with disdain by Doctor Rogé, "the old loon" is a figural representation of Roquentin himself in his nausea and of the real psychological danger he runs with his metaphysical speculations.

There is also *le bonhomme* wearing the large cape (p. 114). In front of a little girl, the old fellow "exposes" himself sexually. Roquentin might have prevented that if he had understood why the pervert was wearing a cape. Only the girl's running away breaks his fascination with their little drama. Roquentin shouts at the man ironically "A great menace hangs over the city" to scare him. The *bonhomme* is an outcast reminding us of all the others.

There is a newspaper story about the little girl Lucienne, who has been raped and killed, her flesh murdered. (She is the reason Roquentin later stabs his own hand — in a ritualistic gesture of commiseration.) As a figura, she recalls our physical fragility and clearly personifies mankind as victim.

The café cashier, rotting from a disease in her abdomen, is a figura of decomposition, of existence, and ultimately of Roquentin's own death.

His notice of these people and their human condition reflects his heightened awareness of life through the nausea. That these eventually point to Roquentin is shown by the painting *The Death of the Bachelor*. The bachelor, like Roquentin, had lived for himself. No one had come to close his dead eyes. The man had died utterly alone. It appears that Roquentin foresees that this will be his own fate.

These peripheral figurae, then, all point to Roquentin's sense of isolation, his loneliness (the lonely notice the lonely), his unspoken anxiety — his nausea before existence which he shares with all human beings aware of death.

In contrast to these solitary figurae, there are those men who live their usual communal lives. Roquentin notices all those who pass their time explaining themselves, recognizing happily they are of the same opinion as others (p. 19). Unlike the sufferers who suffer alone, unlike the dying who always die alone, unlike the artist who must create the melody alone, such men are what Roquentin must not become.

At the café Roquentin observes card players (cf. Cezanne's *Card Players*) who try to fill time, but it is too vast to fill. And he notices a playing card king "come from so far, prepared by so many combinations, by so many disappeared gestures . . ." (p. 39). Here again is a figural representation, for not only will the figures of Bouville disappear from his life but the ceaseless disappearance of the players' gestures reveals to him "the unbreakable chain of circumstances." He realizes he cannot go back in his own life. The aimlessness of the card-playing, like a life without purpose, is a warning to him — that the past is dead, that only the present and future count. He will have to decide to live, to fulfil his destiny.

Roquentin is annoyed by the statue of Gustave Impetraz (pp. 45-46). The women admire the bronze figure, for he was of the *beau monde*, a guardian who upheld the ideals of the bourgeoisie and who wrote on trivial academic subjects. Here too is a figura of what Roquentin will determine not to be.

Roquentin thinks of all the professionals of experience: the doctors, the priests, the magistrates, and the officers who know man as if they had made him (p. 99). They are the ones who have baptized their little obstinations with some proverbs, in the name of experience, but they have never really understood anything, because all the world's past cannot serve to explain anything (p. 101). The irony with which Roquentin treats them in his journal shows that he will not use them as models, for such men believe they have figured out man, but man has in Roquentin's eyes an infinite capacity to change and to create a new destiny.

Moreover, doctor Rogé himself, who plays the role of the successful and experienced man, does so to masquerade the insupportable reality of his own approaching death (p. 102). Hence all such successful men, sure of their rights and of their duties, are figurae of what the artist and thinker must not become. For this reason, Roquentin's words, "So long, bastards" (p. 135).

In general, Roquentin speaks of the bourgeois sarcastically. His rendering of their religious habits, their *coups de chapeau* (their social customs), their pretensions (e.g. *The Illustrated History of Mudville*), their monotonous monologues in the restaurants, their smiles, the gourmandise of the women, their gossipy stories, their hopes, their habits, their Sundays (pp. 63-81) remind us of the lost gestures of the playing cards.

These same bourgeois, with their guarantee of heaven and eternity (*the extreme unction*), believe in the world of order, in cause and effect, in their power to legislate, and in self-adulation (their portraits in the museum). But Roquentin rejects and ridicules their world. The bourgeoisie become figurae of those leading artificial lives, of those having superimposed an absurd order on existence, of squandering their lives in meaningless ritual. They are the figures of the false purposes which the artist and thinker must avoid.

It is M. Fasquelle. manager of the café Mably, who represents the reason men group together. Roquentin notices how, after the café empties, M. Fasquelle, alone, slips into unconsciousness. In fact, the clientele need others and exist only when with one another (p. 16). By contrast, Roquentin slips into consciousness when apart, and he exists only when alone. So is it with the artist and thinker. So must Roquentin's life be in the future.

Beyond these fringe figurae are the central characters Rollebon, the Autodidacte, Anny, and Roquentin. Roquentin's long-standing interest in the historical figure of Rollebon bears particular attention for what it reveals about Roquentin. He first became interested in Rollebon because the man had been accused of treason, been thrown in prison where he died after five years of captivity "without appeal" (p. 24). This shows Roquentin's characteristic interest in a loner like himself, in one unjustly judged like the social outcast and the artist.

After 1801, Rollebon inexplicably changed. The documentation on him (letters, secret reports, police archives) lack firmness and consistency as if they were not talking about the same person. This situation parallels the change that takes place in Roquentin because outwardly the transformation cannot be explained. Rollebon prefigures, but Roquentin will become an artist, whereas Rollebon became a charlatan.

A further parallel between the two is seen in their both being homely or ugly (*laid*). However, Rollebon used his charm to make conquests of the women at court whereas Roquentin sees his own face as something at the edge of the vegetable kingdom. This insight into his relationship with other forms of existence is figural in that it situates Roquentin as an existent. It is interesting to note that while Rollebon is a man continually disguising his motives and acts, Roquentin seeks a motive to live by (pp. 135-36). However, when Roquentin finds he can no longer write about the historical figure, Rollebon dies for him. Roquentin stops living with a fiction (p. 138) when he realizes Rollebon had been his *raison d'être*. Rollebon prefigures what will happen to Roquentin, but the latter will free himself from the prison of existence and of his old life by living for a true purpose — that of art.

The Autodidacte is a definite figura. He tells Roquentin that, if he were ever to travel, he would keep a journal of the smallest traits of his character in order to retrace what he was and what he might become (p. 54). He prefigures Roquentin who does keep a record of his metaphysical metamorphosis,

The Autodidacte would also have adventures happen to him — a series of accidents — in the hope of having "lived" and found meaning. Roquentin has had "stories, events, incidents" really happen to him. He had imagined (like Anny) that at certain moments, as when he heard music in cafes, his life could take on a rare and precious quality (p. 58). And he realizes all at once "What summits wouldn't I attain if my own life made the material for the melody" (p, 60). Hence the Autodidacte in his naive way awakens Roquentin to a life purpose.

Roquentin detects signs of the Autodidacte's pederasty. That the "self-taught" man's figural representation foreshadows the fulfilment of his destiny is shown in the following indications. (The Autodictate's "love" for man as a humanist, while ironically revealing his homosexuality, belies his overt hatred of individuals. In this he is unlike Roquentin who hates abstractions, but feels compassion for individuals).

Roquentin cannot prevent the Autodidacte from making a homosexual pass at the boy in the library just as he could do nothing for Lucie or for the pervert in the public garden. One may ask why. Probably Roquentin felt man cannot prevent anyone from fulfilling his destiny.[16] In a sense all the figurae in the journal are fated because they do not come to terms with existence.

When Roquentin discovers that the Autodidacte is reading his way through the library according to the alphabet, it becomes obvious that order *per se* is absurd.[17] For Roquentin's own later determination to create a work of art would be ridiculous if — unlike the pseudo-orders of science and of the bourgeoisie — he did not confront the absolute absurdity of existence. Roquentin does not want to be like the Autodidacte who, having read all the books, asks "And now?" Roquentin will seek to create an order out of his existence. By uniting and varying his life, he will free himself from suffering and thereby free others from suffering.[18]

Anny provides an example of the figural in her seeking to realize "perfect moments." Such "moments parfaits" had always been preceded by "auguries." Anny explained that the "privileged" situation, could be made into a perfect moment, and the moment was perfect if you were already plunged into something exceptional and you felt the need to put it in order. Anny had sought a kind of revelation or revealed truth in such moments, but now she feels she exists (in Roquentin's sense of the word). In the past Anny had tried to find those instants with passionate people who were carried away by hatred or love. Now she lives surrounded by deceased passions (p. 204) much as Roquentin lives surrounded by the defunct world order of cause and effect, history, scientific law, and bourgeois purposes. Anny has found there are no more perfect moments. She has learned to live without histrionics (p. 202). Hence she is like Roquentin who has learned there are no adventures. They seem to have changed in the same sense.

However, there is a basic difference. When Anny described the perfect moment as an exceptional situation, which she felt called to put in order, Roquentin adds "like a work of art," and Anny replies, "no, like a duty."

Furthermore, Anny wants to see Roquentin and to know he exists unaltered so that she could measure her own changes, assuming in her vain way that he could not change. Yet it is she who has not altered really. For she is still without pity for failures (p. 147), she is still bourgeois in her philosophy of duty. And in giving up her search for perfect moments, she abdicates from seeking to realize her life. It remains for Roquentin to fulfil his existence by choosing freely his own destiny.

In the past Roquentin had modeled himself on two French thinkers. He says that when he was twenty "I was a type like Descartes" (p. 84). Late in the novel he asks "Where is your dignity as a 'thinking reed'"? Here he clearly has the ideal of Pascal before him.

Roquentin's story is the discovery that the past is dead and that he is free to choose his own destiny. It began (under "Monday, January 29, 1932") when he notes in his journal, "it is necessary to choose — either the change is in me or in the room, the city, in nature." This need to choose emphasizes that he will discover the change is *in* him and in all Existence. In short, nothing is immutable, all is undergoing change.

This insight is reinforced when Roquentin observes that he is aware that a whole series of small metamorphoses have taken place (p. 15). Later he reaffirms. "Anything can take place, anything can happen" (p. 111). This is both a patriarchal warning to heed the lesson of existence and a prophecy of things to come. All is changing. and in contrast to men who try to stop time and in contrast to science which seems to fix existence in stable laws, Roquentin will be the first to work *with* time.

When Roquentin says, "I don't think enough of historical research to waste my time with a dead man (Rollebon), . . ." he rejects the past of lived life in order to live more meaningfully now and in the future. This figural tendency is verified when Roquentin remarks, "The sense of adventure would be quite simply that of the irreversibility of time" (p. 84).

The song, "Some of these days, You'll miss me, honey;" causes his nausea to disappear and his body to harden; his arm (symbol of his existence) dances to the music (p. 38). Not only is the Jew who wrote the song a figura of Roquentin, the artist-to-be, but the song itself is a figura in the sense of being the fulfilment of a situation: either the composer or singer has lost a beloved and the song warns the beloved that she will miss him, or in Sartre's ironic sense, we will all miss life one of these days when we have died.

For Roquentin, adventure has meaning only by its death. He wishes ardently he could achieve the summit of the music with his own life (pp. 59-60). Here the motif is to become an artist and to create something durable out of his dying existence.

The keystone to the arch of logic comes in the extinction of Antoine Roquentin as a person (p. 239). Only the anonymous conscience in existence remains and his own cognizance of being a conscience which forgets itself (p.239). This is figural: the old self must nearly die if the new is to be born. Once a historian devoted to the past, Roquentin transforms himself into an artist dedicated to living the present and creating the future. Finally, Roquentin realizes the music does not exist, it *is.* He wants *to be* pure, hard — to compose precise and clean music. In his becoming an artist, the figural prediction is completed. He will become the melody — firm and young in his thought and through the beauty he creates — as his very life dissolves.

SYMBOLIC DESTINIES

Sartre makes a particular point in the novel to identify the instability, the uncertainties, the doubts, the lawlessness and the contingency within the deceptive constancy and immutability of *IS* — within what Western man has thought Existence is. What Sartre demonstrates artistically and metaphysically is how a symbolic truth emanates like a melody out of human anguish. This is seen in the unfolding of the existential situations of various characters into symbolic destinies. Anny's faith that the privileged situation could be made into the perfect moment shows Roquentin the direction he himself must take, for the privileged situation is life itself, and it is up to the individual not merely to suffer, but to create some kind of perfect destiny out of it. This is what is meant by Sartre's dictum, "Existence precedes Essence." This symbolic novel is such a transformation of existence into essence.

To make this question of symbolic destinies even clearer, let us see how Roquentin finds himself in a situation parallel with all the sufferers. All of them are doomed to die. On the other hand, all the other characters are in contrast to Roquentin in the sense that they lead false lives, that they drift through purposeless existences, and that they are inhumane to their fellow men. The truest *figurae* or parallels to Roquentin are peripheral ones — the Negress and the Jew — outcasts who create beauty out of their suffering. The artist must move counter to all who lead mindless, insensitive lives.

Roquentin's searching psyche alternates between fear and determination, hope and desolation. As a seeker, he explores the murky unknown of himself adrift in the world. Only when his life forces find their purpose does his own existence become transformed to take a meaningful direction.

Time shows him its innate power, for it shows man how to attain completion and perfection by revealing to him the possibilities in freedom and in self-realization. Roquentin discerns that man alone can fashion his future, and by doing so, man distinguishes himself from existence. While man is fated as an existent to decay and die like all other living things, he is free to realize his own destiny. This is the ultimate meaning of the melody — it directs its own destiny, even though it dies so the song may be born.

Time also reveals man is guided toward an end or shaped by a purpose. Traditionally this plane of time reveals the plan of Providence. What Roquentin has found is that, in order to make any sense out of existence, it is not in working out pseudo-systems or in self-adulation. Rather, meaning comes from measuring one's own pain and in mitigating the anguish in the world through a work of art.

It is interesting to note how time does change Roquentin. As Antoine confronts everyday realities, the style in his journal is correspondingly realistic. When he considers the sciences and social man, his style is reminiscent of literary naturalism. In his description of men's agonies, Roquentin is expressionistic, but when he expresses his own metaphysical suffering, he creates his true modality.

In fact, the transformation of Antoine's vision of things is translated by his voice. The novel begins with the historian's tone, Roquentin sounding like a man dedicated to Cartesian rationalism. Gradually one hears a Pascalian accent or mystical intonation. The first voice articulates the logic of civilization and science until

Roquentin is faced with man's suffering in a senseless existence, at which moment the utterance changes to express his compassion. The voice of reason becomes a voice full of emotion and mercy. Indeed, the impassioned tone seems to echo voices out of the Bible.

Or is it Dante's influence on Sartre? It is hard to ignore the striking affinities between them, for both condemn and pardon, both damn and show mercy. If we look deeply enough, we cannot fail to see that *The Nausea* embodies a Dantesque hierarchy of values with seven levels of punishment corresponding to the seven forms or degrees of existential transgression: (1) The sins of the flesh are personified by the exhibitionist, the Autodidacte, Lucie, Francoise, and Anny. (2) The impurity or suffering of the flesh is typified by the café cashier, Lucie's tubercular husband, and doctor Rogé. (3) The sin of violence is exemplified in doctor Rogé's contemptuous treatment of the old loon (*toqué*), in the Corsican's smashing in the Autodidacte's nose, in the mutual massacre of the Nazis and Communists, and in the murder of little Lucienne. (4) The sin of mindlessness is represented in the card players, in the simpleton, in M. Fasquelle without his clients; in the aimless gestures, courtesies and activities of the bourgeoisie; in the Autodidacte's asinine, alphabetical reading of his way through the library. (5) The sign of pride is impersonated in men of experience like doctor Rogé; in the bourgeois self-adulation in their portraits and in their projects; in Anny who scorns failures. (6) The sin of malice is in mis-using one's free will to harm others. Rollebon belonged to this class and this is one reason he finally sickens Roquentin. (7) At the deepest level, to complete the suffering of the flesh, there is the suffering of the mind. Curiously the Autodidacte's humility before knowledge is akin to this kind of excruciation, but it is, of course, Roquentin in the deepest pit who grieves for mankind's purposeless suffering in the hell of existence and who actually sorrows for the loss of heaven and of God. As Dante entered the "Inferno" to suffer for those in hell who had lost the way forever, so does Roquentin journey among the lost and lonely, the sure and the cynical, to find his meaning

We now recognize that the impassioned tone of *The Nausea* is like the patriarchal and prophetic voices of the Bible. In the Old Testament the dominant voice is that of Moses. It was he who read the signs of nature (the oncoming pestilence, the sea turning blood red, etc.); it was he who mounted Sinai to receive the ten commandments and consulted his visions to know the promised land. The patriarchal voice seeks to ascertain the truth of daily life, the abiding laws, the revelation of eternal verity, or of the Presence of God here and now. It is the patriarchal voice which predominates Pascal's *Thoughts* and provides the vision of implacable justice in Dante's "Inferno" where the design of destiny is immutable. It is also Roquentin's voice speaking out against the wilderness of Existence.

By contrast, it is a voice of prophecy which fills the New Testament. Although remembered for His parables and his everyday wisdom, Christ's foreseeing His own death and understanding the purpose of His life aroused men's awe. Thus did His daily gestures, words and actions become symbolic of a higher destiny and, in a true figural sense, they prognosticated the fulfillment of a promise for all who would follow His way. Roquentin's voice seems to echo that promise when it urges us to overcome suffering by creating a future of our own.

These alternate voices modulate the meaning of the symbols and figurae which establish man's communion with the ultimate reality of things. If the patriarchal voice translates for us the brutal meaning of existence, the representation of a single *figura*, capable of overcoming the absurdity of death, prophesies for others a future released from present anguish. Sartre's vision of existence is a message of hope for the few who dare to realize the mystical meaning of their symbolic destinies.

CONCLUSION TO
PART FIVE

In order to remove any lingering doubts as to the validity of studying the mystical dimension in literature, let me cite some pertinent observations from A.H. Maslow's *Religions, Values, and Peak Experiences* (1994).

Maslow's Preface states that his book is intended for ". . . thinkers who try to be holistic, integrative, and inclusive." (p.vii) Because ". . . organized religion has forgotten the mystical experience, the illumination, and the great awakening . . ." (p. viii), he sees the need for a new "healthy openness to the mysterious." (p ix)

Based on extensive research, Maslow discovered that many unreligious, common-sense people had extraordinary experiences. "In peak experiences, there are such emotions as wonder, awe, reverence, humility, surrender and even worship before the greatness of the experience." (p.65) Elsewhere, he states that individuals feeling mystic or peak experiences have great insights and revelations. (p.75)

In *La Vita Nuova*, in the presence of Beatrice, Dante's love for her awakened in him a sense of beatitude and of decision to live a new life. The poem is a medieval example of this type of experience.

In *The Old Man and the Sea*, the fisherman marveled at the giant marlin as it rose above his tiny skiff like some Great Spirit.

In *Nausea* Antoine Roquentin is filled with disgust at the evident meaninglessness of life and with the mindless activities of common mankind. But in hearing the American Negress sing the song "Some one of these days, You're going to miss me, honey", he realizes that one day both love and life itself will be gone.

Maslow also observed, "The person himself tends to move toward fusion, integration, and unity and away from . . . conflicts and oppositions." (p.66) Thus the anti-hero Roquentin loses his intellectual cynicism and existential despair when, at last, he is able to identify with humanity. Moreover, *Nausea* illustrates Maslow's observation "The peak experience can make life worthwhile. Such experiences can give meaning to life itself." (p.62) Thus Roquentin comes to realize that the answer to death is creativity, and the response to the meaninglessness of existence is *engagement* in a cause, the need to combat our sense of hopelessness and to live the authentic life.

Maslow defines his key concept in yet another way. "The 'unitive conscience' of peak experiences . . ." yields ". . . a sense of the sacred *in* and *through* the particular instance of the momentary, the secular, the worldly." (p.68)

In *The Old Man and the Sea*, it should be apparent that Santiago, despite his fisherman's simplicity, is aware of the mystical unity of all living creatures in nature. Santiago is a pilgrim in nature and a diviner of her powers, intuitively understanding the vast cycles of sidereal time. His love of the creatures of nature is a mystic's love. Through his lone pilgrimage, he seeks both spiritual purification and ultimate communion with the mysterious meaning of life.

In *Nausea* it should also be manifest that Roquentin has discovered in a particular instance (the song) a truth beyond the secular, worldly existence of everyday life.

But of what consequence are such emotional responses? Maslow reminds us "The intrinsic value of the peak experience is that it enlarges consciousness." (p.80)

✳ ✳ ✳

To substantiate his position, Maslow alludes to Rudolf Otto's *The Idea of the Holy* (1958). Otto described the key attributes of the mystical encounter. One is overwhelmed by the presence of the holy and sacred, filled with humility and gratitude. One is "awed before the *mysterium tremendum*; the sense of the divine; the quality of its sublime nature."(p.54)

It should be self-evident that Dante's *Vita Nuova* expresses the poet's direct experience of the *mysterium tremendum* at the center of the Ptolemaic universe. Dante is a medieval Christian mystic.

The Old Man and the Sea suggests a similar experience when we examine the uncanny, intricate omnipresence of Pythagoran, astrological, and sacred numbers — the three's, seven's, twelve's, forties, four's and finally the mystical one — as Godhead. Somehow they mysteriously seem to influence his destiny. Somehow they seem an awesome mystical hermeneutic to his solitary story.

On the other hand, in *Nausea* it is not easy to perceive the holy, sacred, or the divine. Yet the experience described in the novel has the quality of sublimity. But what is its source? As Maslow points out "The kind of knowledge gained in peak experiences can be gained from desolation experience." (p.74)

Indeed, the sense of desolation calls forth the sublime in all three works studied. The death of Beatrice awakened Dante to the meaning and dedication of his new life.

Although *The Old Man and the Sea* represents secular literature, it also manifests important aspects of the *mysterium tremendum*. Isolated and alone on the vast and silent sea, aware of the great currents and the mysterious depths below, Santiago knows her nature to be nurturing and devouring, maternal and murderous. Under the limitless sky, he lives with rapacious, merciless death at the center of existence. Santiago's spirit is at the center of a universe of death.

Yet his life is a testament. Though alone in his skiff at the focal point of the immense circle of ocean and earth, the giant cycles of nature have taught him what life is. All his lifelong he had sought to conciliate the laws of death with the laws of life. He finally understands that in the face of the predatory laws of nature, because life goes on, the ultimate truth is that the higher power in Creation is female.

In *Nausea*, the desolation is in the atheistic conception of a meaningless universe and a purposeless existence. Yet the awakening of his creative instinct and Roquentin's decision to be *engagé* in the lives of mankind by some form of creativity is the sublime moment rising out of the grave of his existential despair.

Maslow offers a caveat similar to that of *Beyond Literary Theory*, which cautions against using the purpose and methodology of the positivist sciences. Maslow avers that "positivist psychologists pass by entirely the old, rich literature based on the mystical experience." (p.41) Correspondingly, in the 20th century, all too many theorists and critics embraced some form of scientism. As a consequence, they lost contact with the deeper sense of literature, the search for the meaning of human destiny.

Maslow himself justifies his study of peak experiences by stating that scientists and humanists need to learn a lesson that mystery, ambiguity, illogic and transcendental experiences may now be considered to lie within the realm (of the study) of nature.(p.45) The study of peak experiences is not limited to manifestations of the supernatural.

A last comment needs to be made. Maslow contrasted the peak experience to the "plateau experience." The latter ". . . always has a noetic and cognitive element . . . not always true of peak experiences, which can be purely and exclusively emotional." (p.xiv) Indeed, ". . . plateau experiencing can be achieved, learned, earned by long hard work. It can be meaningfully aspired to." (pp.xv-xvi) However, to achieve the "unitive consciousness" characteristic of the plateau experience requires "a lifelong effort [like] the spiritual exercises." The plateau experience comes with ". . . time, work, discipline, and commitment." (p.xvi)

It should be clear to the reader of *Beyond Literary Theory* that such dedication and discipline are necessary: to experience a peak insight into the epiphany of a literary work and to reach the plateau experience that comes only with years of passionate study of unforgettable literature.

GENERAL CONCLUSION

The usual conclusion condenses and recapitulates the major ideas of a discourse. Yet we have already reviewed with care a wide range of literary strategies. Hence it would seem advisable, instead, to caution the reader against pursuing one's own persuasions into strategic blind alleys. Therefore, before committing yourself to a definite approach to literary interpretation , let me first offer two suggestions: (1) *What to Avoid* and (2) *What to be Wary of.*

That done, the third part of the conclusion presents *Facts about Reality*, which hopefully will guide the reader to re-examine seriously his or her most basic assumptions about human existence. The facts derive from 20th century microbiology and ecology. Moreover, the social sciences enlarged our understanding of the significance of spheres of time in human life. In sum, the findings of 20th century biology and the human sciences invite the serious literature specialist to study time, biological nature, and human nature in unfamiliar and creative ways.

Yet beyond such neoteric knowledge, modern mystical experiences in real life and in secular literature prepare us to acknowledge that human destiny does have some immortal meaning.

WHAT TO AVOID

1. Shun the use of the dualistic language inherited from western man's understanding of the nature of reality. The natural world is *not* divided by spiritual powers of light and darkness, spirit versus matter, good versus evil, mind versus body, or essence versus existence. Dualism is pure mythology. It does not exist as a material, empirical, or scientific reality. In whatever form, dualism is a delusion.

2. Discard obsolescent literary terminology. There are no pure genres as epic, drama, or poetry, especially in modern literature. Even where one tendency prevails, one or the other is also present to vivify the human experience created.

   Moreover, any vocabulary which divides, dissects, or "analyzes" the sentient experiences of literature into subjective/objective, content/form, or parts/whole may be of historical interest but of very little interpretive value. Such terms and concepts do not give access to the meaning of experience as it is actually lived. The intent of literature is to evoke life in its various dimensions.

3. Dismiss mechanistic, causal analogies. Any analysis of life or literature as representing some form of causal law in human relations is a reduction ad absurdum of the nature of man and literature. To believe a specific pyschological cause brought about a specific psychological effect is to ignore the many circumstances and conditions which influence human decision and reaction. The infinite mental and moral complexity of human personality and of life itself cannot be reduced to simplistic, sophomoric, causal explanations of human relations.

4. Avoid analogies drawn from the empirical sciences or predicated on methodology not intended to examine the actual, sentient experiences of human beings. Refuse to regard humans (viz., characters) as integers, specimens, "case histories" or examples of racial, religious, sociological, or psychological typology. The "typical" largely ignores the uncommon, distinctive, creative, and exceptional characteristics of the individual in life and in literature.

5. Reject blind adherence or fealty to any particular school of thought or literary philosophy — past or present — because few theories last in popularity more than a few decades. Furthermore, those which disappear and resurface over decades or generations are often contested by antithetical convictions. These test the fundamental argument or epistemological soundness of the theories which they oppose.

BE WARY

1. Be circumspect in your use of any analogy drawn from the Darwinian theory of evolution. It may quite distort the interpretation of human nature which is distinct from animal behavior in raw nature. Though there are undoubted genetic and zoological similarities between man and our simian cousins, yet Homo sapiens have evolved beyond them as is evident in man's worldwide civilizations and cultures.

   Moreover, Darwin's explanation of the evolution of species uses the unfortunate term "mechanisms" to explain "chance" mutations that impelled evolution. In the 20th century the microbiological description of *morphogenesis* and the macrobiological explanation of *symbiosis* and *mutualism* in nature call into question certain aspects of Darwin's otherwise genial exposition. While 19th and 20th century literary naturalism had its day in the sun, the 21st century will surely insist on a deeper knowledge of our biological nature.

2. Be vigilant when using myth to interpret literature, however attractive or illuminating such myths appear to be. Is the myth from so remote a time that a modern interpretation can be trusted? Do we superimpose our sophisticated knowledge upon "primitive" or prehistorical people who may have had minds wholly occupied with surviving another day? Is the myth the product of a single imagination or is it the characteristic expression of a whole culture? *Is our ignorance greater than their knowledge?* Caution is called for.

3. Be guarded when undertaking religious interpretations for at least three reasons: (a) The orthodox, fundamentalist interpretation of Scripture and even of secular literature may be justifiably opposed by heretical insights. (b) Christianity, Judaism, and Islam all have exoteric and esoteric, dogmatic and mystical interpretations of the meaning of scripture and human experience. In all probability, none is totally right or completely wrong. Yet the intransigent claim to possess the absolute truth. (c) Furthermore, different religions hold distinct world views, which

often ignore the beliefs held by other religions. Each is based on a spiritual founder and uses its own symbols to sustain and justify its faith. Yet within any given religion, sects often hold rebellious, heretical views in defiance of the orthodox. The salient danger is to presume a zealot's superiority and assume one possesses the final, definitive truth. Such conviction "empowers" one to judge human life in absolutistic terms of moral good and evil, to decide who is to be "saved" and who to be "damned."

In sum, be distrustful of your own religious intolerance due to your ethnic or racial pride, for it may influence you to misinterpret and misrepresent a fine literary work beyond any recognizable truth or meaning.

4.   Be wary of using any single psychological theory as the basis for understanding literature. Since various psychological theories invite a multitude of literary interpretations of psyche, which to choose? With what justification? Perhaps one should eclectically use them all so as to render the "whole" truth about the particular psyche characterized in a literary work. However, such eclecticism takes very great knowledge of psychology. Moreover, new theories seem to pop up every decade or so. Are we to believe only in the "founder" of a particular psychology, or only in the latest theory to emerge? In other words, the utilization of any human science (sociology, history, psychology, anthropology) requires more than a superficial or casual knowledge of it to do justice to the discipline itself and to the piece of literature thus studied.

5.   The danger of willful or shallow literary interpretation requires us to offer yet another caveat. Are we looking for certainties — as some scientists are want to do — when there may be no such certainty to human life or existence?

It is noteworthy that Chinese scholars over hundreds of years wrote copious interpretations of the *I Ching, Book of Changes*. They recognized existence as manifesting both continual and cyclical change. These scholars eventually devised an ideogrammatic method of interpretation which undertook to respond to the endlessly metamorphizing situations that the human being encounters in life.

Thus their Taoistic interpretation of human experience seems cognizant of the changes of nature and all life. Perhaps for this reason the basic Taoist philosophy seems truly to understand the inner mutability in universal myths, folklore, and literary stories about humankind.

So we need to take care when anticipating permanence in a world where metamorphosis occurs in and around us all the time. The ancient conviction that humankind lived in a permanent world against a backdrop of eternity led man to hope for survival in an afterlife. Perhaps we needed faith in an afterlife to save mankind from total despair at the apparent senselessness of being born only to die.

So modern man as skeptic, agnostic, or atheist is wary of seeking comfort and consolation where they may not exist. Yet we may console ourselves with one thought. If our search for knowledge fails to give us the certainty we hunger for, perhaps through our study of literature, our search for wisdom will teach us to live in the mutable world as it actually is.

FACTS ABOUT REALITY

1. It is time to recognize and acknowledge two fundamental facts about nature, which condition man's understanding of himself and human destiny. The two are the following: (a) The world's appearance of permanence is deceptive. We know today that the earth itself is continually changing. Yet in antiquity the illusion of the earth's permanence and the apparent eternity of the stars was justification enough for ancient man to establish religions based on the "revealed" truth in Scripture. In turn, this foundation led to orthodox and dogmatic interpretations. Only the exoteric was immutable truth. Ironically, even today the scientific search for knowledge is driven by the same need for certainty. (b) Whether short-term, long-term, or cyclical, metamorphosis is manifest through the world of plants and animals, all life forms, all human life.

2.   Darwin's theory of evolution virtually monopolized western man's thinking over the past 150 years. However, by the end of the 20th century, microbiology discovered new natural processes which were bound to affect our understanding of animate nature and of human nature itself.

(a) The most recent discovery of microbiology was that of *morphogenesis* (cf. organogenesis). It directs and governs the entelechy of plant and animal life *from within*. (Note that this visualization of the *inner processes* in forms of life is, in contrast to, yet complementary to Darwin's interpretation of *external* evolution through competition for food, mates, shelter, and prospects of offspring for the successful competitors.) Correspondingly, it is believed *morphogenesis* also shapes and guides the nature of man *from within*.

(b) An earlier 20th century discovery of microbiology was that of *symbiosis*. It designates the union or intimate association of dissimilar organisms. A few thinkers realized that this process probably accounted for the entire inner integration of the organs and life support systems *within* life forms. Contrary to Darwin's evolutionary exposition of nature, symbiosis also indicated that different species actually established non-competitive, mutually beneficial relationships.[1]

In acknowledging these two fundamental facts of animate nature, we come as close to discovering a universal as we may ever expect to achieve in reality.

* * *

I have sketched in these latest microbiological discoveries for the reader interested in re-examining his assumptions about what we habitually call reality. Indeed, these biological breakthroughs may help us to reconsider other aspects of reality and life, which in turn may open our eyes to the presence of dimensions in literature that the student may not yet have considered.

* * *

In 1974, I presented a spherical vision of time. Visualizing time as offering spheres of significance, I discussed and described eight intricately interconnected spheres: the chronometric, biological, social, historical, psychic, entelechal, transcendental, and teleological. The book demonstrates how such spheres of meaning appear throughout modern literature. If interested in a further explanation, see my book *A Philosophy of Literary Criticism (A Method of Literary Analysis and Interpretation).*

* * *

Beyond the use of contemporary knowledge based on these eight concepts, the student may wish to consider studying other spheres of signification.[2] To be sure, as the reader already knows, there are religious and mystical spheres of meaning implicit in many works of literature. Whenever literary works confront the sense of human destiny, there you can expect the author to probe humanity's existential anguish and the individual's mystical experiences. To ignore this sphere of feeling is intentionally to neglect studying man's deepest intimations regarding our purpose in life. It is hoped that the chapters which illustrate the mystical dimension in literature have induced some readers to explore mysticism itself for the wisdom it can bring the adept.

The reader is also invited to be receptive to the spiritual experiences of various religions, ancient and modern, because the lives of the mystics have revealed moments of self-realization unimagined in an age of skepticism, agnosticism and atheism. Before you reject such research as unworthy of your attention, consider the possibility that the exploration of the innermost experiences of human life may lead you to find the secret sanctum of everlasting literature.

* * *

A final observation about studying images, metaphors, symbols, and themes as ideas. The student should be aware that imagery and symbols occur not only in individual literary works or even only in national literatures. As so effectively presented in A. Lovejoy's *The Great Chain of Being*,[3] metaphors, symbols and themes as germinal ideas often appear in the literature of entire continents, as Europe, and can influence man's understanding and concepts across thousands of years. Moreover, solidly researched essays by other eminent scholars have explored such ideas as: skepticism, myth, religion, temperance (*sōphrosynē*), theodicy, good and evil, and a hundred more.

These readable, encyclopedic essays reveal enduring facts about ideas. Over centuries they periodically progress and regress, appear and disappear. These studies note the similarities and differences between the earlier and later use of subjects and themes, thereby facilitating our intimate comprehension of different generations of mankind. Moreover, different ages define archetypal terms (e.g., love, loyalty, morality) in different ways. Variations of definition in succeeding cultural epochs or in diverse civilizations tell us not only a great deal about literature but also their sense of their own humanity.[4] Furthermore, their idealized archetypes of manhood and womanhood help us visualize their gender understanding of human destiny.

In sum, the history of ideas provides a cross-cultural context for literary study. It also enables us to better understand the emotional intelligence of the human race. The history of ideas teaches us to admire humanity, ancient and modern, for its undeniable wisdom.

APPENDIX A
MYSTICAL POETS,
PHILOSOPHERS AND AUTHORS

The list of writers given below does not include any representatives from Asia or the Orient. In as much as Part Five of *Beyond Literary Theory* focused on the direct or indirect mystical influences on Dante, Hemingway, and J.P. Sartre, I confined my selection of great mystical writers accordingly. Hence the five categories list mystics: ancient, Jewish, Christian, Islamic and secular.

However, even this limited list may encourage some readers to study other authors renown for their exploration of the mystical in life. Through ingenious imagery and a consciousness of life's cosmic dimension , poets and creative thinkers are able at times to perceive the ultimate significance of human destiny.

ANCIENT

Epictetus (ca 50 - ca 130)
Heraclitus (ca 544 - 484 B.C)
Hermes Trismegistus (wrote between 3rd century B.C. and 3rd A.D.)
Marcus Aurelius (120 - 180)
Plato (428 - 348 B.C.)
Plotinus (ca 204 - 270)
Pythagorus (ca 575 - 500 B.C.)

JEWISH

Martin Buber (1878 - 1965)
Moses Maimonides (1135 - 1204)
Baruch de Spinoza (1637 - 1677)

CHRISTIAN

Saint Augustine (354 - 430)
Franz Xaver von Baader (1765 - 1841)
Bernard of Clairvaux (1090 - 1153)
Jacob Boehme (1575 - 1634)
Giardino Bruno (1548 - 1600)
Richard Crashaw (1612 - 1649)
Alighieri Dante (1265 - 1321)
Meister Eckhart (1260 - 1327)
Juan Falconi de Bustamente (1596 - 1638)
Francis of Assisi (1181 - 1266)
Hildegard of Bingen (1098 - 1179)
John of the Cross (1542 - 1591)
Philippus Aureolus Paracelsus (1498 - 1546)
Blaise Pascal (1633 - 1662)
Giovanni Pico della Mirandola (1403 - 1494)
Friedrich E.D. Schleiermacher (1768 - 1834)
Pierre Teilhard de Chardin (1881 - 1955)
Thomas Aquinas (1225 - 1274)
Miguel de Unamuno y Jugo (1864 - 1936)

ISLAM

Abdallah Ansari (1006 - 1088)
Farid ad-din Attar (1142 - 1220)
Abd al-Rahman Diami (1414 - 1492)
Omar Khayyam (ca. 1062 - 1123)
Jalal ad-Din Rumi (1207 - 1273)
Moslih al 'Din Abu Mohammed Abdallah Sadi (ca 1200 - 1292)

SECULAR

Pierre C. Baudelaire (1821 - 1867)
William Blake (1757 - 1827)
Khalil Gibran (1883 - 1931)
Novalis (1772 - 1801)
Antoine de Saint Exupery (1900 - 1944)

Alfred Tennyson (1809 - 1892)

NOTES

Notes to Chapter 2

1. M.H. Abrams, *The Mirror and the Lamp* (New York, W.W. Norton & Co., Inc., 1958), p. 241.
2. Ibid., p. 242.
3. Wellek & Warren, *Theory of Literature* (New York: A Harvest Book, Harcourt, Brace & Co., 1956), p. 168.
4. C.K. Ogden and I.A. Richards, *The Meaning of Meaning* (New York: A Harvest Book, Harcourt, Brace & Co., 1946), p. 111.
5. Ibid., p. 235.
6. Wellek & Warren, p. 11.
7. Wolfgang Kayser, *Das Sprachliche Kunstwerk,* elfte Aufl., (Bern u. München: Francke Verlag, 1965), p. 274.
8. Ibid.
9. J.T. Shipley, ed., *Dictionary of World Literature* (Patterson, New Jersey: Littlefield, Adams & Co., 1962), pp. 294-295.
10. Abrams, p. 26.
11. Such critical theory is centered on Aristotle's "Poetics."
12. Herbert Seidler, *Die Dichtung: Wesen, Form, Dasein*, 2. Aufl., (Stuttgart: Alfred Kröner Verlag, 1965), p. 473.
13. Franz K. Stanzel, *Typische Formen des Romans*, 2. Aufl., (Göttingen, Vandenhoeck u. Ruprecht, 1965), p. 3.
14. Ibid., p. 11.
15. Cf. Percy Lubbock's distinctions between "scenic" and "panoramic" in the *Craft of Fiction.*
16. Stanzel, p. 12.
17. Ibid., pp. 12-13.
18. Ibid., p. 17.
19. Wayne C. Booth, *The Rhetoric of Fiction* (Chicago & London: U of Chicago P, 1961), p. 20.

20.   Ogden & Richards, p. 149.

Notes to Chapter 3

1.   Wellek and Warren, *Theory of Literature* (New York: A Harvest
         Book, Harcourt, Brace & Co. 1956), p. 217.
2.   Ibid., p. 218.
3.   E. Staiger, *Grundbegriffe der Poetik* (Zurich: Atlantis Verlag,
         1966), p. 209.
4.   Ibid., p. 78.
5.   Ibid., p. 204.
6.   Ibid., p. 242.
7.   W. Kayser, *Das Sprachliche Kunstwerk* (Bern: Francke Verlag,
         1965) p. 330.
8.   Ibid., p. 331.
9.   Ibid., p. 332.
10.   Wellek and Warren, p. 110.
11.   W. Kayser, p. 332.
12.   H. Seidler, *Die Dichtung: Wesen, Form, Dasein* (Stuttgart:
         Alfred Krönig Verlag, 1965), p. 69.
13.   Ibid., p. 507.
14.   Ibid., pp. 361-362.
15.   Ibid., p. 381.
16.   H. Bonnet, *Roman et Poésie* (Paris: Libraire Nizet, 1951), p. 10.
17.   Ibid., p. 129.
18.   Ibid., p. 261.
19.   A.M. Albérès, *Métamorphoses du Roman* (Paris: Editions Albin
         Michel, 1966), p. 11.
20.   Ibid., p. 37.
21.   P. De Boisdeffre, *Où va le Roman?* (Paris: Editions Mondiales,
         1962), p. 250.
22.   Robert Champigny, *Le Genre Romanesque* (Monte Carlo:
         Editions Regain, 1963), p. 11.
23.   Ibid., p. 32.
24.   *Le Genre Poétique* (Monte Carlo: Editions Regain, 1963), p.
         229.
25.   Ibid., p. 187.
26.   *Le Genre Dramatique* (Monte Carlo: Editions Regain, 1963), p.
         149.

27. Ibid., p. 179.
28. Ibid., p. 180.
29. W.H. Driedrich & W. Killy, eds. *Literatur* (Das Fischer Lexikon, Frankfurt a.m. Fischer Bücherei, 1965), Vol. II on *Gattungen.*
30. Ibid., pp. 237-239.
31. Ibid., p. 242.
32. Alex Preminger, ed., *Encyclopedia of Poetry and Poetics* (Princeton, N.J.: Princeton U P, 1965), article by G.N.G. Orsini, p. 308.
33. Northrop, Frye, *Anatomy of Criticism* (New York: Atheneum, 1966), p. 305.
34. Herbert Muller, *Science and Criticism. The Humanistic Tradition in Contemporary Thought* (New Haven and London: Yale U P, 1943), p. 112.
35. Jean Pucelle, *Le Temps* (Paris: P U de France, 1967), Quatrième Edition, pp. 61-62.
36. Roman Ingarden, *Das Literarische Kunstwerk*, Dritte durchgesehene Auflage, Tübingen, Max Niemayer Verlag, 1965), p. 43.
37. The reader may object that I have omitted the imperative mode. While this is true, I do not believe the imperative plays such a dominant role in apperception as do the subjunctive and indicative in imaginative literature.
38. In this connection, the reader may wish to examine my book, *A Philosophy of Literary Criticism, Volume I, Patterns of Comparison*, Exposition Press, N.Y. 1974.
39. In I.A. Richards, *Principles of Literary Criticism* (New York: A Harvest Book, Harcourt, Brace and World, Inc., 1925), pp. 242-243.
40. To some readers, this may appear a sweeping conclusion. Those who wish further references on this modal approach may refer to my dissertation, *A Subjunctive-Indicative Modality (A Contribution Toward a Theory of Literature)*, Indiana University, Bloomington, Indiana, 1969. In it, patterns of comparison and contrast, intentional distortions and transformations are shown to express and evoke the subjunctive and indicative, which together divulge the design and meaning of fictive experience.

Notes to Chapter 4

1.   J.T. Shipley, ed. *Dictionary of World Literature*, (Patterson, New Jersey: Littlefield, Adams & Co., 1962), p. 219.

2.   Whenever possible I have avoided using the words "objective" and "subjective" because they have become too ambiguous for the scrupulous and sensitive discussion of literary works. For a more precise vocabulary, the reader may wish to look up the terms "indicative" and "subjunctive" as employed in my dissertation *The Subjective-Indicative Modality, A Contribution Toward a Theory of Literature*, Indiana U, Bloomington, Indiana, 1969.

3.   Eberhard Lambert, *Bauformen des Erzählens*, (Stuttgart: J.B. Metzlersche Verlag, 1955).

4.   The reader may wish to explore this subject further in Chapter 8, "Metaphor as Mood, State of Mind, and Symbol" and in Chapter 9, "Metaphor as Bond, Symbol, and Archetype" of my book, *A Philosophy of Literary Criticism, Volume I, Patterns of Comparison*, Exposition Press, N.Y., 1974.

5.   The logical problem is that the genus cannot truly contain the species.

6.   Idea predominates in prose; feeling holds sway in poetry.

7.   A. Preminger, ed., *Encyclopedia of Poetry and Poetics*, (New Jersey: Princeton U P, 1965), p. 833.

8.   cf William Empson, *Seven Types of Ambiguity* (New York: New Directions, 1966).

9.   For most of these symbolic interpretations I am indebted to K. Lipffert's *Symbol-Fibel, Eine Hilfe zum Betrachten und Deuten Mittelalterlicher Bildwerke*, Vierte Aufl. (Kassel: Johannes Stauda Verlag, 1964).

Notes to Chapter 5

1.   Ronald S. Crane, et al., *Critics and Criticism, Ancient and Modern* (Chicago: U of Chicago P, 1952). pp. 7-8.

2.   Ibid., p. 17.

3.   Ibid., p. 23.

4.   Crane, "The Critical Monism of Cleanth Brooks," pp.63-107.

5.   Crane, "I.A.Richards on the Art of Interpretation," pp.27-44.

6. Richards' view of language seems to have evolved from the emotive-referential stance of his earlier writings to a view that meaning arises out of the cooperation and rivalry of contexts, which is essentially a dialectical interpretation.
7. Olson, "William Empson, Contemporary Criticism and Poetic Diction," pp. 45-82.
8. Olson, "An Outline of Poetic Theory," pp. 546-566
9. The latter effort is pursued by such New Critics as I.A. Richards and Cleanth Brooks; Olson, p.55.
10. Olson, pp. 552-3.
11. Ibid., pp. 561-62.
12. McKeon, "Literary Criticism and the Concept of Imitation in Antiquity," p. 149.
13. Ibid., p. 150.
14. Ibid., p. 152.
15. Ibid., p. 160.
16. Ibid., p. 175.
17. McKeon, "The Philosophical Bases of Arts and Criticism," p. 463.
18. Ibid., p. 464.
19. Ibid., p. 465.
20. Ibid., p. 482.

Notes to Chapter 6

1. Alfred Behrmann, "Der Anglo-Amerikanische New Criticism" in Smegac and Skreb's *Zur Kritik literaturwissenschaftlicher Methodologie* (Frankfurt am Main: Athenaum Fischer GmbH Verlag, 1973).
2. Ibid., p. 180.
3. Ibid., p. 181-182.
4. Ibid., p. 189.
5. Wolfgang Kayser, *Das Sprachliche Kunstwerk, Eine Einführung in die Literaturwissenschaft*, elfte Auflage (Bern u. München, Francke Verlag, 1965), p. 14.
6. Ibid., p. 21.
7. Ibid., p. 37.
8. Ibid., p. 160. Obviously this line of reasoning corresponds to the interpretation of perception embraced by phenomenology.

9. Ibid., p. 163.
10. Ibid., p. 239. Compare this idea with the Russian formalist view that form is part of literary "materials."
11. Ibid., p. 234.
12. Ibid., p. 174.
13. Ibid., p. 225.
14. Ibid., "Literarische Wertung und Interpretation" in *Die Vortragsreise* (Bern: 1958).
15. Emil Staiger, *Grundbergriffe der Poetik* (Zurich u. Freiburg i. Br. Atlantis Verlag, 1946) p. 131.
16. Ibid., p. 152.
17. Ibid., p. 242.
18. Ibid., p. 256.
19. Ibid., *Die Kunst der Interpretation* (Zurich u. Freiburg i. Br. Atlantis Verlag, 1955).
20. Karl Otto Conrady, *Einführung in die Neuere Deutsche Literaturwissenschaft* (Reinbek bei Hamburg: Rowohlt Taschenbuch Verlag GmbH, 1966), p. 59.
21. Ibid., p. 58.
22. Werner Krauss, *Grundprobleme der Literaturwissenschaft* (Reinbek bei Hamburg: Rowohlt Taschenbuch Verlag GmbH, 1968), p. 26.
23. Ibid., pp. 91-92.
24. Ibid., pp. 81-82. Krauss quoted K.S. Lawrila.
25. J.O. Carloni and Jean-C Filloux, *La Critique Littéraire* (Paris: P U de France, 1966), Que-Sais-Je? series, cinquième édition revue, p. 5.
26. Ibid., p. 61.
27. Ibid., p. 64.
28. Ibid., p. 70.
29. Ibid., p. 73.
30. Albert Klein und Jochen Vogt, *Methoden der Literaturwissenschaft I: Literaturgeschichte und Interpretation* (Düsseldorf, West Germany: Bertelsmann Universitäts - Verlag, 1971), p. 7.
31. Ibid., p. 44.
32. Ibid., p. 45.
33. Ibid., p. 64.
34. Ibid., p. 11.

35. Ibid., p. 13.
36. Ibid., p. 43.
37. Zdeno Skreb, "Die Wissenschaft der Literaturfoschung" in Viktor Zmegak and Zdenko Skreb's *Zur Kritik Literaturwissenschaftlicher Methodologie* (Frankfurt am Main, West Germany: Athenaum Fischer Taschenbuch Verlag, 1973). p. 27.
38. Ibid., p. 28.
39. Ibid., p. 12
40. Ibid., p. 34.
41. Ibid., p. 17.
42. Edgar Lohner, "The Intrinsic Method: Some Reconsiderations" in *The Disciplines of Criticism: Essays in Literary Theory, Interpretation and History*, edited by Peter Demetz, Thomas Greene, and Lowry Nelson, Jr. (New Haven and London: Yale U P, 1968), p. 148.
43. Ibid., pp. 166-167.
44. Ibid., p. 515.
45. W.L. Guerin, E.G. Labor, L. Morgan, and J.R. Willingham, *A Handbook of Critical Approaches to Literature* (New York and London: Harper and Row, 1966), p. xii.
46. Ibid., p. 3.
47. Ibid., p. 9.

Notes to Chapter 7

1. Bertrand Russell states that the ancient Greeks, in general, relied too much on deduction as a source of knowledge. On the other hand, Aristotle questioned the basis of the first premise from which deduction starts and concluded that it derives from induction. Nevertheless, in his theory of knowledge, Aristotle overestimated the importance of deduction to human reasoning. See Russell's *A History of Philosophy* (London: George Allen and Unwin Ltd., 1947), p. 222.
2. W.J. Bate, *Criticism: the Major Texts* (N.Y. and Burlingame: Harcourt, Brace, and World, Inc., 1952), p. 499.
3. Ibid., p. 490.
4. Ibid., p. 498.
5. Ibid.

6. Ibid., p. 490.
7. Ibid., p. 499.
8. Ibid.
9. Cited in Leo Pollmann's *Literaturwissenschaft und Methode* (Frankfurt am Main, West Germany: Athenaum Fischer Verlag, 1973), p. 95. "Le poète trouve la région où son génie peut vivre et se déployer désormais; le critique trouve l'instinct et la loi de ce génie."
10. There were objections to Sainte-Beuve's approach. Gustave Lanson said, "Instead of using biographies to explain works, he (Sainte Beuve) uses works to make up biographies." Marcel Proust also raised an objection, ". . . a book is the product of another self (*moi*) than that manifest in society." (Bate, p. 499; 498) René Wellek in his *History of Literary Criticism, 1740-1850, Vol. III, Age of Transition* also criticises Sainte Beuve sharply, p. 70ff.
11. Bate, p. 504.
12. Ibid., p. 501.
13. Ibid., p. 502.
14. Ibid., p. 503.
15. Numerous objections have been made against Taine's approach. Sainte-Beuve argued that one cannot *deduce* a literary work of the first order by studying the influence of *race, milieu* and *moment* on it. Carloni and Filloux in *Le Critique Littéraire* (1966) see his determinism and philosophical pretensions degenerating into mere impressions. Finally, René Wellek in his *History of Literary Criticism* (p. 36) shows how Taine's concepts shift in meaning and how his causal explanations prove to be baffling in the end. On the other hand, W.C. Brownwell in *Criticism: An Essay on Function, Form and Method* (pp. 33-34) considers that Taine's philosophic structure amply atones for the misapplication of some of the details.
16. O.B. Hardison, Jr., ed., *Modern Continental Literary Criticism* (N.Y.: Appleton-Century-Crofts, 1962), p. 109.
17. Wellek, p. 67.
18. René Wellek objects, "The analogy between evolution and the life cycle breaks down at every point: it is only a series of metaphors, . . ." Wellek believes Brunetière had made too close a transference of concepts from biology; ". . .literary genres are

not species, and do not transform themselves to higher species." *History of Literary Criticism, Vol. III*, p. 67; pp. 70-71. Thus Wellek argues that Brunetière's analogy served more to confuse the historical interpretation of literature than clarify its development.

19.   Wilheim Scherer, "Die neue Generation" in Viktor Zmegac's *Methoden der deutschen Literaturwissenschaft* (Frankfurt am Main, West Germany, 1972), p. 24.

20.   Scherer, "Zur Geschichte der deutschen Sprache" in Zmegac's *Methoden*.

21.   The three criteria in combination with "reciprocal illumination" apparently have a distinct kinship with diachronic-synchronic linguistic and structuralist studies currently being pursued by European scholars.

22.   Scherer, "H. Hettners Literaturgeschichte des 18. Jahrhundert," in Zmegac's *Methoden*, p. 14.

23.   Scherer's "Geschichte . . ." in Zmegac, p. 19.

24.   Scherer was also inspired by Giambattista Vico's *Scienza Nuova* (1725) when Scherer regards German literary history as cyclical, alternating between male and female dominance in 300 year periods. Furthermore, he applied Darwinian evolutionary concepts to the "growth" of individual works.

Notes to Chapter 8

1.   Ernest Jones, *Hamlet and Oedipus* (Garden City, N.Y., 1954), p. 15.

2.   Ibid., p. 18.

3.   The core of Jones's argument appears on pages 91-103.

4.   Jones seems to have made only a limited use of Freud's theory of psyche to explain how an artwork springs from an artist's mind. Jones insists that the work arises from the *id* whereas an artistic composition is more likely to result from the interaction of *id, ego* and *superego* with the latter predominant. It would seem that the artist's higher consciousness (*superego* or suprapersonality) produces the artwork through sublimation rather than the subconscious. If true, art is the consequence of the healthful drives of the mind's superior functions rather than the manifestation of any complex arising out of the destructive

impulses of a disordered mind.

5.   Indeed, Jones's logic simply disintegrates in the face of the more cogent view of *Hamlet* as a story of retribution. While Jones believes Hamlet's repugnance to revenge his father is due to the youth's *Oedipus Complex*, it must be obvious that revenge by murder must be repugnant to anyone of Hamlet's education and nobility of soul. In other words, Hamlet's task of revenging his father is hindered above all by his highly civilized intelligence and his educated conscience. Furthermore, the prince wants irrefutable proof that the king is a murderer so that Claudius can be brought to public justice. In short, Hamlet must prove to all the world that his uncle is guilty of fratricide — the most repellent crime to a Christian soul because it re-enacts the crime of Cain, which is a theme closer to Shakespeare's upbringing than any conscious use of the *Oedipus Complex*.

Obviously, then, Hamlet wants to bring justice to set the time aright, not to commit murder. This difference makes us realize that Hamlet's moral problem is centered in the distinction between revenge and retribution. Revenge demands destroying an enemy and humiliating him, regardless of the means. Retribution, on the other hand, signifies acting for someone to punish a wrong done onto that person, and since such retribution is often regarded as an act of fate or providence, the agent is obliged to act in a moral way. By seeking vengeance in such a way in behalf of his father, Hamlet is avenging his father, not revenging himself. Hamlet is not a revenge play but a play of retribution.

6.   Robert Emmet Jones, *Panorama de la Nouvelle Critique en France de Gaston Bachelard à Jean Paul Weber* (Paris [1968], pp. 153-86. Further page references are in the text.

7.   Renê Wellek, *Concepts of Criticism* (New Haven & London, 1963), p. 349. Wellek does point out an example of the judicious use of the psychological approach in Edmund Wilson's *The Wound and the Bow*.

8.   R. Wellek, and A. Warren, "Literature and Biography" in *Theory of Literature* (New York 1956), pp. 65-6.

9.   Ibid., "Literature and Psychology," p. 69.

10. Herbert J. Muller, *Science and Criticism: The Humanistic Tradition in Contemporary Thought* (New Haven & London, 1964), p. 155.
11. Ibid., p. 147.
12. Ibid.
13. Carl G. Jung, *Modern Man in Search of a Soul* (New York, 1933), p. 6.
14. This is the main objection of the neo-Aristotelians to the New Critics, who, according to the Chicago scholars, tend to dwell too much on parts (ironies, paradoxes, and the like) to the neglect of structural matters as depicted in Aristotle's *Poetics*

Notes to Chapter 9

1. C.G. Jung, "Sigmund Freud and His Historical Setting," *The Spirit in Man, Art, and Literature*, (Princeton, N.J.: Princeton U P, 1966), p. 33.
2. Ibid., p. 35
3. Ibid., p. 36
4. Ibid., p. 38.
5. Ibid., p. 39.
6. Ibid., p. 40
7. C.G. Jung, "In Memory of Sigmund Freud," *The Spirit in Man, Art, and Literature*, p. 41.
8. Ibid., p. 44.
9. In *Leonardo da Vinci, A Study in Psychosexuality*, Sigmund Freud states, "As artistic talent and productive ability are connected with sublimation, we have to admit that the nature of artistic attainment is psychoanalytically inaccessible to us." p. 119. This statement should stimulate honest and careful thought on the part of literary critics pursuing Freudian interpretations of literature.
10. C.G. Jung, *Modern Man In Search of a Soul*, (N.Y.: A Harvest Book, Harcourt, Brace, and Co., 1933), p. 6.
11. Ibid., p. 21.
12. Ibid., p. 116.
13. Ibid., p. 118.
14. Ibid., p. 57.
15. Ibid., p. 153.

16.		Elsewhere I intend to go into the inadequacies and the obsessive mode of interpretation of Freud's essay *Leonardo da Vinci*. Let it suffice here to say that Freud's reasoning is as tenuous and unsubstantial as smoke. Virtually every scrap of evidence used by Freud and every assertion imputing incipient homosexuality to da Vinci adds up to sheer verbiage. My aim will not be to prove da Vinci's "innocence" of homosexuality. Freud's essay is simply an example of preposterous speculation. Jung's criticism of Freud's inability to conceive or reason in a sound, philosophical way is exemplified by the da Vinci essay.

17.		Jung, *Modern Man in Search of a Soul*, p. 162.

18.		Ibid., p. 168.

19.		Ibid., p. 170.

20.		Ibid., p. 155.

21.		Ibid., p. 157.

22.		Ibid, p. 61.

23.		Ibid., p. 67.

24.		Ibid., p. 120.

25.		C.G. Jung, *The Archetypes and the Collective Unconscious*, (trans: R.F.C Hull), Bollingen Series XX (Princeton, N.J.: Princeton University Press, 1959), p. 82.

26.		Jolande Jacobi, *Complex/Archetype/Symbol in the Psychology of C.G. Jung*, Bollingen Series LVII, (Princeton, N.J.: Princeton University Press, 1974), pp. 21-28.

27.		Ibid., p. 31.

28.		Ibid., p. 34.

29.		Ibid., p. 36.

30.		Ibid., pp. 37-38.

31.		Ibid., p. 50.

32.		Ibid., pp. 74-75.

33.		Ibid., pp. 89-91.

34.		Ibid., p. 100.

35.		Ibid., p. 105.

36.		Ibid., p. 119.

37.		Ibid, p. 123.

38.		C.G. Jung and Ch. Kerenyi, *Introduction à l'essence de la Mythologie, L'enfant divin, La Jeune fille divine*, (Paris: Petite Bibliotheque Payot, no publication date given but the Preface to the new edition gives 1951 as the date it was written.) French transl. from German, H.E. Del Medico, p. 112 p.

39.   Ibid., p. 121.

40.   Ibid., p. 118.

41.   Ibid., p. 120.

42.   Ibid., pp. 122-23.

43.   Ibid., p. 123.

44.   Jung's "Foreword" to Richard Wilhelm's translation of *I Ching or the Book of Changes*, English translation by C.F. Baynes, (Princeton, N.J.: Princeton U P, 1950). The *I Ching* is a book of hexagrams with scholarly commentary and interpretation. Based on a vision of existence as manifesting continuous transformation, the Taoist philosophy supporting the *I Ching* regards the female and male principle, or the powers of dark and light (yin and yang), as effecting the continuous change man experiences in the life around him.

45.   Ibid., p. xxii.

46.   Ibid., p. xxiv.

47.   Matthew Arnold, "Hebraism and Hellenism", *Culture and Anarchy* (1869).

48.   cf. Erich Auerbach's chapter one, "Odysseus' Scar,", *Mimesis: The Representation of Reality in Western Literature* (Garden City, N.Y.: Doubleday and Company, Inc., 1957).

49.   C. G. Jung, *Archetypes of the Collective Unconscious*, p. 28.

50.   Ibid., p. 87.

51.   Ibid.

52.   Thomas Mann, "Freud and the Future" in *Criticisms the Major Texts*, ed., J.W. Bate, (N.Y.: Harcourt, Brace, Jovanovich, Inc., 1970), p. 668.

53.   Ibid., p. 670.

54.   Ibid., p. 671.

55.   Ibid., pp. 671-72.

56.   Ibid. This revaluation of the term "imitation" may be of considerable consequence for students of literature not only in the context of Aristotle's *Poetics* but also in the whole history of mimetic literary theory. Although the first chapter in Erich Auerbach's *Mimesis* is rather clearly archetypal in implications, a good number of other chapters, reflecting various periods of European literature, also lend themselves to a revaluation as archetypal mimesis.

57.   Ibid., p. 672.
58.   Ibid., pp. 672-73.
59.   Ibid., p. 673.
60.   Thomas Mann's *Joseph and his Brothers* (1933-43) also manifests archetypal themes with its recounting of the Old Testament story. Implicit in it is the fact that by recognizing an archetype as God, one's psychic preoccupation with it can lead one to live a life according to the image.

Notes to Chapter 10

1.   All pagination is based on the *Psychologie de la Motivation, Théorie et application thérapeutique*. Paris: Petite Bibliothèque Payot, no date given. However, it was previously published by the P U de France in the "Bibliothèque de philosophie contemporaine," B^e ed. revue, 1969.
2.   See Helen F. North's comprehensive article on *temperance*,pp. 365-378 in the *Dictionary of History of Ideas*, Volume IV. NY: Charles Scribner's Sons, 1973.

Notes to Introduction
to Part Five

1.   I.M. Lewis, *Ecstatic Religion. An Anthropological Study of Spirit Possession and Shamanism*. Harmondsworth, Middlesex, England: Penguin Books, 1971.
2.   M. Eliade, *Shamanism. Archaic Techniques of Ecstasy*. Princeton, N.J.: Princeton UP, 1964.
3.   B. Borchert, *Mysticism. Its History and Challenge*. Trans.Transcript Ltd., York Beach, Maine: Samuel Webster, 1994.

Notes to Chapter 11

1.   All references and pagination from: Dante, *La Vita Nuova*, tr. Mark Musa (Bloomington: Indiana U P, 1962).

Notes to Chapter 12

1. All pagination in parentheses refer to Ernest Hemingway's *The Old Man and the Sea* (New York: Charles Scribner's Sons, 1952).
2. Carl G. Jung, *The Archetypes and the Collective Unconscious* (New York: Pantheon Books, Inc., 1959), Bollingen Series XX, transl. by R.F.C. Hull, p. 173.
3. Ibid., p. 56.
4. Ibid., p. 82.
5. Ibid.
6. Ibid., 81.
7. Ibid., p. 82.
8. Ibid., in the Appendix, p. 387 ff.
9. This conflict is at the core of 19th and 20th century existentialism where the contingencies of existence and the absurdity of human destiny taunt man's mandala rationality.
10. Op cit., p. 82.
11. I am indebted to Jean Pucelle's *Le Temps*, (Paris: P U de France, 1967) for his excellent philosophical discussion of time in its manifold rhythms and cycles.
12. Jung, p. 169.
13. Mircea Eliade, *Le Mythe de l'Éternel Retour, Archétypes et Répétition*, (Paris: Gallimard, 1969), pp.ll4-127. To Eliade it is the great value of Christianity to have transformed suffering from a negative state to a positive spiritual meaning.
14. Jung, p. 82.
15. Ibid., p. 212.
16. Ibid., footnote on p. 137.
17. Ibid., p. 114.
18. The *Webster's Seventh Collegiate Dictionary* (Springfield, Mass: G. and C. Merriam Co. 1965), gives the following definition of anthropology: "teaching about the origin, nature and destiny of man esp. from the perspective of his relation to God." p. 38.
19. The 1952 Scribner Library edition of *The Old Man and the Sea*.
20. It is a curious fact that *to orient* also means to bury a body with the feet pointing eastward.

21.   A number of basic characteristics described on pilgrimages are derived from Romain Roussel's *Les Pèlerinages.* (Paris: P U de France,1972, the *Que-Sais-Je?* series, No. 666. On pp. 126-127 he furnishes an excellent bibliography of related works.

22.   How different in this occult view from Einstein's formula for the velocity of light and his esoteric description of relativity in the universe?

23.   Perhaps the Latin word for number *numerus* and the Latin word for divine will or divinity *numen* give us a clue. In the mind of antiquity, that affinity between number and divine will seemed a sufficient correspondence for numerologists to exercise their ingenuity.

24.   To be sure, mythical and mystical associations centered on the number four occurred before the advent of Christianity. For instance, there were four rivers around the Greco-Roman Hades; the four human races (black, white. yellow, red); four ages of humanity, according to Hesiod; and the four Pythagorean virtues (health, beauty, vigor, and finesse of the senses). For a fascinating and a relatively thorough review of associations of numbers, the reader should refer to Georges Polti's *L'Art d'Inventer les Personnages* (Paris; n. d.), pp. 120-3; 163-73.

25.   Henry Corbin in *Histoire de la philosophie islamique, des origines jusqu'a la mort d'Averroës: 1198* (Paris: 1964) draws the analogy between this four level exegesis of the Bible and the hermeneutic of the Koran. He states there is no Koranic verse which does not have four meanings: the esoteric (*zahir*) the esoteric (*batin*), the limited sense (*haad*), and the divine plan (*mottala*) p. 20. It is also of interest to note that two principal branches of Shiism (the Iranian version of Islam) are the duodenary, which originally derived from the twelve zodiac constellations, and the septenary Imamology, which originated in the seven planetary heavens and their mobile stars.

26.   Obviously the number twelve has mythical and mystical dimensions beyond immediate Biblical connotations. To mention a very few, the Chaldeans divided the day into twelve double hours; the Egyptian calendar was twelve months of thirty days. In ancient Persia, there were six light (good) and six dark (evil) months. There were twelve ancient Greek gods and twelve Indian gods whose general character and powers corresponded

to the same months of the year of the Olympians. Confucius had twelve disciples. There were twelve tables of the law for ancient Rome. Under Charlemagne, there were twelve orders of chivalry. And in contrast to the twelve articles of faith symbolized by the Apostles, there were twelve heresies.

27.   The 1952 Scribner Library edition of *The Old Man and the Sea* (1952).

28.   It may well be argued that the boy Manolin has much heart in his concern for and love of the old man. Thus his heart is implicit in the story, in which case four hearts could correspond to the four gospels that ware concerned with interpreting the true story of Jesus of Nazareth, fisherman of men's souls.

29.   Op. Cit.

30.   C.G. Jung, *The Archetypes and the Collective Unconscious*, p. 82.

31.   Again, I am indebted to Jean Pucelle's *Le Temps*, (Paris: P U de France, 1967).

32.   C.G. Jung, p. 169.

33.   Ibid., p. 171.

34.   Ibid., pp. 389-390.

35.   Ibid., p. 114.

36.   If a reader finds the symbolic interpretation of this article disconcerting, let him see Jessie L. Weston's *From Ritual to Romance* (Garden City, New York: Doubleday & Co., Inc., 1957) pp. 113-136. Miss Weston points out convincingly that fish and fisher are life symbols of immemorial antiquity and that the fisher has from the earliest ages been associated with Deities who are connected with the origin and preservation of life (p. 125). Not only is the sacramental fish meal common to Jewish, Christian and Mystery cults (p.130). ". . . the central point of Jewish Fish symbolism is the tradition that, at the end of the world, Messias will catch the great Fish Leviathan and divide its food among the faithful . . ."(p. 128). This brings new light to Santiago's belief that no one is worthy to eat the marlin.

    Of broader consequence, of course, is that fish symbolism is shared by both Occident and Orient. For instance, in Indian cosmogony Vishnu is represented as the golden fish which saved the Vedas from the underworld. "The Fish Avatar was afterwards transferred to Buddha." (p. 126) In the

Māhāyana scriptures, Buddha is seen as the fisherman who draws fish from the sea of Samsara to the light of Salvation (p. 126). Finally, in funeral rites in India and China, the fish is employed as a symbol of resurrection (p. 127).

Notes to Chapter 13

1. P. van Tieghem, *Let Grandes Doctrines Littéraires en France* (Paris, 1965), p. 249.
2. Jean Paul Sartre, *La Nausée* (Paris, 1938), p. 247. All specific quotations and paraphrases are from this edition of the novel. References are indicated in the text.
3. Van Tieghem, p. 251.
4. Ibid., p. 252.
5. Ibid., p. 257.
6. Norman Friedman's article on "symbol" in *Encyclopedia of Poetry and Poetics* edited by Alex Preminger (Princeton, 1965), p. 833.
7. The English titles of these works by Sartre are: *Sick at Heart, The Flies, Closed Doors, The Devil and God,* and *Being and Nothingness.*
8. Erich Auerbach, *Mimesis: The Representation of Reality in Western Literatures* (Garden City, N. J., 1953), pp. 64-66.
9. Ibid., p. 64.
10. Norman Friedman's article on "imagery" in Preminger's *Encyclopedia*, p. 368.
11. Auerbach, p. 101.
12. Ibid., p. 171.
13. Ibid., p. 172.
14. Ibid., p. 175.
15. Ibid., p. 490.
16. This inability to prevent anyone from fulfilling his destiny is comparable to the helplessness of those around Oedipus to stop him from bringing about his own doom.
17. Indeed, the Autodidacte's use of the phrase "*À nous deux, Science Humaine,*" not only comically recalls Rastignac in Balzac's *Père Goriot* and Flaubert's *Bouvard et Pecuchet* but is also an ironical figural comment. I have largely omitted the ironies in *The Nausea* aimed at all things social, orthodox, and

religious. Their intent is to arouse the reader's skepticism at absurd human activities which repeat the senseless processes and self-reproduction of nature. Such ironies express and evoke a contrapuntal pattern to the dominant melody of symbols I have explicated.

18. By this child-like self-teaching, the Autodidacte reminds us of Pascal's concept of "natural ignorance" whereas Roquentin recalls the man of "learned ignorance." Put another way, the Autodidacte is the naive man, Roquentin the nauseated man.

Notes to General Conclusion

1. See Koprotkin's *Mutual Aid* for original research in this field with vast sociological implications.

2. The psychic sphere of time is discussed on pages 43-66 in my 1974 publication. In addition, a more detailed description appears in chapter 10, "Paul Diel's *Psychology of Motivation*" in *Beyond Literary Theory*.

3. A. Lovejoy, *The Great Chain of Being*. Cambridge, Mass: Harvard UP, 1932.

4. In addition, by way of studying the etymology or history of words, a college level dictionary precedes the definition of a word by reference to its origins in Sanskrit, Latin, Greek, Old French, Old German, Old English as well as other languages.

Bibliography

The following bibliography separates works written in English, French, German and Spanish for the convenience of the reader. You will note that there are not only multiple references to literary theory and methods for studying literature. In addition, in keeping with the range of subjects covered in various chapters, there are useful reference works on the following: anthropology, religion (Judaism, Christianity, Islam), epistemology, Gnosticism, the history of ideas, mythology, mysticism, psychology (Freud, Jung, Diel), rhetoric, and esoterism.

English

Abrams, M.H. *The Mirror and the Lamp*. N.Y.: Norton, 1958.

Auerbach, A.M. *Mimesis. The Representation of Reality in Western Literature*. Princeton, N.J.: Princeton UP, 1953.

Bate , J.W., ed. *Criticism: The Major Texts*. N.Y.: Harcourt, Brace, Jovanovitch, 1970.

Biedermann, H. *Dictionary of Symbolism*. Hertfordshire, U.K., Wordsworth, 1996.

Bizzell, P. & Herzberg, B. *The Rhetorical Tradition. Readings from Classical Times to the Present*. Boston: St. Martin's P, 1990.

Bodkin, M. *Archetypal Patterns in Poetry. Psychological Studies of Imagination*. London: Oxford UP, 1934.

Booth, W.C. *The Rhetoric of Fiction*. Chicago & London: U of Chicago P, 1961.

Burke, E. *A Philosophical Inquiry into the Origin of Our Ideas of the Sublime and the Beautiful,* 1757.

Campbell, J. *The Hero with a Thousand Faces*. Bollingen Series XVIII, Princeton, N.J.: Princeton UP, 1973.

Corn, A. *The Metamorphoses of Metaphor*. N.Y.: Viking, Penguin, 1987.

Crane, R.S. *Critics and Criticism: Ancient and Modern*. Chicago: U of Chicago P, 1956.

Dante. *La Vita Nuova*. Trans. Mark Musa. Bloomington,Indiana: Indiana UP, 1962.

Demetz, Greene, & Nelson, eds. *The Disciplines of Criticism. Essays in Literary Theory, Interpretation and History*. New Haven: Yale UP, 1968.

Eliade, M. *Shamanism. Archaic Techniques of Ecstasy*. Princeton, N.J.: Princeton UP, 1964.

Epstein, V. *The Way of the Jewish Mystic*. Boston: Shambala, 1988.

Ferguson, G. *Signs and Symbols in Christian Art*. Oxford UP, 1961.

Freud, S. *Leonardo da Vinci. A Study in Psychosexuality*. trans. A A. Brill, N.Y.: Knopf & Random House, 1947.

Frye, N. *Anatomy of Criticism. Four Essays*. Atheneum, N.Y.: Princeton UP, 1966.

Geurin, Laber, Morgan, & Willingham. *A Handbook on Critical Approaches to Literature*. N.Y.: Harper & Row, 1966.

Groden,M. & Kreisworth, M. *The John Hopkins Guide to Literary Theory and Criticism*. Boston & London: John Hopkins UP, 1994.

Hemingway, E. *The Old Man and the Sea*. N.Y.: Scribner's Sons,1952.

Hawkes, T. *Metaphor*. London: Methuen, 1972.

Hornstein, Percy & Brown. *The Reader's Companion to World Literature*. N.Y. Holt, Rinehart & Winston, 1984.

Jacobi, J. *Complex/Archetype/ Symbol in the Psychology of C.G. Jung*. Princeton, N.J.: Princeton UP, 1974.

Jones, E. *Hamlet and Oedipus*. Garden City, N.J.: 1954.

Jung, C.G. *Modern Man in Search of a Soul*. N.Y. Harcourt Brace, 1933.

_____. *The Archetypes and the Collective Unconscious*. Trans. R.F.C. Hull. Princeton, N.J.: Princeton UP, 1959.

_____. *The Spirit in Man, Art and Literature*. Princeton, N.J.: Princeton UP, 1966.

_____. *Mandala Symbolism*. Trans. R.F.C.Hull. Princeton, N.J.: Princeton UP, 1972.

Lakoff & Turner. *More than Cool Reason. A Field Guide to Poetic Metaphor*. Chicago: U of Chicago P, 1989.

Maslow, A.H. *Religion, Values and Peak Experiences*. Harmondsworth, Middlesex, England: Penguin Books, 1964.

Monk, S.H. *The Sublime: A Study of Critical Theories in XVIII-Century England*. Ann Arbor, Michigan: U of Michigan P. 1960.

Moon, B., ed. *An Encyclopedia of Archetypal Symbolism*. Boston: Shambala, 1991.

Muller, H.J. *Science and Criticism: The Humanist Tradition in Contemporary Thought*. New Haven: Yale UP, 1964.

Ogden, C. K. & Richards, I.A. *The Meaning of Meaning*. N.Y.: Harcourt, Brace, 1946.

Müller-Vollmer, K. *Towards a Phenomenological Theory of Literature. A Study of Wilhelm Dilthey's Poetik*. The Hague: Mouton, 1963.

Perkins, D. *Is Literary History Possible?* Baltimore & London: John Hopkins UP, 1992.

Preminger, A. ed. *Encyclopedia of Poetry and Poetics*. Princeton, N.J.: Princeton UP, 1965.

Strauch, E.H. *A Subjunctive-Indicative Modality. A Contribution Toward a Theory of Literature*. Doctoral dissertation. Bloominton, Indiana: Indiana University, 1969.

_____ . *A Philosophy of Literary Criticism. Volume I. Patterns of Comparison*. N.Y.: Exposition P. 1974.

_____ . *How Nature Taught Man to Know, Imagine, and Reason. (How Language and Literature Recreate Nature's Lessons)* N.Y.: Peter Lang, 1995.

Weistein, V. *Comparative Literature and Literary Theory. Survey and Introduction*. Trans.W. Riggan. Bloomington & London: Indiana UP, 1973.

Wellek, R. & Warren, A. *Theory of Literature*. N.Y. Harcourt Brace,1956.

Wellek, R. *Concepts of Criticism*. New Haven & London:Yale UP, 1963.

Weston J.L. *From Ritual to Romance*. Garden City, N.J., 1957.

Wiener, P.P., Ed-in-chief. *Dictionary of History of Ideas, Vols. II, III*, and *IV*. N.Y. Scribner's Sons, 1973.

Wilhelm, R. Trans.C.F.Baynes. *I Ching or the Book of Changes*. Princeton, N.J.: Princeton UP, 1950.

FRENCH

Albérès, A.M. *Métamorphoses du roman*. Paris: Éditions Albin Michel,1966.

Benoist, R. *L'Esoterisme*. Paris: PU de France, 1975.

Blanche, R. L'Épistémologie. Paris: PU de France, 1972.

Bernis, J. *L'Imagination*. Paris: PU de France, 1975.

Bonnet, H. *Roman et poésie*. Paris: Librairie Nizet, 1951.

Bouthoul, G. *Les Mentalités*. Paris: PU de France, 1971.

Corbin, H. *Histoire de la philosophie islamique des origines jusuq'a la mort d'Averroës*: 1198. Paris, 1964.

Diel, P. *Psychologie de la Motivation*. Paris: Petite Bibliothèque Payot, 1969.

Dilthey, W. *Théorie des Conceptions du Monde. Essai d'une Philosophie de la Philosophie*. Trans.L. Sauzin. Paris: PU de France,1946.

Eliade, M. *Le mythe de l'éternel retour. Archetypes et répétition*. Paris: Éditions Gallimard, 1969.

Emmet, Jones R. *Panorama de la Nouvelle Critique en France de Gaston Bachelard à Jean Paul Weber*. Paris: 1968.

Gardet, L. *La Mystique*. Paris. PU de France, 1970.

Jung, C. G. & Kerenyi , Ch. *Introduction à l'Essence de la Mythologie , l'enfant divin, la jeune fille divine*.Trans. H.E. Del Medico. Paris: Petite Bibliothèque Payot, 1951.

Otto, R. *Le Sacré. L' élément non rationnel dans l'idée du divin et sa relation avec le rationnel*. Paris: Petite Bibliothèque Payot. No date.

Pucelle,J. *Le Temps*. Paris: PU de France, 1967.

Roussel, R. *Les Pèlerinages*. Paris: PU de France, 1972.

Sartre, J. P. *La Nausée*. Paris, 1938.

Van Tieghem, P. *Les Grandes Doctrines Littéraires en France*. Paris: PU de France, 1965.

GERMAN

Conrady, K.O. *Einführung in die neuere deutsche Literaturwissenschaft.* Reinbek bei Hamburg: Rowohlt Verlag, 1966.

Dilthey, W. "Die Einbildungskraft des Dichters. Bausteine für eine Poetik." (1887).*Gesammelte Schriften VI Band.* Stuttgart: B.G. Tuebner Verlag, 1962.

Frenzel, E. *Stoff-, Motiv- und Symbolforschung.* Stuttgart: Metzler, 1966.

Herman,J. *Literaturwissenschaft und Kunstwissenschaft. Methodische Wechselbeziehungen..* Stuttgart: Metzlersche Verlag, 1971.

Kayser, W. *Das Sprachliche Kunstwerk. Eine Einführung in die Literawissenschaft u. Interpretation.* Bern U.München, Frankl Verlag,1965.

Klein A.& Vogt, J. *Literaturwissenschaft l: Literaturgeschichte und Interpretation.* Düsseldorf: Bertelsmann Universitätsverlag, 1971.

Kraus, W. *Grundprobleme der Literaturwissenschaft.* Reinbek bei Hamburg: Rohwohlt Verlag, 1968.

Lipffert, S. *Symbol-Fibel. Eine Hilfe zum Betrachten und Deuten Mittelalterlicher Bildwerke.* Kassel, Germany: Johannes Stauda Verlag, 1964.

Rothacker, E. *Logik u Systematik der Geisteswissenschaften.* Bonn: Verlag Bouvier, 1947.

Seidler, H. *Die Dichtung: Wesen, Form, Dasein.* Stuttgart: Kröner Verlag, 1965.

Smegac & Skreb. *Zur Kritik Literaturwissenschaftlicher Methodologie.* Frankfurt am Main: Atheneum Verlag, 1973.

Staiger, E. *Die Kunst der Interpretation.* Zurich u. Freiburg: Atlantis Verlag, 1955.

————. *Grundbegriffe der Poetik.* Zurich u. Freiburg, Atlantis Verlag ,1946.

Zmegac, V. *Methoden der deutschen Literaturwissenschaft.* Frankfurt am Main Germany: Atheneum Fischer Verlag,1973.

SPANISH

Balmes, J. *El Criterio*. decimoseptima edition. Mexico: Espasa-Calpe, Mexicana, 1989.

CHAPTER-BY-CHAPTER
SUMMARY INDEX

This Chapter-by-Chapter Summary Index is intended to complement the standard alphabetical index. The purpose of this is fourfold: 1) to introduce preeminent French, German, British and American scholars' writing about the aims and methods of literary criticism; 2) to demonstrate the scope and limits of rational and scientific theory in the analysis and interpretation of literature; 3) to offer the reader an overview of the text's major concepts and themes; and finally; 4) to help the reader perceive the significant changes that took place in literary theory in 19th and 20th century Europe and America.

To be more specific, these changes emerge as a pattern of transitions:

1) There was a shift from exclusive rational exposition of literary theory to the admission that logical descriptions of literary forms were limited. The intrinsic nature of literature transcended logic.

2) There was a shift from literary study emulating impersonal scientific theory and practice to a recognition that the human sciences could offer more tangible, germane insights into literature.

3) Twentieth century psychology changed from Freud's causal and deterministic explanation of the subconscious psyche to the Jungian exposition of the influence of archetypes on our racial unconscious and our ethnic conscience. In turn, this phase became Paul Diel's elucidation of how our evolution, as a species, affected the psyche's biogenetic destiny. As evoked in myth, religion and literature, Diel's psychology argues that the psyche displays an evolved supraconscience. Thus these shifts in psychological theory directly and indirectly influenced literary analysis and interpretation.

4) In sum, transformations of world view became manifest: from logical to dialectical reasoning about literature; from scientism to depth psychology; from atheistic existentialism to solid anthropological evidence that humanity needed spiritual experiences; from worldly skepticism to a late century realization that humanity's emotional intelligence, as portrayed in literature, includes the search for the mystical meaning of human destiny.

For these reasons, the final part of *Beyond Literary Theory* offers three *explications de texte*, which examine the mystical dimensions inherent in memorable literature.

PART ONE
THE HISTORICAL SEARCH
FOR A LITERARY AESTHETIC

Chapter 1
The Traditional Perspective: Literature as Beauty, Truth, Meaning and the Sublime

Chapter 5
The Neo-Aristotelian Analysis of Literature and the Limits of Logic, 75-88

Chapter 6
European Criticism of Anglo-American Formalism, 89-98

PART THREE
LITERARY THEORY AS HUMAN SCIENCE

Chapter 7
The Search for a Science of Literary Criticism, 101-114

The three purposes of this chapter:
   To review ideas of early, methodical thinkers, 101
   To retrace the attempt to transform criticism into a science, 101
   To provide a list of maxims and methods to pursue more effectual research, 101

Science seeks to understand *how* and *why* of phenomena, 101
   Francis Bacon
      defined induction, 101
      its aim to detect connections between phenomena, 101
      beware of "idols," i.e. false assumptions and misleading prejudices, 101-102
      test hypotheses to uncover law governing facts, 102
   French Theory and Criticism
      René Descartes
         sought solid system of thought, 102
         practiced systematic doubt till he could not doubt act of doubting, 102
         result: "*cogito ergo sum*," "I think, therefore I am," 102
         his *Discourse on the Method* outlined four principles of reasoning, 102-103
      Lavoisier
         provided concept and method of *analysis* and *synthesis*, 103
      Montesquieu
         studied spirit of the laws, its constitution, climate, religion, mores, 103
      Diderot et al, the *Encyclopedia*, 103-104
         demonstrated range of human knowledge, 103-104
         described each science, trade, and art, 104
         its aim: to convert common ways of thinking to rational thought, 104

PART FOUR
THE PSYCHOLOGICAL
INTERPRETATION OF LITERATURE

Chapter 8
The Scope and Limits of the Freudian Psychoanalytical Approach to Literature, 117-132

There is a psychic function named the *subconscious*, manifesting
   mental illness, 158
Psyche also manifests a *supraconscious*, which is foreshadowed in
   ancient mythologies and man's notions of divinity, 158
Life has a biogenetic sense, 158
Demons and powers of darkness manifest the *subconscious*, 158
Gods and powers of light are signs of man's *supraconscious*, 158
The Subconscious, 159-161
   the vital sin is to exalt false desires and to fail to satisfy the vital
      need of the essential desire, 159
   the exalted imagination destroys clarity of thought, and through
      exalting multiple desires destroys the essential desire, 159
The Supraconscious, 161-163
   the Essential Desire, 161
      suffering can be sublimated and spiritualized by pursuing
         the essential desire, 161
      the supraconscious guides us to realize a meaningful destiny
         by pursuing a lifetime purpose, 161
   the Vital Need, 162
      the vital need is to create a sensible plan of life, 162
   the sublimated and spiritualized imagination, 162-163
      sublimation means to convert instinctual impulses into
         socially acceptable attitudes, 162-163
      spiritualization means to purify self in the sense of sacred
         and religious values, 163

European philosophies and medieval moral concepts are the roots of
   Diel's psychology of motivation, 163
   Stoicism and Diel's psychology, 163
   Epicureanism and Diel's psychology, 163-164
   The Theme of *Hybris* and *Sōphrosynē*, 164-166
      hybris and *sōphrosynē* are moral concepts converted to the seven
         virtues and seven deadly sins of the Middle Ages, 164
      psychomachia is the struggle between virtue and vice that runs
         throughout European literature, 164
   Hybris, 164-165
   Sōphrosynē, 165-166
      meant temperance, the avoidance of immoderate or irrational
         behavior, 165

PART FIVE
THE MYSTICAL DIMENSION
OF LITERATURE

Introduction, 177-182
  Secular, imaginative literature can be studied for its mystical dimensions, 177
  Because twentieth century literary theories were limited by methods of logic and science, such theories became remote from the quality and intensity of life's experiences, 178
  Today skeptic and atheist can admit that mysteries still exist which may lead us to understand life's mystical meanings, 181

Conclusion, 181-182
  The mystical dimension in literature testifies to potentials of a more humane humanity, 182

Chapter 11
Dante's *Vita Nuova* as Riddle: A Medieval Meditation on the Numinous

This chapter offers a medieval world view, which reflected a mystical vision of existence. The *Vita Nuova* illustrates Dante's poetic search for the direction and meaning of his life. That quest led him to face life's ultimate riddle. Dante explored the numinous meaning of numbers and used hermetic language to express his deepest insights. The poem is the meditation of a medieval mystic.

Vita Nuova
  Its Faults and Affectations, 185
      if faults and affectations abound in Chs. I-XIV, the poet's sincere inspiration, derived from Beatrice's death, transformed Dante and his subsequent poetry, 185
  It is unified by Dante's retrospective insight into the direction and meaning of his life, 185
  It has a prophetic voice and telological purpose, 185
  It is a poetic microcosm with Beatrice at its center as the Holy Trinity is the hub of the medieval Ptolemaic universe, 185-186
  Riddles of Time, 188

Chapter 12
Four Dimensions of Signification in *The Old Man and the Sea*

The four dimensions in the novel show how the mature Hemingway came to terms with life's mystery:

Chapter 13
The Mystical Dimension in J.P. Sartre's *Nausea*

There also exists a kinship between Sartre and Dante. *Nausea* is remarkably similar to Dante's *Inferno*. Both describe the hopelessness of destinies devoid of purpose and meaning. The whole aim revealed to medieval man by God was to love man and to practice the commiseration of Christ and the mercy of Mary, 240

Time provides the ultimate form and mystical meaning of Sartre's symbolic novel. Eric Auerbach describes how religious literature united past, present and future through the representation of *figurae* who connect figures and events over time. So too the figures in *Nausea* prognosticate Roquentin as an archetype whose decision leads to the authentic, creative life, 240-241

What medieval *figurae* divulge is a Presence within reality, an Essence sustaining and directing human existence. Time is the medium through which men may convert existence into essence. Sartre's characters become figural representations of such a possible conversion, 242

Roquentin's notice of the alienated, the sick and dying heighten his awareness of life through the nausea, 242-244

There are multiple affinities between the peripheral *figurae* and the central characters, 244-248

Roquentin recognizes how he has also changed intellectually. When he was twenty, he was like Descartes. Later like Pascal, he asked himself "where is your dignity as a 'thinking reed'?" Roquentin rejects historical research as a waste of time. He realizes that soon life itself will be gone. The lyrics of the song tell him this. "Some one of these days, You'll miss me, honey" causes his nausea to disappear and his body to harden. For Roquentin, it becomes important to create something durable out of his dying existence, 248-249

Symbolic Destinies, 249-250

Symbolic truth emanates like a melody out of human anguish. The unfolding of the existential situations of various characters becomes symbolic destinies. For Roquentin, the privileged situation is life itself, and it is up to the individual to create some kind of perfect destiny out of it. That is what is meant by Sartre's dictum "Existence precedes Essence." This symbolic novel is an example of the transformation of existence into essence, 249

To make the question of symbolic destinies clearer, let it be said Roquentin's situation is parallel with all the sufferers. All are doomed to die. On the other hand, all the other characters lead false lives, drift through purposeless existences or are inhumane to their fellow men, 249-250

He must move counter to all who lead mindless, insensitive lives, 250

Time shows man the possibilities in Freedom and in self-realization. In existence, man alone can fashion the future. Man is *free* to realize his own destiny, 250

If we look deeply enough, we find *Nausea* embodies a Dantesque hierarchy of values with seven levels of punishment according to seven forms or degrees of existential transgression. At the deepest level is the suffering of the mind, 251

The impassioned tone of *Nausea* is like the patriarchal and prophetic voices of the Bible. These alternating voices modulate the meaning of the symbols and figurae, which establish man's communion with the ultimate reality of things. Sartre's vision of existence is a message of hope for the few who dare to realize the mystical meaning of their symbolic destinies, 251-252

ALPHA INDEX

T

Taine, H.A. (see literary criticism as science) 106-107
telling vs. showing 48-52
testament (see Hemingway) 218-226
textimmanent (see formalism and Kayser) 91-92
themes in literature: disintegration and integration (see Diel) 171-172
Taoism (see Jung) 146-147
tragedy (see Aristotle and Nietzsche) 75, 77, 147-148
truth (see poetics) 10-21

V

van Tieghem, P. 231-232
Verlaine, Paul 231
Viëtor, K. 95
vital need (see Diel) 162
vital sin (see Diel) 159-161
voice (see Ogden and Richards) 46, 52-53
von Wiese, Benno 95

W

wechselseitige Erhellung (see "reciprocal illumination" Scherer) 110
Wellek, René 125, 276-277
Wellek and Warren (see intrinsic and extrinsic) 46-47, 55
Weston, Jessie L. (see symbolic interpretation in Hemingway) 285

Wilhelm, Richard (see *I Ching* in Jung) 146-147
Wordsworth, William 7, 15

Y

Young, Edward (see originality) 34

Z

zodiac 213
Zola, Émile (see literary naturalism) 108